Gilles Deleuze: Affirmation in Philosophy

Gilles Deleuze: Affirmation in Philosophy

Jay Conway

First published 2010 by
PALGRAVE MACMILLAN

Palgrave Macmillan in the UK is an imprint of Macmillan Publishers Limited,
registered in England, company number 785998, of Houndmills, Basingstoke,
Hampshire RG21 6XS.

Palgrave Macmillan in the US is a division of St Martin's Press LLC,
175 Fifth Avenue, New York, NY 10010.

Palgrave Macmillan is the global academic imprint of the above companies
and has companies and representatives throughout the world.

Palgrave® and Macmillan® are registered trademarks in the United States,
the United Kingdom, Europe and other countries.

ISBN: 978-0-230-27658-1 hardback

This book is printed on paper suitable for recycling and made from fully
managed and sustained forest sources. Logging, pulping and manufacturing
processes are expected to conform to the environmental regulations of the
country of origin.

A catalogue record for this book is available from the British Library.

Library of Congress Cataloging-in-Publication Data

Conway, Jay, 1971–
     Gilles Deleuze : affirmation in philosophy / Jay Conway.
        p. cm.
     Includes bibliographical references and index.
     ISBN 978-0-230-27658-1
     1. Deleuze, Gilles, 1925–1995. I. Title.

B2430.D454C69 2010
194—dc22   2010027499

10 9 8 7 6 5 4 3 2 1
19 18 17 16 15 14 13 12 11 10

Transferred to Digital Printing in 2011

For my parents, Jean Elizabeth Falls and John Turner Conway

Contents

Acknowledgments

In *Proust and Signs*, Deleuze describes how philosophical apprenticeships require time and encounters. A chance encounter with a book, then more books, led me to write my own. And this project took considerable time: time filled with not only detours, dead-ends, and frustration, but also great excitement. I thank the late Gilles Deleuze for his beautiful and inspiring work.

No one could ask for a more patient, more encouraging community than the one that accompanied me on this road. I want to thank my mother Jean Falls for encouraging my pursuit of philosophy from day one. I want to thank my father John Conway and Tammy Conway for their deep commitment to my well-being and to the life of this project. I want to thank Duane Wright for opening up his home to me. I want to thank my sister Margo Radovich along with Rob Radovich and Kayla Radovich for their love and support. For his help with this manuscript, for allowing me to try out applications of Deleuze's concepts in our daily life, and for his solidarity in all matters philosophical I thank Carlos Brocatto. For believing in this book I thank Priyanka Gibbons and the good folks at Palgrave Macmillan.

I want to acknowledge the tireless support, helpful suggestions and humor of Georgia Warnke. David Glidden's sensitivity and appreciation for crime fiction helped me play both sides against the middle. No one validated my decision to work on Deleuze's philosophy more than Carole Fabricant. Her fierce love of books and ideas encouraged me to go past the cliché to the concept and the street. For their acts of kindness I want to thank Donna Balderrama, Michelle Bloom, Bernd and Lore Magnus, Stephen Daniel, and Mark Balaguer. I thank my students past and present, especially those who attended my lectures on the work of Deleuze, Spinoza, and Bergson. For kind words along the way I thank Todd May, Constantine Boundas, Mike Davis, Sandra Harding, and Erika Suderberg. Many years ago I overheard Rosi Braidotti recommend the book *Empiricism and Subjectivity*; I am indebted.

My introduction to philosophy occurred while I was a student at the University of South Florida. One could not ask for a better, more challenging, and more accommodating group of instructors than Jim Bell, Roy Weatherford, Willis Truitt, Linda Lopez McAlister, and Stephen Turner. The lectures, kindness, and friendship of Joanne Waugh inspired me to pursue philosophy. I want to thank Butler Waugh as well.

I embrace my creative and loyal friends: Joe Tsambiras, Gloria Bryan, Jeff Le Comte, Cixous Le Comte, Diego Le Comte, Megan Dailey, Richard Bryan, Tracy Bryan, Brittany Bryan, Alex B., Gloria's folks, Fernando Ruiz, Rosa Maria Ruiz, Isabel Pearson, Richard Pearson, Zack Fish, Cindy Wheeler, Richard Dellifraine, Tom Donovan, DJ T-bird, Bethany Kraemer, Sophia Brocatto, Mireya Brocatto, Anthony Brocatto, Mario Berlinguer, Nicolas Deantoni, Felipe Caceres, Yolanda and her mother, Catherine Newman, Uaratiex Mendoza, Elizabeth Venable, Beth Lauritis, Richard Reynoso, Maria Cornejo, Pacal Cornejo-Reynoso, Aitzin Cornejo-Reynoso, Josh Lewis, Leah McClimans, Kalani Pahoa, Kathy Saylor and family, Rue Herbert and Richard Herbert, Autumn Hjort and Evan Hjort, Ellis Gesten, Ray Horn, and Stephanie Kay.

John Imboden can no longer write. I write in his memory. At my side is Colette.

Introduction

Among the more pronounced features of Gilles Deleuze's work is a sustained discussion of the demands and joys of reading philosophy. Whether the concept is that of "becoming," middle," or "actualization", whether the metaphor is that of the portrait or the double, the reader understands that the idea of interpretation as the simple relocation of a fixed meaning from one chain of signifiers to another has been left far behind. Equally noticeable, however, is the fact that Deleuze never frames his discussion of reading philosophy as a critique of the signified. In contemporary theory the critique of the signified has assumed a variety of forms: the claim the signified is itself a signifier (an interpretation is itself a text); the celebration of the reader's role in the production of meaning; the assertion that multiple, valid interpretations of the same text are possible; the notion of *différance*. But *Anti-Oedipus* finds Deleuze, along with Guattari, distancing himself from this entire current of thought (what could be called the valorization of the signifier).

For Deleuze the popular and noisy drama of signifier versus signified obscures certain truths. One is the marginality of the very idea of deep meaning: meaning requiring attention, diligence, perhaps even a method to uncover; meaning whose identity is debated and deemed worthy of debate. *Anti-Oedipus* includes a nostalgia-free description of how, under capitalism, this experiential prerequisite to exegesis has been severely eroded. When Deleuze and Guattari declare "writing has never been capitalism's thing" they are not making a statement concerning the status of the printed word relative to the image.[1] Rather, their point is that the question "what is the meaning of X?" rarely mediates the consumption of inscriptions, utterances, or images within the cultural landscape: the workplace memo, a piece of reportage, a television show, a course textbook. If the authors are correct, then the critique of the signified could hardly qualify as a subversive gesture. In fact, by inflating an obsolete target it could serve to misdirect critical and creative energies.

For Deleuze the debate surrounding the practice of interpretation also conceals an important feature of the philosophical profession. Within the disciplinary apparatus of philosophy, the fanfare surrounding the possibility of multiple legitimate interpretations can restrict our awareness of the high degree of uniformity characterizing discussions of individual philosophies. For Deleuze it is important to recognize the existence of dominant interpretations, and it is important to recognize that the dominant interpretations are typically superficial and misleading. Work on a philosophy always occurs within a situation—a situation partially defined by the current interpretations of that philosophy. What Deleuze suggests is that the typical situation is one in which the worst conceivable interpretations (less readings than nonreadings) exert the greatest influence.

Just as Deleuze's discussion of reading philosophy breaks with, but is not a critique of the signified, so his philosophy breaks with, but is not at bottom a critique of traditional notions of substance and essence. This means that Deleuze's philosophy does not conform to the popular image of a philosophy of difference. Consider, for example, the case of deconstruction. Within this orientation, difference is not a thing (an object spatially and temporally present) and thus resists naming or straightforward description. Difference is the way absence prevents any presence from being fully present, any identity from being self-identical. The Derridean variations on this theme of absence, nonpresence, or *différance* have become familiar: signifying chains *do* routinely convey determinate meanings, but they do so because their forms can operate in the absence of those meanings (iterability); experience of what is present in consciousness is shaped by what was present (but now absent) as well as by what we anticipate will be present (the phenomenological notion of primary retention and anticipation); perfect identities or essences are nothing but appearances engendered through the conceptual oppositions of discourse.

Under the heading of "the politics of deconstruction" this theme of difference as nonpresence often becomes indistinguishable from an older and more influential line of criticism. This is the quasi-nominalist or anti-essentialist critique of the way general terms (especially those at the center of nationalistic, supremacist, or patriarchal discourse) conceal the heterogeneity of the concrete. The concrete is depicted as either a collection of unrelated entities or as a site of intersecting forces (e.g. the individual as the site of the extra-individual forces of class, race, gender, and sexuality).

At first one might confuse Deleuze's theory of difference with this critique of general terms. This is because the critique of ready-made conceptions of unity and difference – a critique that is at times connected to a consideration of language – is a thread running through each of Deleuze's books. For example, in *Empiricism and Subjectivity*, Deleuze highlights Hume's contention that there is no demonstrable correspondence between, on the one hand, the use of the first- person pronoun, general terms, or the word "cause," and, on the other hand, a substance, essences, or internal connections. Similarly, Deleuze highlights areas in Bergson's, Spinoza's, and Nietzsche's work in which taxonomic categories are analyzed as abstractions, distortions, or impediments to grasping particular forms of difference.

Understanding Deleuze's thought, however, requires recognizing the exact place this strand of criticism occupies within his overall project. Succinctly put, antiessentialism or the critique of the appearance of self-identity is never Deleuze's ultimate concern. Thus, Deleuze's interest in Hume's philosophy resides less in the critique of familiar locutions, than in Hume's account of the process that lies behind the speaking-subject. This is the formation of habits through the unconscious association of heterogeneous elements. The theme of concealed heterogeneity (or of the non-existence of internal relations) sets up a consideration of how a system is formed out of external relations. In this way, the critique of a specific way of thinking unity (unity as a principle of identity beneath difference) paves the way for an alternative (unity as an order composed of difference). The focus of Deleuze's study of Bergson's work is not the idea that natural kinds are unreal. Rather, it is the specific reality Bergson affords kinds: it is natural for humans to perceive the world as comprised of discrete entities belonging to kinds, because this is the form of perception required for action and survival. Additionally, Deleuze is interested in how Bergson's analysis of this real, natural form of perception—where difference is the difference between entities—is developed alongside of concepts that break with established ways of thinking unity and difference. These are the concepts of duration, qualitative multiplicity, pure memory, and evolution. In his reading of the *Ethics*, Deleuze shows how Spinoza's depiction of natural kinds as imaginary is accompanied by a consideration of individual bodies as dynamic, albeit relatively stable, organizations embedded in concrete environments. A body is envisioned as a complex society (or organization of smaller bodies), one possessing a porous border and defined by what it does (by the way its power to act and be acted upon is actualized). Similarly, in Nietzsche's writing Deleuze finds a critique of substance, but, more importantly, he finds a vision of entities as mobile arrangements of disparate (or nonequivalent) forces.

Given what Deleuze amplifies in his presentation of these philosophies, it should come as little surprise that in *Difference and Repetition* and *Logic of Sense*, his critique of familiar conceptions of unity and difference is more nuanced, and more far-reaching than the antiessentialist gestures that have become commonplace. Deleuze wants to think difference in a way that evades a host of intellectual tendencies. These include the tendency to think difference as negation or opposition; as the difference between substance and the other Aristotelian categories; as specific difference (i.e. difference as the difference between natural kinds); as the difference between members of one and the same kind; as the difference between entities; as the difference between an original and its representations; as the different representations of an original; as the difference between this world and transcendent, other-worldly principles; as the absence of order (or chaos). Alternatively, one can say that Deleuze wants to think unity, order, or systematicity, but in a way that breaks with or overhauls the traditional notions of substance, essence, universal, or ground. Deleuze's theory of difference is not an answer to the deconstructionist question, "What are the conditions of signification?" Deleuze's theory of difference is not an answer to the question, "How do the categories of class, race, gender, and sexuality intersect?" Rather, Deleuze's theory of difference is an answer to the metaphysical question "What is an entity?" or "What is a body?"

In perhaps his most provocative move, Deleuze's critique of Platonic essences or Ideas paves the way for a new theory of essences or Ideas – one that breaks with the logic of representation. In Deleuze's *Difference and Repetition* and *Logic of Sense*, anti-Platonism is indistinguishable from a reworking of Platonic notions. Is Deleuze a Platonist or anti-Platonist? Is he a philosopher of difference or a philosopher of unity? Like the figure of the schizo in *Anti-Oedipus*, Deleuze scrambles "all the codes" and possesses a "unique system of co-ordinates for situating himself." One grasps these coordinates and Deleuze's concepts by resisting the urge to classify his thought—by resisting the urge to see his philosophy as an example of a pre-existing position.

A commentary can and should display an awareness of the subject matter's practical implications. This includes the implications the material has for the practice of commentary. Thus, commentaries on deconstruction frequently begin by mimicking the *sous rapture* (or "under erasure") style of Derrida's writing. Just as Derrida's work is loaded with qualifiers accompanied by their theoretical justification (e.g. scare quotes are surrounded by parentheticals defending their necessity), so a persistent feature of work on deconstruction is the construction of a preface qualifying the subsequent commentary. The commentator begins by interrogating the "very idea of a preface," by cautioning the reader against regarding their analysis as definitive, by apologizing for synthesis and clarity of presentation as if these traditional virtues diminished the disruptive quality of their theoretical subject. Such an opening move should not be confused with the time-honored practice of an author assuming responsibility for any and all mistakes. Here the rhetoric suggests misgivings about the very practice of exposition.

The incommensurability of Deleuze's philosophy of difference and deconstruction entails that such a preface would be entirely out of place here. To begin a commentary on Deleuze's philosophy with a statement like "what follows is but one way of interpreting Deleuze's philosophy," would obscure how Deleuze's attack on the valorization of the signifier encourages us to regard such statements as uncontroversial and thus gratuitous. Similarly, a statement along the lines of "to even speak of Deleuze as having *a* philosophy or a philosophical system is in tension with his emphasis on difference" would obscure one of the fundamental impulses of Deleuzian thought. Deleuze's theory of difference is not advanced as a critique of unity, identity, and systematicity but as a rethinking of unity, identity, and systematicity. The principal target is not the belief in unity per se, but the belief that the real only possesses unity and structure if its infrastructure conforms to the traditional notions of essence or substance.

Of course the justification deconstruction provides for writing *sous rapture*, is that language-use is inescapably logocentric. The use of a noun is linked to the belief in essences, while the subject-predicate form (or the use of the word "is") is linked to the notion of substance. Even linear, straightforward presentation is, according to Derrida, entangled with the search for origins or first principles. For Deleuze, however, any philosophy of difference that is, at the end of the day, a critique of general terms tends to exaggerate the connection between expressions and ontological commitments. With this exaggeration comes a reduction of social criticism to the perpetual critique of language. I encourage the reader to think of Deleuze as a figure determined to keep philosophy from getting stuck in the practice of demystification. Deleuze is a philosopher who feels it is far easier to get unstuck from traditional notions of identity than the perpetual destroyers of the appearance of self-evidence would have you believe. Does the use of the word "I" without qualification presuppose a commitment to substance? Does the statement "tomorrow the sun will rise" without scare quotes contain an assumption of necessary connection (not to mention a warped cosmology)? Deleuze's answer to these questions can be found in the opening paragraph of *A Thousand Plateaus*:

> it's nice to talk like everybody else, to say the sun rises, when everybody knows it's only a manner of speaking. To reach, not the point where one no longer says I, but the point where it is no longer of any importance whether one says I.[2]

Writing *sous rapture* resembles a confession of guilt ("I regret having to use these words") and is intimately tied to criticism packaged as criticism of the philosophical tradition. In sharp contrast, Deleuze characterized his own practice of philosophy as innocent. One expression of this innocence was his unequivocal identification with the term "philosophy."[3] Deleuze does not present his work as an internal critique of philosophy or as an internal critique of language. Deleuze analyzes and utilizes the concepts of other philosophers non-defensively, he introduces his own concepts non-defensively, *as if* he was not surrounded by critiques of philosophy (Heideggerian, Derridean, Marxist, psychoanalytic, and structuralist critiques of philosophy). But Deleuze describes innocent thought and writing as a point to be reached. Innocence is hard won and Deleuze wins it for us by producing a conception of philosophy that bears little or no resemblance to the target of anti-philosophers.

That Deleuze's work does not encourage commentary *sous rapture* does not mean that it lacks a serious discussion of the challenges and responsibilities facing the interpreter. Anyone considering writing on Deleuze should examine this area of his work very carefully. In particular, one needs to identify the concrete demands Deleuze's account of reading has for those writing on Deleuze. A convenient place to begin this task is with the fact that, for Deleuze, not every interpretation of a philosophical text is itself philosophical. There are artistic, scientific, and historiographic ways of encountering philosophical writings, just as there are specifically philosophical ways of utilizing literature, science, and historiography.

More importantly, for Deleuze, many discussions of philosophical writings are best seen as counterfeit philosophy. Though presented as philosophy, they represent the diminishment of philosophy's power.

This distinction between philosophical and counterfeit readings was a feature of Deleuze's thought from the very beginning. In one of the few sections of *Empiricism and Subjectivity* (1953) where Deleuze operates at a distance from Hume's concepts, he raises the question of understanding and evaluating philosophical writing. He does so while arguing that most objections to philosophical texts are based upon patently erroneous readings (readings that frequently omit the most visible, the most obvious features of a philosophy). In this unlikely context, Deleuze appeals to the orthodox distinction between a theory's origin and its value. What follows displays his penchant for reworking the familiar philosophical lexicon: truth, necessity, eternity, essence, substance, Idea, etc. Ordinarily the origin/value distinction is associated with the practice of justification where justification is a matter of correspondence. A theory is construed as a set of propositions; the question of a theory's value is the question of whether these propositions fit the facts. But Deleuze invokes the origin/value distinction in the course of arguing that, in philosophy, truth-value should be understood as a property of problems rather than propositions.[4]

Following this Bergsonian move (for Bergson problems can be true or false), Deleuze incorporates Baconian language (truth as a function of coercion) in order to latch the question of a problem's truth-value onto the question of a problem's power.[5] The effect this connection has is easy to miss. Familiar senses of "value" are blurred: value can be considered an intrinsic property of an object, value can be considered a property bestowed upon an object, and value can be regarded as the outcome of something done to an object. There is the identification of value, there is the assignment of value, and there is the act or circumstances through which something becomes valuable or increases in value. Representational accounts of theory turn upon the first sense of value. The representational value of a theory (construed as a propositional system) is something one discovers rather than gives or makes. But when Deleuze says a problem's value is its power he is saying a problem's truth is not simply demonstrated, it is something created through demonstration. The meaning of Deleuze's origin/value distinction is that true problems (and thus true philosophies) are made true. The connection between value and power means making a philosophy true is inseparable from demonstrating its power (i.e. from showing what it can do).

We are now in a position to appreciate Deleuze's distinction between philosophical and counterfeit readings. In *Empiricism and Subjectivity*, the position of counterfeit reading is occupied by the objection based upon caricature. By defining individual philosophies as unique problems,

Deleuze suggests that the systemic misrepresentation of a philosophy often takes the form of ignoring incommensurability, creativity, or difference within the history of philosophy. In other words, instead of being grasped as the articulation of a new problem, the philosophy is presented as a new way of answering a preexisting problem, as a position within a conversation, or as a side in a larger debate.

The specific way Deleuze connects value to power (a philosophy is made valuable by being put in action) implies that philosophies do not have fixed truth-values. Philosophical reading resembles Deleuze's characterization of love in *Proust and Signs*: at any point in time certain philosophies stand out to us, certain philosophies force their way into our lives and increase our power to think, certain philosophies obsess us, certain philosophies strike us as instruments with which we can accomplish things. Most philosophies do not. Thus for Deleuze, one genuinely philosophical response to philosophical texts consists of placing most of them off to the side. Deleuze's philosopher only writes on what fills him or her with a sense of urgency.

Empiricism and Subjectivity, as well as Deleuze's other commentaries on individual philosophers, gives us a clear sense of what it means to write from this place of urgency. Deleuze does not write on these philosophies as external objects, but as objects he inhabits. For Deleuze, to write on a philosophy philosophically is to participate in its life—to maintain, restore, or increase its vitality.

This requires detailing the complex movements within and between the concepts comprising the philosophy. A philosophical commentary is one that truly rescues its subject from systematic misrepresentation. At the same time, a philosophical commentary is one that could never be confused with the writings of the philosopher under consideration. You do not participate in the life of a philosophy by simply re-presenting what already exists. Clearly the ready-made concepts of "old" and "new," "identity" and "difference" are of little use for describing such a relationship between a commentary and its subject. The Deleuzian term for the process of composing such a commentary is actualization, or differenciation, or becoming. In place of the critique of a signified, Deleuze will speak of philosophies as Ideas or Problems, where to be an Idea or Problem is to be irreducible to any one actualization. In place of the assertion that different, legitimate interpretations of an individual text are possible, Deleuzian thought gives us a practical imperative: actualize or differenciate a philosophy.

Once again sensitivity to the nuances of Deleuzian metaphysics is critical. The re-actualization of a philosophy should not be confused with preexisting notions such as the realization of hidden potential or the uncovering of possibilities. This is because Deleuze's use of the term virtual incorporates Bergson's critique of the logic of possibility or potentiality.[6] For Bergson, philosophers who explain the present or the future using the notions of potentiality or possibility are still operating within the Platonic notion of representation. The position of timeless essences is occupied by a realm of possibilities or potentiality; the representations of timeless essences become the realization of possibility or potentiality. In each case what happens in time is explained in terms of preexisting principles (a preexisting essence, a possibility that already exists as a possibility). The Bergsonian alternative to this logic, is to think of the whole of the real as not already given – in a deep sense, the future is unwritten. Similarly, Deleuze argues individual philosophies should not be reduced to what already exists. Thus, he distinguishes between the actual and the virtual side of a philosophy. To say a philosophy has a virtual side is not to say it has unrealized potential. The future of a philosophy has to be created or invented, not realized or uncovered. An actualization is the production of real difference. This difference has to be radical (a difference added to the world) without it being a difference between two things (the commentary is less about a philosophy than it is part of a philosophy's identity or life). In short, a philosophical commentary is a creation rather than a representation, but a creation immune from the charge of misrepresentation. Little surprise, then, that Deleuze's reflections on reading philosophy exist alongside a profound consideration of those figures within the philosophical tradition (Duns Scotus, Hume, Spinoza, Bergson, Nietzsche) who help us think of difference, not as a difference between things, but as a difference within a thing – within a one that, because of this difference, can no longer be thought of as one in the traditional sense.

What would it mean to write on Deleuze in a Deleuzian manner? Sensitivity to the profound discord between Deleuze's philosophical enterprise and the most influential ways of classifying and describing it would be required. One would be required to identify Deleuze's fundamental meta-philosophical and metaphysical concepts: problem, plane of immanence, concept, component, neighborhood, conceptual persona, Idea, the virtual, actualization, and incorporeal. Each concept would have to be described, not as a simple position or proposition, but as a complex movement of thought. To be adequate these descriptions would have to capture the originality of these movements – to show how they embody radical novelty and difference within the history of philosophy. The concepts would have to be construed as the expression or solution of a new rather than preexisting problem. Similarly, one would need to show how whenever Deleuze uses an unusual word it is precisely because other, more familiar expressions carry with them undesirable connotations. There would be the challenge of showing how Deleuze's utilization of others' concepts are re-actualizations rather than re-presentations. Last but not least, such a commentary would itself have to be an actualization of Deleuze's philosophy. To be an actualization it would have to be a strong display of fidelity and creativity. To be an actualization such a commentary would have to be written from within Deleuze's philosophy, but could not resemble or mimic any of Deleuze's own writing. My goal in writing this book was the production of just such a commentary. Deleuze's own books on Hume, Spinoza, Nietzsche, Bergson, and Foucault were my inspiration. Therefore, the pages that follow are intended to re-actualize as well as document Deleuze's original and important vision of philosophy.

The following study consists of three parts. Part I is a consideration of Deleuze's endorsement and practice of system building. What, according to Deleuze, is a system? A constant in Deleuze's writing is the idea that philosophy is the practice of producing problems. Deleuze uses the word "problem" because it immediately suggests the history of philosophy contains moments of great novelty and creativity. True philosophers do not solve pre-existing problems, they create new ones. True philosophers do not debate, they invent. If we are not careful, though, this elegant definition of philosophy will lead us astray. For Deleuze the invention of a philosophical problem should not be confused with the act of posing a question. Therefore, it is not enough to say that Deleuze regards philosophies as problems, one must come to understand his theory of problems. Through no small amount of engineering (Hume, Spinoza, and Bergson are important mediators) Deleuze arrives at the view that a philosophy or philosophical problem is a differential structure: an arrangement of intellectual tendencies. This arrangement permits radically different expressions. Additionally, Deleuze characterizes a problem as an abstract machine or immanent cause in order to capture how it exists within rather than outside of its diverse, concrete expressions.

At first glance, this definition may seem unnecessarily difficult, if not impenetrable. In fact, it is Deleuze's powerful and necessary response to the concrete experience of reading and writing philosophy. Alternative views of philosophical systems do not fare well. For this reason, I argue it is the best guide for coming to understand Deleuze's own system. A well-known but misunderstood feature of Deleuze's work is his departure from habitual or ready-made conceptions of unity and difference. All too often, though, the relationship between Deleuze's different books is explained using models reflecting precisely these habits. I suggest a more Deleuzian beginning is in order. Thus, Part I concludes with an account of the tendencies comprising the differential structure of Deleuze's philosophy.

For Deleuze every philosophical problem is simultaneously a theatre. A philosophy is expressed through characters (or "conceptual personae") that interact in precise ways. In Plato's dialogues this dramatic or theatrical side of philosophy is on full display. It is also on full display in Deleuze's writings. Part II introduces the reader to the array of characters populating Deleuze's system: there are a couple of structuralists and phenomenologists; there is an artist, a scientist, a detective, an Anglo-American philosopher, a French philosopher, a pervert, and a schizo. Most importantly there is the Deleuzian equivalent to the Platonic figures of Socrates and poet: the personae of the philosopher and the academic.

By referring to such characters as conceptual personae Deleuze suggests they have to be understood as elements within specific conceptual systems. To get to know the characters you have to get to know the system which is their home. What about the relationship between Plato's or Deleuze's personae and lives outside of their system of thought? For Deleuze, the question of the relationship between personae and persons is part of the more general question of the relationship between a philosophical system and its outside. Deleuze insists we need to acknowledge both the radical creativity of philosophical thought, and the fact that this thought is connected to an outside. Philosophical systems are both responses to the world and they act within it. The notion of representation is wholly inadequate for this task: it suggests transcendence (a philosophy exists apart from the world it represents), passivity (a representation is an image rather than a creative act), and sterility (a representation is an interpretation rather than an intervention). New concepts are needed to think through the precise relationship between a philosophy and its outside. The one Deleuze engineers goes by the name of counter-actualization.

Part III is a more or less linear journey through the two registers of Deleuze's system: his metaphilosophy and what I call his ethico-political metaphysics. I tackle consistently ignored passages in which the first is folded into the second. A familiar, comfortable move is to understand a philosopher's contribution to metaphysics in the light of their metaphilosophy. That is, we are accustomed to the idea that understanding a philosopher's discussion of the world requires familiarity with how he or she views the practice of philosophy (in particular the practice of making ontological commitments). But, to grasp Deleuze's conception of philosophy requires familiarity with his metaphysics. This is because Deleuze consistently treats philosophy (and thus philosophical concepts) as part of the world. A basic axiom of Deleuze's philosophy is that any theory of reality that fails to account for the place and function of philosophy within that reality is unacceptable. Similarly, theorists who bracket metaphysics are unable to account for the precise reality of their practice of theorizing.

Much of Part III is taken up with the task of analyzing Deleuze's philosophy of difference and unity. I show how Deleuze's most well-known metaphysical distinctions – the distinction between virtual and actual and the distinction between corporeal mixtures and incorporeals – are, in fact, secondary distinctions within his system. Commentators often cite Deleuze's claim that the mission of contemporary philosophy is the reversal of Platonism. His subsequent assertion, however, is ignored: the reversal of Platonism should preserve some of its fundamental characteristics. I argue that it is precisely the combative, ethico-political dimension of Plato's metaphysics that Deleuze wants to preserve. The reversal, however, entails that this preservation will be a reconfiguration and redirection of the Platonic battle lines.

For Deleuze, metaphysics is supposed to engender effects in the world. As he remarked in *Difference and Repetition* his aim was to "put metaphysics in motion," "to make it act, to make it carry out immediate acts."[7] Despite the political character of all of Deleuze's writing, the phrase "the politics of Deleuze" tends to evoke the volumes of *Capitalism and Schizophrenia*. Part of the beauty of that project is the way Deleuze and Guattari's writing frustrates the practice of attribution. Nevertheless, it is unfortunate that Guattari's name often gets lost in Deleuze scholarship. That being said, while I acknowledge Guattari's labor, my references to *Capitalism and Schizophrenia* reflect a specific goal: a portrait of Deleuze's philosophy. The accents and connections would be entirely different if I were providing an account of Deleuze and Guattari's project, or an account of Guattari's theoretical-political trajectory. My hope, though, is that my efforts will inspire others to thoughtfully and energetically engage with the work of both writers.

Part I
Deleuze and Systematic Philosophy

Any writer, especially one whose aim is the elucidation of a theoretical framework, wrestles with the question of the appropriate point of departure. How to lead oneself and others into the details of a philosophy? Here in Part I, my strategy is to identify the most general features of Deleuze's thought. The first such feature is that Deleuze's philosophy is systematic. The second is that Deleuze's system is a Problem or Idea, a differential content permitting heterogeneous expressions. Moreover, this problem or differential content *is* its past, present, and future expressions. The third general characteristic is a slogan moving across the system's surface – that of the middle. The fourth is a description of the acts of thought or ways of thinking comprising the differential content itself.

1 The shape of systematic philosophy

Deleuze should be taken at his word when he describes his theoretical labor as the construction of a system. This self-description is part of Deleuze's larger, influential defense of systematic philosophy past and present:

> It's become commonplace these days to talk about the breakdown of systems ... There are two problems with this idea: people can't imagine doing any serious work except on very restricted and specific little series; worse still, any broader approach is left to the spurious work of visionaries, with anyone saying whatever comes into their head. Systems have in fact lost absolutely none of their power.[1]

Describing Deleuze's work as systematic, though, only gets us so far. After all, the history of philosophy contains numerous forms and conceptions of systematicity. In fact, as a prolonged meditation on unity, order, or structure, Deleuze's work contains countless images of systematicity. These, however, can be divided into three basic types, where each type represents an alternative to habitual ways of thinking unity and difference.

In *A Thousand Plateaus*, the word "rhizome" is intended to evoke the philosophical penchant for thinking systematicity through botanical imagery: the image of the rhizome is opposed to the more familiar one of the roots, trunk, and branches of a tree (the so-called tree of knowledge).[2] In contrast to the linear, vertical derivations or species-genus catego-ries characterizing the root or tree, a rhizome is a de-centered network comprised of a myriad of external relations between multiple, disparate points of unification. In *Anti-Oedipus*, this opposition between rhizome and root takes the form of a distinction between two types of construc-tion. On the one hand, there is desiring-production: desire as the mobile production of connections between partial objects. On the other hand, there is the repression of desire, where repression is itself a form of pro-duction: a rigid whole or organism is formed through the restriction and coordination of its parts or organ-machines. In *Difference and Repetition*, Deleuze extracts from the early history of calculus an alternative to the view that identity is the support for difference. This is the view that iden-tity itself is a differential or complex curve connecting multiple singular points.[3] *Empiricism and Subjectivity* finds Deleuze distinguishing between a unity formed through multiple acts of synthesis, and a unity comprised of internal relations. Whether given the name "rhizome," "desiring-production," "differential," or "synthesis," the image is that of a system composed of multiple centers and relations – a system that is less a thing than an activity.

A second picture of a system is the logic of expression Deleuze finds in Spinoza's metaphysics.[4] In his *Ethics*, Spinoza argues that the essence of substance (or God) is expressed through an infinite number of attributes each of which is conceived through itself; that every modification of this substance is expressed as an infinite number of modes (one for each attribute), and, that the coextensive nature of God's power of thought and action implies an infinite number of individuals each of which is expressed as an idea under the attribute of thought and as a body under the attribute of extension.[5] In each case, the operative form of difference is not a difference between things, but between different expressions of the same thing (substance, a modification, or an individual). Spinoza's notion of expression combines strict correspondence or unity (between the attributes and between the modes of the different attributes) with heterogeneity (there are no relations of efficient causality between the attributes). Additionally, substance, modifications, and individuals are not principles existing outside of their expressions. A substance, modification, or individual *is* its radically different expressions.

In *Difference and Repetition*, this logic of expression reappears as the concept of Problem or Idea.[6] A problem permits an indeterminate number of distinct expressions, "actualizations," or "differenciations." When, in *What is Philosophy?*, Deleuze and Guattari characterize philosophical problems as planes of immanence, they are saying that philosophical problems should not be confused with explicitly delivered, interrogative sentences. A philosophical problem does not exist outside of its expressions, and these expressions are bodies of concepts.

The mediator of Deleuze's third image of systematicity is the philosophy of Bergson. Central to Deleuze's treatment of this philosophy is the distinction he finds between two forms of multiplicity.[7] A major theme of Bergson's *Time and Free Will* – and of his philosophy in general – is the claim that reducing perception to ordinary or natural perception reduces the real to the category of quantitative multiplicity, and in so doing engenders false problems or debates (freewill vs. determinism, materialism vs. idealism, nominalism vs. realism, the one vs. the many). Bergson defines a quantitative multiplicity as one in which the elements are discrete, discontinuous, or juxtaposed.[8] There is, in other words, a clear border separating the various elements. This general definition enables "quantitative multiplicity" to serve as a shorthand for a variety of ways of thinking difference: difference as the difference between things, difference as the different members of a kind, difference as the difference between kinds, difference as a measurable difference or difference in degree (one element is greater than a second or an element is greater now than it was), and difference as the return of the same. Bergson argues that consciousness is typically absorbed in the pragmatic task of disclosing our immediate environment in a manner useful to action: we experience an object as discrete, as a kind of thing, and as permitting specific types of interaction. The state of consciousness disclosing our surroundings, and the specific way our surroundings appear in such a state, are labeled quantitative multiplicities.[9]

According to Bergson, grasping a qualitative multiplicity (or duration) requires an empiricism based in less pragmatic, less typical, less "human" experiences.[10] The elements of a qualitative multiplicity are described as fused or confused; they anticipate and lean into one another like the steps comprising a graceful dance.[11] At the same time Bergson describes these elements as radically different. A qualitative multiplicity is the process of producing states that are genuinely new but continuous with one another. Reflecting the highly tactical expository style of *Time and Free Will*, qualitative multiplicity or duration is first presented as consciousness in its entirety, then as one region of consciousness (the notion of a deep self), and finally as moments in our life in which we simultaneously think, feel, *and act* differently (Bergson's notion of freedom). Following *Time and Free Will,* the movement of duration increasingly comes to occupy the position of substance (or infrastructure of the real) within Bergson's metaphysics.[12] Bergson would come to compare quotidian human experience to a snapshot. The world as duration is frozen and framed – experienced as a collection of discrete, relatively stable object belonging to kinds – for the sake of action.

Summarily put, the three images of systematicity are the notion of a movement connecting or synthesizing heterogeneous points, the idea of a thing *as* a series of radically different expressions, and the notion of a sequence of radically new, interpenetrating states. Each image demonstrates the inadequacy of one of the most popular questions within Deleuze's scholarship: "Is Deleuze a philosopher of difference, of oneness, or both?" The question should not be answered but rejected. What is important is to see how Deleuze consistently breaks with all of the familiar ways of thinking unity and difference or the one and the many.

Deleuze's ultimate answer to the question, "What is a philosophical system?" should be seen as a combination of these three images. For Deleuze, each philosophy is a unique problem. As an extraordinary invention a philosophical problem is neither the meaning of an interrogative sentence (the familiar sense of question) nor the content of a set of propositions. Rather, the content of a problem takes the form of a differential, a complex curve, or a rhizome. This differential content permits different expressions and *is* its different expressions. Each expression is itself a rhizome, a network of relations within and between concepts. As for philosophical concepts these are best located on the threshold of a problem and its expressions. Reading a philosophical text we often find ourselves wondering, "are these different concepts or the same concept?" On the one hand, the concept could be compared to a modification or individual receiving multiple expressions. In this case, the concept is located on the side of the differential content; one could speak of a concept's multiple actualizations. On the other hand, a concept could be compared to one of the specific modes expressing a modification or individual. In this case, there are not multiple expressions of the same concept, but multiple conceptual expressions of the same problem.

The relationship between a philosophical problem and its expressions is not the relationship between a preexisting principle of identity and its multiple representations. Nor is it the relationship between a preexisting reservoir of potential or possibility and the realization of this potential or these possibilities. The problem is a differential, and like Spinoza's God it is immanent to its expressions. Like the continuous elements of a qualitative multiplicity, each of these expressions is a genuine creation – it is radically new.

A new actualization is radically new, but not *a new thing* (a separate philosophy). Unlike Descartes, for Spinoza radically different attributes does not entail multiple substances. For Bergson radically different moments does not entail multiple entities or things. For Deleuze radical novelty in philosophy does not always take the form of a new philosophy. Philosophical systems are, in a strong sense, open-ended. Their identity is not simply created but re-created. And no actualization or re-creation has to be the last one.

Earlier I indicated how Deleuze identifies with systematic philosophy. We have seen three of the images of systematicity contained in Deleuze's work and how his conception of a philosophical system pulls them together. The remaining step is to recognize that Deleuze's own thought is systematic in a precise sense – the Deleuzian sense. Therefore, it is not enough to ask questions such as "What is Deleuze's concept of problem or plane of immanence?" One must ask "What is Deleuze's own plane of immanence?" "What is Deleuze's problem?"

Deleuze's metaphysical conception of system should be seen as a response to the very real challenges of understanding philosophies in their concreteness. Any reader of Deleuze is struck not only by how each of his books (even his short essays) seems to encapsulate his entire philosophy but also by the range of topics he explored in his work, by the dramatic transitions within and between his texts, and by how the wave of concepts grew with each book (until the tidal wave of *Capitalism and Schizophrenia*). Descriptions of the relationship between Deleuze's various books, however, are often governed by the most banal, most habitual images of development, unity, and difference. The first consists of locating in a chronological sequence of texts, *the book*, the one embodying a philosophy's core. The second model consists of locating within the sequence of texts, a break separating one philosophy from another. The third model consists of treating, not just specific concepts but a philosophy as something that emerges gradually, piece by piece over time. Nearly every one of Deleuze's books has, at one time or another, been marketed and positioned as *the* key to understanding Deleuze's philosophy. Similarly, the great rupture dividing Deleuze's thought into two philosophies has been located just about everywhere: between his study of Hume and Bergson, between his philosophical portraits and the books *Difference and Repetition* and *The Logic of Sense*, between *Difference and Repetition* and *The Logic of Sense*, and between his work prior to meeting Guattari and *Capitalism and Schizophrenia*. A brief, progressive narrative in *Difference and Repetition* – one concerning the notion of univocity in the work of Duns Scotus, Spinoza, and Nietzsche – is routinely projected onto his books on Hume, Bergson, Spinoza, and Nietzsche. This sequence is represented as the story of the gradual, piece by piece formation of Deleuze's philosophy.

But when the representations governed by these habitual models are placed alongside of Deleuze's writings, it is clear that something has gone wrong. We sense that a deep continuity of objectives and concerns has been lost. But we also sense that a massive reduction of Deleuzian thought has occurred. In Deleuzian terms, what went wrong was trying to capture the experience of reading Deleuze using ready-made concepts of unity and difference: where strong difference means discontinuity, where continuity means homogeneity, where a work that fully expresses a philosophy must occupy a foundational position relative to the others, and where development and growth are always a gradual accumulation of pieces. Deleuze's conception of systematicity is such that radical difference is linked to philosophical continuity. A work can express a philosophy's defining problem without being foundational (because there are other expressions of the problem), and both philosophies and actualizations are unpredictable events. A new philosophy is a dramatic, open-ended addition to the world. Through the production of new actualizations a philosophy grows (i.e. becomes more and more expressive) over time.

2   Deleuze's slogan of the middle

At this point we have identified two of the most general characteristics of Deleuze's thought: the fact that Deleuze is a systematic philosopher and the basic shape of his philosophical system. Remaining at this level of accurate generality, I want to now examine a notion found in many of Deleuze's writings: that of the middle. The Deleuzian middle is less a concept than a slogan. By "slogan" I mean a highly malleable phrase, one that ripples across the surface of a philosophical system. What a slogan lacks in precision it gains in distance. Consider the diverse contexts in which Deleuze uses the expression. Without beginning or end, the rhizome is described as all middle.[13] The life and thought of Sartre is remembered as always in-between, always growing from the middle ("like all creative things and people").[14] Deleuze does not describe his work with Guattari as a communication or exchange of ideas, but as a middle.[15]

The words "slogan" or "sloganeering" often carry negative connotations. But in referencing Lenin's famous text "On Slogans," Deleuze and Guattari suggest a good slogan operates in opposition to clichés and intellectual laziness.[16] If clichés are the type of thing "one says" in a given situation (Deleuze and Guattari's term for this is "major language"), a good slogan should serve to energize practice. Deleuze's slogans (not only "the middle," but also "relations are external," "no one knows what a body can do," and "no one knows what thought can do") create the atmosphere within which the rest of his system unfolds, and condense his thought into a call to think and live differently.

How exactly does the phrase "the middle" secure the atmosphere of Deleuze's system? This question can only be answered by seeing how Deleuze contrasts his slogan with an entirely different kind of middle: "The middle is by no means an average; on the contrary, it is where things pick up speed."[17] By "average" Deleuze means the way identification with familiar, preexisting reference points diminishes thought's power. In other words, Deleuze's use of "average" carries with it both the word's numerical and normative connotations.

Deleuze's distinction between philosophical events and "debate" illuminates the middle as average. An established position anticipates, and in this sense preestablishes, its inverse. A debate is initiated when someone identifies with this inverse. Others then participate in the debate through identification with one of the two positions. For Deleuze, those most responsible for turning the debate into an obligatory reference point are the ones who position themselves as reconcilers: it is the compromise, the "average," or "middle-of-the-road" position, that establishes "what we call orthodoxy."[18] Part of what Deleuze means by "dialectical" is this interminable logic and practice of position and counter-position, reconciliation and opposition to the reconciliation, and so on.

In contrast to the middle as average, Deleuze's "middle" indicates, albeit in an ambient fashion, thought freed from the goal of explanatory closure. For Deleuze this goal is in reality a series of illusions which lead philosophy to fulfill its creative vocation in a diluted manner. The rhizome grows from the middle in the sense that none of its elements are intended to be terminal points (origins or final causes) in an epistemological chain of propositions. Additionally, Deleuze's "middle" encourages us to cultivate an attitude of critical indifference toward the fashionable, attention-seeking gesture of declaring a beginning or end. What do social criticism and the history of ideas gain by mimicking the drama and rhetoric of an obituary: the end of history, the end of philosophy, the end of theory, the end of ideology, the end of man, the end of literature, the end of the book, the end of cinema, the end of the intellectual?

3   The middle as becoming

A wave rolling across Deleuze's system, the slogan of the middle is shaped and reshaped by the contours of the various conceptual reefs it travels across. By surrounding a particular concept the slogan takes on a positive character (i.e. becomes irreducible to critique). In the case of the concept of becoming Deleuze and Guattari write: "A line of becoming is not defined by points that it connects, or by points that compose it; on the contrary, it passes *between* points, it comes up through the middle."[19]

Nothing prepares readers for their first encounter with Deleuze's concept of becoming. That includes the knowledge that Bergson used "becoming," "duration," and "qualitative multiplicity" interchangeably. After all, Bergson does not write about becoming a child, becoming an animal, or becoming a rock. At first it can seem as if Deleuze is advocating some enigmatic process of transmogrification. Evidence to the contrary is provided by numerous concrete examples, especially in his work with Guattari.[20]

Since becomings are described as in-between we should identify what they are between (what they are in the middle of). Term number one, the so-called subject of the becoming, is in fact the middle as average: a well-defined, dominant organization. This organization can be a regimentation of thought, of bodies, of perception, or discourse; it can be a rigidly structured life or the rigid side of a life. In Deleuze and Guattari's work, these entrenched structures are often labeled "territories," "organisms," or "majoritarian" formations – language that cuts across the distinction between thoughts and bodies, an individual and a group.

One of the great themes of Deleuze's philosophy is life's irreducibility to dominant territories. Becomings *are* the thoughts and deeds that exceed entrenched structures. Becomings have as their first terms the organizations they displace to varying degrees. But a becoming should not be confused with the inverse or negation of this first term. While the first term is the "subject" of the becoming, the concept of becoming does not fit comfortably within the theme of the death of the subject. The difference of becomings is irreducible to opposition, transgression, or contradiction: "a social field does not contradict itself, but first and foremost leaks out on all sides."[21]

A becoming is a process comprised of disorganization *and* reorganization. The second term – the "zone of proximity" or "medium of becoming" – plays a crucial role in this reorganization. The names Deleuze and Guattari give to becomings (e.g. "becoming-animal") reflect the standard way of classifying the second term (an external object). But a "becoming" is not a matter of the first term becoming equivalent to the second. Additionally, describing a becoming as a matter of the first term pretending to be the second obfuscates the innovation at work. Mimicry is a strictly negative definition of a becoming (to say that x is pretending to be y is to say that x is not y). In reality, a "becoming" is the construction of an organization heterogeneous to the first term accomplished using the second term as a point of reference. Becomings can be ephemeral or lasting, cautious or reckless. From a political standpoint they can be consequential or inconsequential. At the same time, genuine change presupposes and implies becomings. Becomings are a necessary condition for and index of any reorganization of social life.

Two documentaries – Werner Herzog's *Grizzly Man* and Judy Irving's *Wild Parrots of Telegraph Hill* – are useful for understanding what a becoming (in particular a becoming-animal) involves, as well as for differentiating becomings from pseudo-becomings. Herzog's subject – the doomed Timothy Treadwell – heads into the wilderness. Once there, he films and anthropomorphizes the inhabitants while narcissistically and erroneously elevating himself into the role of protector of the bears. That Herzog gravitates toward Treadwell's story is explained by his own conception of the creative process: the overcoming of extreme obstacles in the name of a personal vision. In many respects – cinematography, narration, the music, and so on – Herzog's film is the superior of the two. However, in a Deleuzian sense, Treadwell's story is devoid of a middle, a becoming, or a voyage. There is only the geographical movement of a subject with all of his neuroses.

In contrast, there is the quiet but moving story of Mark Bittner. Irving's film relays how, following a fortuitous urban encounter and subsequent encounters with a flock of wild parrots, Bittner gradually reorganizes his entire life. This reorganization – this becoming-animal – unfolds in the middle of his previous life and the inspiring flock. Friends and strangers bear witness, but at the same time the quiet, nontheatrical character of the becoming confers upon its imperceptibility: "The man of becoming: to look at him, one would notice nothing."[22] Irving's subject obsessively discerns rather than fabricates the mannerisms and physical qualities of each bird. Instead of elevating his importance to the flock he declares (before the city council) that, in his absence, the animals should be left alone. The birds can care for themselves.

For Deleuze philosophical apprenticeship takes the form of becomings. We encounter objects that force us to think differently. For the student of philosophy, some of the most important objects are the books provided by the history of philosophy. Like any becoming, philosophical becomings should not be confused with critique or transgression (i.e. they are not simply the negation of our established way of thinking). Like any becoming, philosophical becomings should not be confused with imitation. An encounter with Deleuze's philosophy, not to mention a reactualization of Deleuze's philosophy, has nothing to do with imitating Deleuze's language.

Thinking and writing in the middle involves a precise ideal, one obscured by the distinction between interpretation and misinterpretation, as well as by the distinction between banal misreading and creative misreading. Each of Deleuze's formulations of this ideal brings together two notions often regarded as mutually exclusive: fidelity and invention, repetition and difference. On more than one occasion, Deleuze declares the history of philosophy should be a practice akin to portraiture: "You can do the portrait of a thought just as you can do the portrait of a man."[23] He defines a portrait as the production of a likeness in a different medium. Similarly, Deleuze states a good commentary should function like the figure of the double. In literature, the figure of the doppelganger combines repetition with a maximum degree of difference: "One imagines a *philosophically* bearded Hegel, a *philosophically* clean-shaven Marx, in the same way as a mustached Mona Lisa."[24] A third formulation of the ideal is that commentaries should be perverse, surprising affairs: "I saw myself as taking the author from behind and giving him a child that would be his own."[25]

Implicit in each analogy are the two styles of reading to avoid. On the one hand, one should avoid producing interpretations in which the subject could just as well have been some other figure: "It was really important for it to be his own child, because the author had to actually say all I had him saying." Similarly, asked about his book on Foucault, Deleuze declares: "I've tried to do a portrait of his philosophy. The lines or touches are of course mine, but they succeed only if he himself comes to haunt the picture."[26] On the other hand, one should avoid producing interpretations that confuse the need for mediators or "zones of proximity" with mimicry or representation: "But the child was bound to be monstrous too, because it resulted from all sorts of shifting, slipping, dislocations, and hidden emissions that I really enjoyed."[27]

4 Deleuze's problem, differential, or abstract machine

A philosophical problem is grasped through the practices of reading and writing. On the one hand, one encounters one or more of the philosophy's expressions and thinks the philosophy through these expressions. On the other hand, one can create a new, written expression of the philosophy. In fact, the two practices are mutually dependent. Poor readers produce caricatures, never actualizations. The philosophy's identity is irreducible to its present actualizations; the problem possesses a future, a future not already given (i.e. determined by present conditions). This irreducibility to the actual is not grasped through contemplation, but through a highly disciplined creative act (the production of an actualization).

I want to end Part I by defining Deleuze's problem. This task is best accomplished by focusing on one of the problem's expressions. The one I am choosing is Deleuze's first becoming or portrait.[28] In *David Hume: His Life and Work* (1952), *Empiricism and Subjectivity: An Essay on Hume's Theory of Human Nature* (1953), and *Instincts and Institutions* (1953), Deleuze engineered a Humean expression of his problem. As a differential, rhizome, or complex curve the problem cannot be conveyed through a question or proposition. The problem is an assemblage of five acts of thought or ways of thinking: the thought of incommensurability, the subordination of critique to production, the reformulation of identity and difference, the act of thinking the social positively, and the act of thinking the body as a concrete mixture of heterogeneous series of organizations. In Deleuze's writings this differential is actualized in diverse ways. Whenever any of its components are ignored, Deleuze's philosophy is severely distorted.

4.1 The thought of incommensurability

Hume's skeptical demonstrations (of reason's inability to found values or trigger action, of the absence of necessary connections within sensation, etc.) are often discussed independently of what he referred to as his "skeptical solutions to these doubts" (i.e. his skeptical solution to skepticism).[29] The omission is regrettable given Hume's consistent and elegant refusal to play the part of devil's advocate in either ethics or epistemology, not to mention the fact that many of the skeptical arguments commonly attributed to him were already present in the writings of Berkeley and Malebranche.[30]

A striking feature of Deleuze's treatment of Hume is the extent to which he undermines this influential caricature of Hume as an essentially negative thinker. Deleuze convincingly presents the skeptical side of Hume's project as simply the destructive prerequisite for the formulation of a new problem and new concepts. As Deleuze would later make clear in a 1972 essay on Hume, his objective is to depict Hume and rationalism (or Hume and Descartes) as incommensurable.[31] Deleuze repudiates the tendency to define empiricism as rationalism's inverse: Hume does not argue that the intelligible is reducible to the sensible (he does not argue that the understanding is reducible to experience). In *Empiricism and Subjectivity*, philosophy is defined as the practice of inventing problems, individual philosophies are defined as problems, and Hume's thought is associated with a specific problem (a curve whose more dramatic points are the view that the subject is constructed, the definition of the subject as a system of habits, and the idea that a habit is produced through the association of disparate impressions and ideas of sensation).

In Bergson's work the distinction between false and true problems is, at the same time, the distinction between preexisting problems (or debates) and the creation of a new problem and its solution: "stating the problem is not simply uncovering, it is inventing."[32] Unlike the answer to an exam question (an answer that already exists in the instructor's solution manual) or the solution to a preexisting problem (a solution that already exists as a possible way of solving the problem), the solution to a true problem is radically new. Echoing Bergson, Deleuze describes philosophy as the invention of problems because it immediately suggests that the history of philosophy is marked by incommensurability and novelty.

Deleuze's study of the literature of Sacher-Masoch relative to de Sade parallels his treatment of Hume relative to Descartes. In *Coldness and Cruelty*, Deleuze argues these two bodies of literature as well as their nominal derivatives (sadism and masochism), represent incommensurable, incompatible universes.[33] De Sade's protagonists do not find their complement in the masochist any more than Masoch's protagonist in *Venus in Furs* is searching for a genuine sadist. Similarly, in *Difference and Repetition*, Deleuze presents Platonism and Aristotelianism as incommensurable by subordinating their answers to the question, "What is a universal?" to their fundamentally distinct practices of division.

He cautions us against "trying to understand Platonic division on the basis of Aristotelian requirements."[34] On the one hand, there is the hierarchical division of particulars into representations and pseudo-representations (or simulacra). On the other hand, there is the determination of a generic concept through the identification of its species.

While the thought of incommensurability is one of the defining features of Deleuze's problem or differential, it is simply one component. Deleuze's philosophy is not adequately defined as a philosophy of incommensurability. The incommensurability of different philosophies does represent a radical difference within the history of philosophy. But Deleuze does not think that radical difference within the history of philosophy is always a difference between philosophies. For Deleuze an individual philosophy is itself a radical difference: the problem is a differential structure, and the problem permits heterogeneous expressions. Then there is the peculiar status of portraiture. Deleuze's philosophy is not Hume's philosophy. At the same time, one expression of Deleuze's philosophy is the portrait of Hume's philosophy. And this portrait of Hume's philosophy is not something external to the philosophy. Deleuze's portrait is a new actualization of Hume's philosophy. Two philosophies can be radically different and can converge. This convergence, however, does not take the form of a conversation, let alone a debate. Just as individuals come together and share moments of their life, so the lives of two philosophies can share an actualization.

4.2   The place of critique

Aspects of Deleuze's work on Hume's philosophy can be seen as anticipating what currently goes by the name of anti-foundationalism, poststructuralism, or theoretical postmodernism. Let me briefly summarize the relevant portions of Deleuze's interpretation. First, he presents Hume's bracketing of origins as a rejection of representation. Hume's argument that impressions of sensation should be regarded "as if" they were innate becomes a challenge to the belief that the understanding consists of the mind duplicating nature. Second, the contention that the understanding's habitual relations are not derived from the episodic impressions and ideas of sensation becomes in Deleuze's hands a critique of interiority. Third, Hume's description of general ideas as constructions becomes the position of antiessentialism. Fourth, Deleuze contests the view that Hume's distinction between relations of ideas and matters of fact is a forerunner to the analytic/synthetic distinction. Deleuze's Hume undercuts the doctrine of analyticity by treating every relation as a synthetic act, canceling in the process the idea of self-explanatory judgments. No less than "matters of fact," the act of asserting a "relation of ideas" cannot be explained without remainder by the content of the terms. Acts of reasoning are a function of ends established by passion or sentiment.

This plausible and intriguing portrait of Hume as anti-foundationalist plays a strictly preliminary role within Deleuze's act of portraiture. Hume the opponent of representation, internal relations, essences, and transcendent values is subsumed under a more general portrait of Hume as the engineer of a tremendous positive undertaking. From the absence of relations within impressions and ideas of sensation we move to the existence of relations as impressions and ideas of reflection (from atomism to associationism). From the attack on representational conceptions of understanding (sensations as copies of a mind-independent world) we move to the intelligible as a system of habitual relations. The rejection of values transcending human reality gives way to an account of how human sentiment along with a naturally partial, natural sympathy is the true source of value (i.e. Hume repudiates the rationalist *and* skeptical tendency to frame the debate over the existence of moral principles in terms of an opposition between transcendent principles and human emotions). The denial of transcendent values becomes in Humean ethics an examination of the basis for the general, artificial rules comprising the social.

Deleuze locates Hume's singularity in the way his skeptical impulse is the groundwork for a separate, constructive endeavor. This facilitates us grasping how Deleuze consistently thinks of critique as subordinate to production. Recognizing this tendency as a second component of his problem or differential is crucial for understanding his relationship to the themes of anti-philosophy and anti-foundationalism.

In their book on the literature of Kafka, Deleuze and Guattari combine a question with an invitation:

> Is there hope for philosophy, which for a long time has been an official, referential genre? Let us profit from this moment in which anti-philosophy is trying to be a language of power.[35]

On the one hand, the anti-philosophical climate is presented as an invaluable resource and unique opportunity. On the other hand, the phrase "language of power" provides a measure of distance between the goals of the authors and this environment. This ambivalence can be developed by way of a modest detour through the logic of desire and its repression developed in *Anti-Oedipus*. Drastically recasting the language of desire, Deleuze and Guattari's notion of repression has little or nothing to do with barring mental contents from consciousness or with preventing the transparent, outward expression of a preexisting, natural principle. The repression of desire is for Deleuze and Guattari the production of docile subjects through a series of mechanisms referred to as desire's paralogisms. Just as Kant used the notion of paralogism to come up with a positive account of metaphysics (i.e. metaphysics is not simply defined as false or unjustified belief), so Deleuze and Guattari employ the notion of paralogism to capture the production of a climate of resignation under advanced capitalism. The name they give to this climate is "Oedipus."

Along the same lines "desiring-production" or the "machinic unconscious" is not a natural substance (a "lost totality") awaiting liberation.[36] For Deleuze and Guattari the unconscious is a project, something that must be created rather than a preexisting interior: "the issue is to produce the unconscious."[37] Here, the use of the word "unconscious" serves the unorthodox, materialist purpose of delegitimating every account of desire that severs it from the issue of the organization of bodies ("unconscious" means irreducible to interiority). Artaud's screams and references to the body-without-organs, the connections Klossowski establishes between Nietzsche's thought and physical condition, Spinoza's conjoining of the mind's power and the body's all pave the way toward understanding desire as the simultaneous reorganization of a body and lived experience.

What does this theory of desire have to do with Deleuze's relationship to foundationalism and its inverse? In the course of an interview, Deleuze remarked that philosophy, while relatively insignificant from the standpoint of repression, does have its own version of the "Oedipus complex."[38] This comment needs to be given real weight. We should ask: "What form do the Oedipal paralogisms assume within philosophy?" I would argue that many of the gestures associated with a robust sense of "foundationalism" operate precisely according to Deleuze and Guattari's paralogisms of desire. Most of all, I suggest Deleuze and Guattari's reference to anti-philosophy becoming a "language of power" is a proposal that we prevent the critique of foundationalism from itself operating as a paralogism of desire within philosophy.

More than any other paralogism of desire it is the double-impasse that evokes the logic of foundationalism.[39] According to Deleuze and Guattari, psychoanalysis implements this paralogism through its menu of unattractive existential options: psychosis or neurosis, the chaos of nondifferentiation or the established lines of determination (male body possessing active/masculine gender seeks female body possessing passive/feminine gender; female body possessing passive/feminine gender seeks male body possessing active/masculine gender). More generally, the "double-impasse" describes the manner in which dominant organizations maintain an air of legitimacy through the construction of a fraudulent outside. Similarly, a foundationalist account is a rhetorical movement through which a perspective is advanced as the only legitimate account, the only genuine solution. "Look at things this way or be in error." Historically *logos* is figured as a double-impasse when two and only two directions for thought are granted: either thought is oriented toward universals (thought as logos), or it is devoid of all rigor, precision, and order. Names given to this chaotic state include "nonsense," "the irrational," "relativism," and "poetry." The notion of the double-impasse highlights the fact that these names are not so much inhabited positions, as they are an outside intrinsic to and fabricated alongside of foundationalist theories.

A related, institutional form of the double-impasse is academic philosophy's imposition of obligatory reference points. Here, the paralogism of the double-impasse incorporates three others: extrapolation, biunivocal application, and the afterward.[40] Deleuze and Guattari describe how psychoanalysis posits a foundational center of desire ("extrapolation"), imposes familial coordinates on every social investment ("biunivocal application"), and treats an analysand's present discontent as an expression of an unresolved past ("the afterward"). Similarly, when academic philosophy operates as Oedipus it establishes a canon of major works or prerequisites; all other texts are positioned as minor or secondary. Deleuze describes his own experiences with this technique of diminishing philosophy's power:

> I belong to a generation, one of the last generations, that was more or less bludgeoned to death with the history of philosophy. The history of philosophy plays a patently repressive role in philosophy, it's philosophy's own version of the Oedipus complex: "You can't seriously consider saying what you yourself think until you've read this and that, and that on this, and this on that."[41]

Against this use of philosophy's history, Deleuze encourages positive, rigorous reactualizations of philosophy's past. This past includes theories deemed canonical. But reactualizations of these are becomings (i.e. they are lines of flight relative to professional philosophy).

A final form of foundationalism's double-impasse within philosophy occurs whenever a particular mode of writing is elevated to the status of a norm. "Write in this fashion or be guilty of irresponsibility or nonsense." The most obvious flaw with this gesture is that it is predicated upon an amnesia of sorts. Either the history of philosophical writing is assumed to be homogeneous, or philosophers' words are treated as mere accoutrement for groups of propositions.

There is a sense in which, among contemporary thinkers, Deleuze places the least emphasis on a philosopher's choice of words and syntax including his own. He does, however, have a specific term for the lexicon and form of a philosophical text – taste.[42] "Taste" denotes the diverse linguistic strategies employed in the course of baptizing concepts. If we conventionally refer to philosophical texts as if they inhabit natural languages (the original language and the language of translations), we should also take note of how the philosopher's conceptual production makes these languages stammer or take flight. Just as Plato incorporated moments of confusion within the drama of his dialogues (Socrates' conversations being illustrations of a particular way of speaking or writing philosophy), so philosophical texts, bearers of new concepts, invariably disorient the reader. Sometimes this disorientation is immediate; sometimes, as a result of the employment of a conversational idiom, it is deferred.

This notion of taste is important because it erases every rigid differentiation of form and content (concepts have names, philosophies are actualized within peculiar texts), because it casts light on the diverse array of tastes exhibited within the history of philosophy (the idea that there is *a way* of writing philosophy is inane), *and* because it prevents philosophies from being construed as simply modes of writing. Deleuze distinguishes between taste and style in philosophy. The philosophical justification for a particular taste (its "strange necessity") can only be the modest role it plays in advancing a philosopher's style. "Style" involves taste but is not taste. "Style" denotes the movement of thought through and between concepts on a plane of immanence. Style in philosophy is the substitution of a new problem for the old, the production of a movement of discontinuity or incommensurability within philosophy.

More than any other philosophical movement, tracing the first instance of the double-impasse within philosophy has been the province of deconstruction. Some have never forgiven Derrida this sin of demystification – the sin of identifying the movement through which a text engenders an aura of self-evidence. Little surprise that in recent times the second and third forms of the double-impasse have been directed toward deconstruction more than any other orientation. The lazy represent deconstruction as thought's hostile, irrational, relativistic, nonsensical, exterior.

But as I have hinted Deleuze and Guattari suggest anti-philosophy is not itself immune from becoming a language of power – a device for restricting philosophical creativity. What would this involve? Here the last of desire's paralogisms – disfigurement or displacement – comes into play. Deleuze and Guattari describe psychoanalytic interpretation as not simply misinterpreting desire, but as repressing it through misinterpretation. Given the constructionist character of their theory, this is equivalent to saying that psychoanalytic discourse ("the repressing representation") reduces physical and intellectual creativity ("the repressed representative") through fraudulent, oedipal representations ("the displaced represented").[43] Anti-foundationalism, an absolutely indispensable internal critique of philosophy, becomes a mode of repression (a repressing representation), when it shuts down philosophical production (the repressed representative) through the image of foundationalism (the displaced represented). This involves collapsing positive, affirmative modes of philosophical address – be it metaphilosophy or metaphysics – onto the territory of foundationalism. Just as the psychoanalyst construes the body's actions as symptoms of familial desire, so the anti-foundationalist labels every positive form of thought a symptom of foundationalism. As a result of this move, only one nonfoundational form of creation appears viable. The only legitimate form of creativity is a creative critique of foundationalism. Deleuze's incommensurability lies in the way his philosophy encompasses anti-foundationalism, without being, at bottom, a reply to foundationalism. Instead of being a critique of self-evidence, Deleuzian thought challenges common sense all the while assigning philosophy an affirmative (albeit still anti-foundational) mission.[44]

4.3   Rethinking identity and difference

Against interpretations foregrounding Hume's atomism (his critique of the idea that cause-and-effect, necessity, and general kinds are internal relations), Deleuze emphasizes the notion of the externality of relations. Hume does not reject the language of causality and necessity, he shifts its basis. There are no impressions of sensation corresponding to expressions such as "necessarily," "always," and "cause" (there is no sensation corresponding to a necessary connection). But our continued use of the expressions – even in the face of skeptical arguments – reflects the fact that their true nature and origin lie elsewhere. The expressions denote habits formed when the principles of association synthesize the disparate impressions and ideas of sensation.

The principle theme of *Empiricism and Subjectivity* is that, in Hume's philosophy, the critique of internal relations exists alongside of this theory of external relations. The norm is to position the outside of a particular structure (be it intellectual or social) as chaos or the lack of order. The Deleuzian message is that structure, unity, order, or systematicity can be thought in any number of ways. By extension, there is no single way to think difference or the relationship between identity and difference. Typically identity is envisioned as a simple principle lying beneath difference (as in the traditional notion of substance or species-essence). But, for Deleuze, identity can and should be thought of as a principle composed of difference.

4.4 The social as site of invention

The distinction between instincts and institutions is a constant in Deleuze's writings from the early 1950s. Initially the analysis accompanying the distinction seems to situate Deleuze's thought in a distinctly humanistic arena. Both the concept of instincts and that of institutions seem to turn upon the idea of innate human tendencies striving for gratification.[45] The notion of instinct is the idea of natural drives directly and naturally satisfying themselves. In contrast, institutions, in the sense of institutionalized modes of behavior, are defined as indirect, oblique, or artificial means of satisfying natural tendencies. Reading carefully, however, one can discern how, for Deleuze, the concept of institution facilitates a specific form of antihumanism in the area of social theory.

Deleuze locates the concept of institution in Hume's account of the artificial or social virtues and in the related notion of general rule (conformity to general rules are the artificial virtues). In the unique ethical-political horizon that is Hume's philosophy, a general rule is a rule of conduct deemed beneficial to the public good (at least most of the time). Natural instincts, in particular our natural sociability, are a necessary condition for the general rule. For Hume, we are naturally concerned about the welfare and happiness of others, we know others are similarly concerned, and we know everyone's natural sympathy is naturally partial (i.e. each is more concerned about some than others). But according to Hume this natural sympathy does not account for the specific character of general rules and thus of society proper. He identifies the gap between the social and natural instincts with the cultural and historical relativity of customs and laws:

> I need not mention the variations, which all the rules of property receive from the finer tunes and connexions of the imagination, and

from the subtleties and abstractions of law-topics and reasonings. There is no possibility of reconciling this observation to the notion of original instincts.[46]

For Deleuze, the importance of the concept of institution lies precisely in the way it restricts the explanatory power of the notion of human nature. Deleuze, like Hume, represents the social as a plurality of institutions. What this means is that natural drives, even a natural concern for the public good, cannot account for a single social norm. As Deleuze writes in *Empiricism and Subjectivity*:

> Take, for example, *one* form of marriage, or *one* system of property. Why *this* system and *this* form? A thousand others, which we find in other times and places are possible.[47]

Deleuze also distinguishes between a theory of the institution and a theory of the law.[48] Theories of law are associated with negative conceptions of the social (whether Hobbesian or psychoanalytic). The social is defined as a contractual restriction, transfer, or sublimation of natural rights or powers. In sharp contrast, the concept of institutions affords a positive depiction of the social. Theorizing a social practice as an institution means that even when the institution is presented as a means to a natural end, it is simultaneously presented as irreducible to this function. The social cannot be explained in terms of a logically prior, pre-social, natural state (be it human nature or a state of nature).

Just as Deleuze finds in Hume a positive conception of the social (one in which negativity is secondary), so Deleuze's own social and political theory is eminently positive. Failure to recognize this fourth component of Deleuze's differential has led to horrendous readings of *Anti-Oedipus*. In terms introduced above, these readings mistake Deleuze and Guattari's theory of desire for a theory of law. The reasoning behind this error goes something like this: Deleuze and Guattari refer repeatedly to "desire;" moreover they contend that capitalism, the nuclear family, and psychoanalysis all "repress desire;" therefore, Deleuze and Guattari believe in a natural, preexisting substance called "desire" that is then suppressed by the social machine of capitalism.

But in the early pages of *Anti-Oedipus*, the authors make abundantly clear that the notion of desiring-production and its repression is a theory of institutions rather than a theory of law. Desiring-production, the revolutionary unconscious, or "the body-without-organs" is "not an original primordial entity" or "lost totality" outside of or preceding the social; it is something that must be invented within the order of advanced capitalism.[49] Deleuze and Guattari's account of the repression of desire is elucidated as a different, "transcendent" use of the same syntheses constituting desiring-production. In short, the capitalist social field is depicted, not as the negation of a preexisting substance, but as a battleground of conflicting institutions, or better yet, as two heterogeneous series of institutions.

4.5   The body as site of creativity and risk

In a section of *Instincts and Institutions*, Deleuze suggests the reader might consider the distinction between law and institution to be a political yardstick.[50] The ratio of tyranny to democracy is directly proportional to the ratio of laws to institutions. But I just referred to the social as the site of competing institutions, not as a mixture of laws and institutions. That Deleuze's distinction between laws and institutions is ultimately replaced by the distinction between kinds of institutions is easy to miss.

Perhaps the most famous feature of Hume's notion of general rules is his critique of the idea that their genesis can be explained in terms of a verbal agreement. For Hume, a more satisfactory and concrete explanation draws upon the numerous instances in which human beings coordinate their actions independently of a verbal promise. Hume, however, simply replaces one abstract scenario with another. His explanation of norms and laws is textbook ideology: abstract individuals invent rules for the sake of the common good. Most of the time Hume's references to human happiness serve to conceal inequality and authoritarian structures. However, at other times, he directly legitimates these structures by describing how reason checks our initial disapproval of them. Hume as the voice of reason "reminds" the readers that history and experience show that absolute equality is ultimately harmful to the public good.[51]

In signature fashion Deleuze's portrait bypasses all of the flaws, the abstractions, and reactionary arguments in Hume's thought in order to radicalize the concept of general rule. This is first accomplished by treating the social as a positive field. Because it is comprised of rules that are invented, the social is through and through a creation. Then, in the following passage from *Instincts and Institutions*, Deleuze erases Hume's abstract justification for general rules:

> What is more, if needs find in the institution only a very indirect satisfaction, an oblique satisfaction, it is not enough to say the "institution is useful," one must still ask the question: useful for whom? For

all those who have needs? Or just for a few (the privileged class)? Or only for those who control the institution (the bureaucracy)?[52]

In this way, the explanation of institutions is made to require a discussion of different groups, and the political yardstick becomes not the ratio of laws to institutions but the ratio of different institutional series.

In another key passage from the same text, Deleuze defines the institution as a "model of action" inscribed "on our bodies."[53] Distinguishing between the different institutional series is therefore a matter of distinguishing different modes of organizing bodies. The dominant institutional series involves the perpetual construction of organisms or closed functional systems (what Foucault calls "docile bodies"). The second institutional series is comprised of what Deleuze would come to call "becomings" or "bodies without organs." Every institution as an institution is thoroughly positive. Every institution is an invention. No institution can be adequately represented as an instantiation of a pre-existing, natural order. But only some institutions embody creativity in a richer sense of the word. These are the institutions or organizations that demonstrate life's irreducibility to normalizing classifications and directives.

Deleuzian thought encourages us to perceive the social as a perpetually open, nontotalizable system comprised of dominant institutions as well as cracks or leaks in the form of alternative institutions. As becomings these leaks may contain moments of straightforward opposition and antagonism but are ultimately modes of organization discontinuous with the first series. Deleuze turns Spinoza's declaration "no one knows what the body can do" into an ethico-political slogan. Our bodies are a particular ratio of organism to body-without-organs. Deleuzian thought encourages us to cautiously increase the proportion of the latter relative to the former.

Part II
Theatre of Operations

Three categories have governed the dominant, academic reception of Deleuze's thought: "postmodernism," "post-structuralism," and "continental philosophy." But the association between Deleuze and these categories tends to go in one direction. While the name "Deleuze" frequently evokes the categories, the categories do not typically evoke the name "Deleuze" (or do so with considerable less frequency than they do the names "Derrida," "Foucault," or "Lyotard"). Moreover, references to Deleuze within discussions of the categories have rarely been accompanied by an engagement with his philosophy. The name "Deleuze" appears as a vacant conjunct: "and Deleuze" or "Deleuze as well."[1]

How should one who believes in the importance and unique qualities of Deleuze's project respond to this impoverished reception? The obvious remedy is the production of scholarship that engages directly with Deleuze's philosophy. But should this remedy include or exclude references to the categories of "postmodernism," "post-structuralism," and "continental philosophy?" I would argue for their provisional inclusion. The goal should not be a better, more complete formulation of the categories. Nor should the goal be that of latching Deleuze's name more securely to fashionable expressions.

As Sartre would say, to write is to write in a situation. Writing on a philosophy, one's situation is partially defined by preexisting interpretations, and some of these interpretations exert more pressure than others. One can accept or contest a dominant interpretation; one can propose an alternative to a dominant interpretation. What one should not do is pretend that the dominant interpretations do not exist.[2] Deleuze's assertion that the typical reading is closer to a nonreading is an intervention. His intention is to foster an awareness of the way clichés obscure the most prominent features of philosophies – in short, to make us better readers. The clichés surrounding Deleuze's work are particularly tenacious. When teaching Deleuze's philosophy one quickly discovers the need to acknowledge the habitual associations at the outset, if only, so they may be securely placed in abeyance.

The dominant reception of Deleuze's thought is simply one manifestation of a classificatory machine within the disciplinary apparatus of philosophy. The categories of "postmodernism," "post-structuralism," "continental philosophy," as well as their accompaniments ("analytic philosophy," "Anglo-American philosophy," "critical theory," and "hermeneutics") shape how philosophy is envisioned, read, and practiced. They influence the titles of courses offered by departments and shape how professional philosophers market themselves and their work.

The classificatory machine positions Deleuze's work as peripheral. At the same time, the machine does not have a monopoly on how Deleuze's philosophy is experienced. There are also encounters with Deleuze's philosophy. In *Proust and Signs*, Deleuze defines "encounter" by stating that every encounter is the encounter of a sign. The Deleuzian sign is less a thing than an atypical form of disclosure.[3] To show up as a sign is to show up as *atopos* or as something exceeding recognition: "I recognize this is a madelaine, but there's something peculiar about it."[4] The sign is an interruption of spontaneous, habitual ways of thinking.

Reworking philosophical modalities, Deleuze describes the encounter as a necessary condition for necessity. Thought's power does not increase by becoming free of outside influence. Against the notion of the "goodwill of thinking," Deleuze argues that necessary thought is always under the influence. It is under the influence of a sign or Outside: "impressions that force us to look, encounters that force us to interpret, expressions that force us to think."[5] To be necessary is to bear the mark of urgency: "Now that was a book that *had* to be written," or "I *had* to put everything down on paper." Conversely, unforced, spontaneous thought is contingent: "truths remain arbitrary and abstract so long as they are based on the goodwill of thinking."[6] Reflecting not a Deleuzian middle but an average, these are the texts that strike us as superfluous. They are contingent in the sense they could just as well not have been written, and perhaps should not have been.

Deleuze describes love – the experience of falling in love – as the collision with a sign:

> It may be that friendship is nourished on observation and conversation, but love is born from and nourished on silent interpretation. The beloved appears as a sign…the beloved expresses a possible

world unknown to us, implying, enveloping, imprisoning a world that must be deciphered, that is, interpreted.[7]

Falling in love with Deleuze's philosophy, the thought is not "Deleuze is a postmodernist" but "What is this thing?" One comes under the influence; one reads obsessively; one is painfully aware of being outside of the system, of not yet being a part of the philosophy's life.

In Part I, Deleuze's philosophy was described as a signature problem – an abstract differential that was actualized in diverse ways throughout his body of work. Here in Part II, Deleuze's thought will be described as a sign relative to a specific structure (the average, professional way of thinking what philosophy is and could be). When Deleuze's work is encountered, thought organized by the classificatory machine assumes the position of a subject of becoming: the established organization that is destabilized. Deleuze's philosophy is the becoming's second term: a reference point. Not for imitation, but for the disruption and creative reorganization of thought. This second account of Deleuze's system is in the middle of, or in-between the classificatory machine and Deleuze's thought.

Explaining how and why Deleuze's system serves as a mediator of becoming will at the same time throw into relief the system's characters. Deleuze asserts that every philosophy is populated by "conceptual personae."[8] Little surprise, then, that Deleuze's own philosophy is a heavily populated affair. There is the philosopher, the academic, the scientist, the historian, the artist, the pervert, the schizo, the neurotic, the noble structuralist, the slavish structuralist, the noble phenomenologist, the slavish phenomenologist, the detective, the American novelist, the American philosopher, and the French philosopher. These are the players in Deleuze's philosophical theatre. Their relationship is not always one of peaceful coexistence. Deleuze's theatre is a theatre of operations: he produces a drama and engages in combat. He invokes the stage *and* guerilla warfare.[9]

1   The exclusive disjunctive synthesis of professional philosophy

Anti-Oedipus and *A Thousand Plateaus* include a detailed analysis of the practice of identification or classification. More precisely, they include an analysis of two basic forms of identification or classification: the inclusive and exclusive forms of desire's disjunctive synthesis. The schizo is described as possessing a unique recording apparatus. Despite the risks involved, there is a refusal to identify with dominant categories *or* there is a subversive use of those categories: "It might be said that the schizophrenic passes from one code to the other, that he deliberately *scrambles all the codes*."[10] Spinoza is the exemplary schizo philosopher: Is he an atheist or the author of a coherent theism, is he the destroyer of Cartesianism or the advocate of consistent Cartesianism, is he a heretical materialist or an extreme idealist? These are useful questions *if* the disjunctions are presented as inclusive disjunctions. Deleuze's code or disjunctive synthesis is similarly inclusive: is Deleuze a philosopher of difference or a philosopher of unity, does Deleuze destroy or redirect the notion of substance, does Deleuze undo or redirect essentialism, is Deleuze the demolisher of Platonism or its proponent? Only by answering "yes" to each part of each question are we able to approximate Deleuze's philosophy.

In contrast, Oedipus or repression is the exclusive or restrictive use of desire's disjunctive synthesis. Identification is equivalent to negation: x or y but not both, to be x is to not be y. Things are put in their place (assigned to a "molar term"). We put ourselves in place. This mode of classification is so entrenched ("we are so molded by Oedipus") we regard it as classification in general: we find it "hard to imagine" a disjunction "that remains disjunctive, and that still affirms the disjoined terms."[11]

Molar classification or exclusive disjunctive synthesis possesses a totalizing impulse. Every object must have its category, its proper place. There may be moments of uncertainty. But this does not mean the object is positioned as radically other: "A ha! It's not a man and it's not a woman, so it must be a transvestite."[12] The classificatory machine rests upon an unspoken metaphysical assumption: the absence of radical novelty. Granted, the philosophy does not belong to this category; it must, however, belong to some category. It must illustrate some preexisting orientation, realize some preexisting possibility or potentiality.

The exclusive use of the disjunctive synthesis does not simply take the form of binary division (x belongs to this category, y to that category). Molar terms often have a built-in standard. This standard is either the average of all members or the average of the ideal members. Thus the category of European has as its standard that of "your average ordinary White Man."[13] Members are then ranked in relation to their proximity or distance from this standard.[14] An object is not simply assigned to a category, it is assigned a place within that category.

1.1   The average post-structuralist, the average postmodernist

According to Deleuze, professional philosophy has its own versions of Oedipus or repression. These include discipline-specific exclusive disjunctions. "Postmodernism," "post-structuralism," and "continental philosophy," are each defined through opposition. These oppositions can be, but are not necessarily, hierarchical ones. Nevertheless, each category is organized hierarchically on the inside. Reconstructing or making visible the operative standards is challenging precisely because they are averages rather than members of their respective categories.

One might expect post-structuralism's opposing term to be structuralism. That the expression "post-structuralism" contains the word "structuralism" is not the only reason for this. In his majestic, two-volume history of structuralism, Francoise Dosse charts the emergence and dissemination of the expressions "structure" and "structuralism" in France. They grew to be ubiquitous features of intellectual life. Because of this, it would not have been surprising to find, in the same climate, the appearance of a category such as "post-structuralism." Moreover, one would even expect the category to be applied to precisely those thinkers who are typically classified as post-structuralist. After all, Derrida selected structuralist anthropology for deconstruction in "Structure, Sign, and Play in the Human Sciences," while Foucault stated "Neither Deleuze, nor Jean-Francois Lyotard, nor Guattari, nor I ever do structural analyses; we are absolutely not structuralists."[15]

But the category of post-structuralism is a North American invention. None of the French authors classified as post-structural ever identified with the category (not that this disqualifies it). The environment in which the category developed was one in which the term structuralism, not to mention the ideas associated with structuralism, had nowhere near the currency they did in France. This was particularly true for the discipline of philosophy. The exclusive disjunction is not "post-structuralist" or "structuralist" but "post-structuralist" or something else.

Unlike "post-structuralism," the notion of postmodernism does circulate in Europe. Nevertheless, as a term it is still for the most part a North American invention exported to France, the rest of Europe (in particular Germany and Italy), and parts of Central and South America. At very specific junctures within their intellectual itineraries, Lyotard and Baudrillard identified with the signifier "postmodern." Derrida and Foucault never did. Althusser, in his memoir *The Future Lasts Forever*, distinguishes the work of Derrida and Foucault (which he praises) from postmodernism (which he associates with political quietude).[16] Similarly, Guattari used "postmodern" as a pejorative, where, like Althusser, the central target was the work of Baudrillard. Sylvère Lotringer writes of Deleuze and Guattari: "They despised Baudrillard's ideas for 'demobilizing' people, turning them away from political action."[17]

The relationship between "postmodern" and "modern" parallels that between "post-structuralism" and "structuralism." Jameson's, Lyotard's, Habermas', and Huyssen's competing juxtapositions of theoretical post-modernism and cultural modernity represent exceptions rather than the rule. When "postmodern" denotes a way of theorizing rather than an architectural, literary, or cinematic style it does not typically involve an opposition to, or even consideration of cultural modernism. At first there was no consensus on how the categories postmodernism and post-structuralism (a later invention) should be related. The second was treated as a synonym for, as a subset of, and as incommensurable with the first.[18] But in the discipline of philosophy, the two terms quickly coalesced and become more or less interchangeable. "Postmodernism" and "post-structuralism" became indistinguishable molar terms. They became one term of an exclusive disjunction the other term of which was neither structuralism nor modernism. The average postmodernism, the average post-structuralism, is defined through opposition to foundationalism: postmodernism or foundationalism, post-structuralism or foundationalism.

Within anti-foundationalist discourse, "foundationalism" has two related senses. Because Cartesianism is commonly used to illustrate each form of foundationalism the exclusive disjunction "postmodernism" or "foundationalism" routinely becomes that of "postmodernism" or "Cartesianism" (the same goes with "post-structuralism"). A philosophy is labeled foundationalist if it incorporates or is claimed to provide the ideal of explanatory closure. As such this first sense of foundationalism is understood to have a metaphysical side (the commitment to essences, universals, and first principles), an epistemological side (the claim to have methodically grasped these first principles within consciousness), and a linguistic side (the image of the text as a transparent medium for the propositions derived from these acts of knowing). When the philosophy of language operates in a foundationalist manner, the registers of metaphysics and epistemology are collapsed into the linguistic. Essences are no longer first causes, universals, and so on, but determinate meanings; distinguishing the true from the false becomes distinguishing sense from nonsense. Thus, the average postmodernism or post-structuralism is a critique of the notion of grounding a body of propositions through the apodictic disclosure of first principles, and a critique of the view that the identity of philosophical texts is reducible to this propositional content.

"Foundationalism" also denotes the belief that philosophy, by engaging in foundationalism in the first sense, is capable of serving as a tribunal for the propositions engendered outside philosophy. As Richard Rorty points out in *Philosophy and the Mirror of Nature*, the chief occupants of this position during the twentieth century were Husserlian phenomenology and logical empiricism. For Husserl, knowledge or science was radically nonsubjective – the idea of science advanced in the *Logical Investigations* is that of a coherent body of fully justified, objective propositions. Nevertheless, such a science does have a subjective side, namely the acts of knowing providing evidence for the propositional content's veracity. Phenomenology, as a science of consciousness and thus of the knowing subject, is positioned as the legitimating ground for other research.

As for logical empiricism, one of its principal objectives was the bifurcation of discourse into regions of sense and nonsense, propositions and pseudo-propositions, by way of the principle of verification. The first region was in turn divided into sentences conveying analytic propositions (propositions verified through a consideration of the meanings of the words in the sentence) and sentences conveying synthetic propositions (propositions identified through a consideration of sentential meaning, but verified through a consideration of the proposition's empirical import). Following Carnap's reading of Heidegger, the logical empiricist treated the sentences in the second region as sentences possessing, at best, emotional or poetic significance.[19] Predictably, the meaning of "poetry" was not specified.

The most obvious vestige of the logical empiricist approach are current attempts at purifying philosophical discourse of "nonsense." In the language of Deleuze and Guattari's political theory, these diatribes are examples of a subjected-group instantiating the paralogism of the double-impasse. That is, it is a matter of groups attempting to restrict taste and creativity by presenting every type of writing outside of a narrow range as indeterminate or chaotic. The important difference between these groups and the earlier logical empiricists is that their denunciations are not attached to any explicit criterion of sense or rigor. They lack the logical empiricist courtesy of stating what makes a text meaningful or properly structured. A.J. Ayer in his 1987 reassessment of the classic *Language, Truth, and Logic* acknowledges the defeat of the verification principle, acknowledges the nonviability of the analytic/synthetic distinction, but he continues by saying: "I am still of the opinion that many of the utterances of such fashionable philosophers as Heidegger and Derrida are simply non-sensical."[20]

An anti-foundationalist in this second sense of foundationalism can insist upon a new nonvertical, understanding of philosophy's relationship to other disciplines and practices. The average, however, is the idea that the very idea of philosophy as a distinct, relatively autonomous practice should be eliminated. Quine's critique of logical empiricism included the idea that philosophy should move in the direction of natural science. The postmodern or post-structuralist critique of foundationalism is associated with two other options: calls for the overcoming of philosophy and the view that philosophy be regarded as literature or as an analogue of literature.

The average postmodernism or post-structuralism is a strictly negative affair. Thought's vocation is restricted to criticism. In this regard, the figure closest to the standard within the categories is neither Derrida nor Foucault, but Richard Rorty. To read a text of Derrida's or Foucault's as post-structuralist or postmodernist is to read it as if it were authored by Rorty. Alternatively, one does not read the work of Derrida at all, only Rorty interpreting the work of Derrida.

Beginning with his introduction to the *Linguistic Turn*, Rorty delivered a series of effective assaults on foundationalist pretensions. Moreover, in these writings an association is established, often quite explicitly, between the practice of formulating positive theories and foundationalism. This association plays a pivotal role in the composition of the typical Rorty text as figures are assigned to a center, periphery, or exterior of relevance. Rorty's conceptual personae (the distinct characters within *his* writings) emerge within each of these ranks. The center is occupied by the purely negative, strong anti-foundationalist; the periphery by the incomplete, overly positive, anti-foundationalist; the exterior is equivalent to the position of the thoroughly positive foundationalist (the uncritical philosophical dinosaur). The average Rorty text is defined by a movement between center and exterior (the inside and outside of relevance) as well as a movement between center and periphery.[21] The second movement is as important as the first. It is initiated in the *Linguistic Turn* through the opposition of Waismann and Wittgenstein, then reiterated through subsequent juxtapositions: Dewey versus Peirce, James versus Peirce, Derrida versus Foucault, Derrida versus Deleuze, and Derrida the critic of logocentrism versus the Derrida who mistakenly believes that such a critical enterprise requires a theory of language.

1.2   The average continental philosopher

"Continental philosophy" also operates as the term of an exclusive disjunction. The opposing term is either "analytic" or "Anglo-American." In fact, "Anglo-American" and "analytic" are often treated as synonyms, despite the latter's birth in Vienna. In this way "Anglo-American" simultaneously suggests and belies a conflation of philosophy's geography with the geography of nation-states or continents. Complicating things further, "continental philosopher" can denote an individual born in the States, living in the States, who reads and writes on the books deemed "continental." These books may be composed, for the most part, in languages other than English, but the American "continental philosopher" typically reads and comments on them in English.

The distinction between analytic and continental operates as an exclusive disjunction when it suggests the existence of two, hermetically sealed compartments of thought. Each compartment is associated with a set of texts, although as we have seen, the region and original language of a text is neither a necessary nor a sufficient condition for being included in a particular compartment. The disjunction can establish a hierarchy between the two terms. Self-identified "analytic" philosophers have employed "continental" as an epithet (usually it means work devoid of rigor or sense). Self-identified "continental" philosophers have employed "analytic" as a term of dismissal (usually it means work that is dull and sclerotic). At the same time, there are many ways the disjunction can be configured as horizontal. Individuals who identify with one signifier can make a point of stating their nonhostility toward the other. Departments can pride themselves on being a hospitable environment for both. Commentaries can be written that demonstrate the existence of certain cross-compartmental affinities. All that defines the average is the belief that one is dealing with two compartments, two traditions. There can be antagonism, neutrality, even resemblance. What there cannot be is interpenetration.

The positive definition of "contemporary continental philosophy" construes it as a larger phenomenon of which postmodernism or post-structuralism is simply one part. In short, "contemporary continental philosophy" carves up thought into three species: postmodernism (or post-structuralism), critical theory, and hermeneutics. As species-terms, differentiation proceeds by way of contrast. To be a critical theorist is to charge hermeneutics with an uncritical deference toward tradition, and postmodernism with being irrational or relativistic. To be a postmodernist is to charge hermeneutics with preserving the traditional view of interpretation through its privileging of textual unity. To identify with hermeneutics is to charge critical theory with a reductive view of tradition, and postmodernism with conflating unity as a horizon or precondition for understanding with a determinate signified. Deleuze's discussion of the middle as average highlights how these debates are cemented into place as the discursive parameters of "continental philosophy." This occurs when commentators assign themselves the task of reconciliation, arbitration, or mediation: Rorty's thought is missing a dash of Foucault, Habermas and Lyotard need one another.

2 Affirmative philosophy

The privileging of criticism, the subordination of construction to criticism, is a feature of the average postmodernism and post-structuralism. Creativity is reduced to stylistically creative criticism of foundationalism. But in Part I, Deleuze's abstract differential was shown to include the separation of critique from production and the subordination of critique to production. There are, in fact, three strikingly affirmative areas of Deleuze's philosophy: portraiture, metaphilosophy, and metaphysics. Little wonder, then, that the classificatory machine has consistently positioned Deleuze's philosophy on the periphery *or* the ability of this philosophy to function as a sign (as a catalyst for becomings within philosophy).

Portraiture produces texts that are extremely positive surfaces. They lack the critical annotations and reservations that are the hallmark of traditional philosophical summaries. In fact the only explicit criticism is directed toward the clichéd representations of the subject. Deleuze does not critique his subject, but the caricatures of his subject. His stunning portraits are isomorphic to book-reports rather than "critical essays."

The second register is that of metaphilosophy. Deleuze offers a strictly positive definition of philosophy: philosophy is the practice of inventing problems and concepts. By juxtaposing the Deleuzian and Derridean use of the word "concept" we can grasp the deeply affirmative character of the former. Deleuze does not simply affirm or advocate the creation of concepts; he offers a positive or affirmative definition of the concept.

Derrida insists that his most celebrated notion, *différance*, is not a concept.[22] What does this mean within Derrida's image of thought? For Derrida, "concept" carries the metaphysical connotation of essence (the concept as a concept of an essence), the epistemological connotation of representation (the concept as the mental representation of an entity), the subjective connotation of pure presence (the concept as an idea that is spatially and temporally self-enclosed), and the linguistic connotation of perfect determinacy (a signifying chain is nothing but the vehicle for a particular concept). *Différance* is not a thing for which there can be a concept; it is not an object spatially and temporally present, but the role of absence in signification and disclosure. Additionally, the fact of *différance* forecloses the existence of pure presence or self-identity. Therefore, *différance* precludes the very existence of concepts in the above senses of "concept." Finally, Derrida declares *différance* is not a concept in that the expression does not serve as a textual center of the essay of the same name. The word *différance* does not pull the passages of the essay *Différance* together into a linear or self-identical text. As with the practice of writing *sous rapture*, Derrida justifies the episodic or "wandering" character of his essay by linking linear exposition to what *différance* challenges: the ontological commitment to substance, essence, or self-identity.[23]

The deconstructionist view of concepts could be summarized in a couple ways. On the one hand, it could be said that Derrida's position is that there are no concepts, only words. To be a concept is to be a concept of an existing essence. If there are no essences, then there are no concepts, only words packaged as concepts. On the other hand, it could be said that Derrida's view is that concepts are words such as "Idea" "substance," "cogito," "essence," or "telos," but that these concepts are not what they appear to be. The concepts are presented as representations of an epistemic or metaphysical ground, but there is no such ground. The appearance of self-evidence is generated by the rhetorical interplay of these concepts and their supplements (their opposing terms).

However one chooses to formulate the deconstructionist position, everything turns on a negative definition of the concept: purported concepts are not, they are simply words; a concept is packaged as but *is not* a representation of an essence; the identity of a concept is a function of negation (of it *not being* its conceptual supplement). Deleuze's work encourages us to see the deconstructionist definition of the concept as part of a larger trend. Themes such as anti-philosophy, overcoming philosophy, or the critique of the history of philosophy go hand in hand with a negative definition of concepts: "Philosophers claim their concepts represent essences, first principles, points of pure presence, but they do not." Deleuze's goal is to provide a positive definition of the concept. This definition must be nonfoundational (i.e. immune from anti-foundationalist criticism) *and* it must be able to operate retroactively. Granted Plato's concept of Idea does not correspond to real, immutable entities. But this only tells us what the concept is not. What *is* Plato's concept? What *is* a concept?

In his *Ethics*, Spinoza goes to great lengths to distinguish ideas from images: an idea is not "some dumb thing like a picture on a tablet."[24] Confusing having an idea with having a picture reduces knowledge to the imagination (you reduce what can be thought to what can be visualized). Every finite idea is a determinate expression of Nature's power of thought and is typically a complex structure (i.e. comprised of multiple ideas).[25] Echoing Spinoza's definition of an idea, Deleuze characterizes the concept as an act or movement of thought.[26] And, for Deleuze the fact that a concept is an act means it is not constituted through negation. The identity of a word may be constituted through negation; we may commonly think through negation; an act of thought may be described through negation; Deleuze may even employ negation in defining an act of thought (the identity of an act of thought *is not* formed through negation). But the act of thought itself is fully positive. And like Spinoza, Deleuze depicts the act of thought as incredibly complex. This is why true definitions of philosophical concepts (e.g. the definitions Deleuze gives for Spinoza's concepts in *Practical Philosophy*) bear no resemblance to one-sentence dictionary style definitions. A concept is a movement comprised of movements (within the concept components are organized into various neighborhoods or relations), and a movement related to other movements (the other concepts populating the philosophical system).

These combined movements are the expressions of a philosophical problem. As a differential this problem is comprised of heterogeneous acts of thought. As an immanent structure, it exists within rather than outside of its concrete, heterogeneous expressions. Each expression is a rhizome: a system of concepts. Each expression is a plurality of pathways through which the complex movements called concepts are brought into relation.

A third, positive register within Deleuze's philosophy is that of metaphysics. The very fact he refuses to use "metaphysics" as a pejorative suggests the incommensurability of Deleuze's thought with both terms of an exclusive disjunction. After all, the theme of challenging or overcoming metaphysics has postmodern and analytic instantiations.

Echoing Heidegger, Derrida presents his own work as the contestation of philosophy as metaphysics. Similarly Rorty uses the term "metaphysics" to mark the center, periphery, and exterior of relevance. In *Consequences of Pragmatism*, Foucault and Deleuze are characterized as too metaphysical (i.e. they are placed on the border between a strong anti-foundationalism and metaphysics):

James and Nietzsche make parallel criticisms of nineteenth-century thought. Further, James's version is preferable, for it avoids the "metaphysical" elements in Nietzsche that Heidegger criticizes, and, for that matter, the metaphysical elements in Heidegger that Derrida criticizes. On my view, James and Dewey were not only waiting at the end of the dialectical road which analytic philosophy traveled, but are waiting at the end of the road which, for example, Foucault and Deleuze are currently traveling.[27]

Granted the logical empiricist critique of metaphysics is not the same as the postmodern one. In fact each side has leveled the charge of metaphysics against the other. The childish depiction of Derrida's work as nonsense is rooted in Carnap's treatment of Heidegger's *Being and Time*. On Carnap's interpretation Heidegger confused grammatical correctness with logical correctness; the result is a series of pseudo-propositions around the pseudo-problem of being.[28] Conversely, for Derrida the analytic practices of identifying meanings (matching up hypothetical locutions to corresponding meanings), positing criteria of sense, even the practice of stipulating meaning, are seen as metaphysical to the extent they contribute to iterability's concealment.[29]

At the same time, we should not ignore the ways in which the postmodern and logical empiricist picture of metaphysics converge. For both parties "metaphysics" includes the belief in substances and essences. And for all parties, "metaphysics" is associated with a theory of the real. For Heidegger theories of the real define being as an entity which serves as an epistemological and/or metaphysical foundation. Conflating being with *a being* (an entity) obscures being as disclosure or unconcealment. Similarly, Derrida attacks theories of the real for promoting the illusions of self-identity or pure presence. Logical empiricism privileges natural science, not because it is a representation of the real, but because it is a meaningful discourse about appearances (in fact the very distinction between reality and appearance is labeled nonsense). In contrast, Deleuze frequently and unapologetically talks about the real. And Deleuze, like Spinoza and Bergson, is not allergic to words such "substance," "essence," "universal," or "Idea." Words are words; what matters is the concepts – the dynamic movements – they name. Rorty is right to accuse Deleuze of traveling on a metaphysical path. Deleuze knows he is doing metaphysics. Unlike Rorty, Deleuze does not regard the end of this path as negation (the realization that metaphysics is wrong or pointless). For Deleuze, the path of metaphysics has no end. Philosophy has no end.

In Part III, I show how Deleuze's metaphysics is an ethico-political metaphysics. No less than Plato or Spinoza, Deleuze's metaphysics is inseparable from ethics and social theory. Just as ignoring the politics of Plato's theory of the real turns Platonism into a contemplative affair, so ignoring the politics of Deleuze's theory of the real turns it into a vague discourse on the reality of the virtual. Additionally, it should be noted that Deleuze's problem is expressed in heterogeneous theories of the real. Deleuze's medium of becoming varies; his philosophy is expressed using the language of Bergson, then Nietzsche, then Stoicism, then, in *Capitalism and Schizophrenia*, through a complex assemblage of languages. To confuse one of these expressions, any one of these concrete theories of the real for Deleuze's problem – to conflate the differential with one of its actualizations – leads to the view that Deleuze has more than one philosophical system.[30]

3   Three conceptual personae: the Anglo-American philosopher, the French philosopher, and the logician

Deleuze and Guattari invent the concept of "geophilosophy" to highlight the complex nexus of philosophy, language, and geography.[31] The word suggests a disparity between the geography of thought and the geography of space. Philosophical time is distinct (i.e. philosophy moves forward by moving back, or moves back to move forward); philosophical space is no less so. The first is obscured whenever a distinction is drawn between philosophy and the history of philosophy, or between doing philosophy and reading philosophy. The second is obscured whenever the map of nation-states and continents is mistaken for the map of philosophy: British empiricism, French Feminism, Anglo-American philosophy, Continental philosophy.

Belying expectations some have of "continental philosophy," Deleuze frequently articulates his own position by identifying with figures popularly associated with Anglo-American philosophy (in particular, the Scotsman David Hume).[32] This does not mean we should classify Deleuze as a continental analytic philosopher (in the way people speak of American continental philosophers). What matters is that we see how Deleuze, like his conceptual persona of the schizo possesses his own recording apparatus, one that scrambles all the familiar codes. One powerful display of this inclusive disjunctive synthesis is Deleuze's production of three conceptual personae: the Anglo-American (or analytic) philosopher, the French philosopher, and the Logician. The interactions of these characters on the stage of Deleuze's philosophy produce two normative questions: "How can we be Anglo-American thinkers and writers rather than French?" and "How can we be analytic philosophers without being logicians?" Obviously these questions only make sense if we recognize we are dealing with specific figures within Deleuze's system.

In Deleuze's references to the Anglo-American or analytic philosopher the reader should immediately recognize his portrait of Hume. Of course Hume has frequently been invoked as the major antecedent to the analytic tradition. Supposedly one can find in his work the analytic/synthetic distinction (minus the Kantian category of the synthetic *a priori*), the fact/value distinction, and a critique of metaphysical principles (substance, the world independently of experience, etc.). But Deleuze's portrait and thus the conceptual persona of the analytic philosopher bears little resemblance to this reading of Hume's philosophy. By foregrounding Hume's theory of passions and action, Deleuze demolishes the idea that either the fact/value or analytic/synthetic distinction can be located within the former's thought. For Hume, the basis of value is human nature and circumstance. The source of morality is a special class of human sentiment the motor of which is the natural mechanism of sympathy. The creation of diverse institutions (general rules) extends or compensates for the naturally partial character of this natural sympathy.[33] Against the notion of analyticity, Deleuze's Hume argues every relation is an act of relating and the content of the terms related are never sufficient conditions of the relations established between them (i.e. all relations are synthetic or external).[34] As for the Humean critique of metaphysics, Deleuze's portrait consistently presents it as the groundwork for a more constructive endeavor: "Given the absence of internal relations, how is the subject (a system of habitual relations) constituted?"

Deleuze's character the Anglo-American thinker (sometimes called the "empiricist") represents a fusion of his portrait of Hume's philosophy with currents of the pragmatic tradition (James, Dewey, and Peirce). A vital intermediary in the construction of this conceptual persona was the work of Jean Wahl. In *The Pluralist Philosophies of England and America* (1925) and *Vers Le Concret* (1932), Wahl examined with favor the work of Russell, Moore, Whitehead, Peirce, James, and Dewey. The style, display of synthesis, and thematic content of these books greatly anticipate the writings of Richard Rorty. Deleuze recalls, "Apart from Sartre...the most important philosopher in France was Jean Wahl. He not only introduced us to an encounter with English and American thought, but had the ability to make us think, in French, things which were very new."[35] Wahl's influence can be discerned in Deleuze's persistent identification with the expressions "empiricist," and "pluralist;" in the positive references to Whitehead, James, and Russell scattered throughout his corpus; and in the specific image of thought he finds in the work of Hume. In fact, Deleuze's reconstruction of Hume's empiricism can profitably be seen as an alternative to the one Wahl provides in *Pluralist Philosophies*. Wahl defines Hume's philosophy as atomistic, opposing it to James' style of circumventing the distinction between the one and the many. In contrast, Deleuze attempts to show that, prior to pragmatism, we can find in Hume's philosophy a theory of relations permitting us to rethink unity, a critique of representation, and a redefinition of truth as useful habits. In this way Deleuze inscribes Hume's philosophy on Wahl's image of pragmatism. Rorty suggests that the founders of pragmatism may be waiting at the end of the Deleuzian road. But these writers were Deleuze's companions from the very beginning.

Deleuze's conceptual persona is completed by references to Anglo-American literature (Whitman, Lawrence, Miller, Kerouac). Whenever Deleuze speaks of the superiority of English literature, it is these writers he has in mind.[36] The appraisal is linked to specific parallels Deleuze establishes between the literary works and his portrait of Hume. The Anglo-American writer displays a sense of the externality of relations, displaces the opposition between the one and the many, privileges movement over roots, and privileges action and the outside over representations of interiority. Along with Wahl's interpretation of pragmatism, Deleuze's portrait of Hume and this treatment of literature coalesce in the first character – the Anglo-American thinker. The second character – the French thinker – is initiated simultaneously through opposition. The French philosopher or writer is obsessed with internal relations, organic conceptions of unity, and interiority.[37] Obviously, the question immanent to Deleuze's philosophy – "How can we increase the proportion of Anglo-American thought relative to French thought in our lives?" – has nothing to do with national character.

What about the character of the logician? This conceptual persona is the star of the sixth chapter of *What is Philosophy?* entitled "Prospects and Concepts." The distinction in the title suggests Deleuze and Guattari's intention to differentiate philosophy (associated with concepts) from science, logic, and phenomenology (all of which are associated with prospects or propositions). For now, I want to focus exclusively upon the distinction between philosophy and logic. Our question is "What are the qualities of the conceptual persona of the logician?" Within Deleuze and Guattari's answer, the reader can spot many of the positions associated with the logical empiricist program: first philosophy, the rational (i.e.

logical) reconstruction of science, and the distinction between genuine propositions and meaningless, pseudo-propositions. For this reason, it is useful to juxtapose this chapter of *What is Philosophy?* with two better known challenges to logical empiricism: the one mounted by Quine in essays such as "Two Dogmas of Empiricism" and "Epistemology Naturalized," and the one delivered by Rorty in his book *Philosophy and the Mirror of Nature.*

Quine argues logical empiricism is epistemologically untenable by challenging the analytic/synthetic distinction.[38] "Analyticity" itself resists analysis and no statement in isolation represents states of affairs (the thesis of holism). Therefore, a statement by statement distribution into the categories "analytic" and "synthetic" is impossible. By extension, a statement by statement translation of scientific discourse into logical discourse is impossible. For Quine, the failure of first philosophy indicates the need to naturalize epistemology. Instead of serving as a foundation, philosophy will join the sciences of linguistics and psychology in order to explain the acquisition of language and the genesis of truth claims.[39] The critique within the *Philosophy and the Mirror of Nature* is more populated and far-reaching. Drawing upon the internal critique of analytic philosophy (Quine, Sellars, Hanson, Goodman), pragmatism (Dewey and James), and European theory (Heidegger and Sartre), Rorty forges an original account of the rise and fall of both senses of foundationalism (authoritative explanations and first philosophy).[40]

The critique in *What is Philosophy?*, has an entirely different feel than these two texts; the focus is not on the viability of first philosophy, but the power of philosophy. For Deleuze and Guattari, it is crucial we see the epistemic elevation of philosophy as the diminishment of its power. The true consequence of first philosophy is not the reduction of science to philosophy. Scientist's go about their business, more or less indifferent to the philosophy of science. The true consequence is the reduction of philosophy, the separation of philosophy from its power to act: "a real hatred inspires logic's rivalry with, or its will to supplant philosophy."[41]

Unlike Quine's or Rorty's argument, Deleuze and Guattari's requires a positive definition of philosophy and the philosophical concept, a sharp distinction between philosophical concepts and scientific functions, and a distinction between both of these and logical functions. The thrust of this argument is that logic turns the invention of concepts into the invention of propositional functions intended to double for scientific propositions and for the propositions of ordinary language. In their account of the project of clarifying a natural language through logical functions, Deleuze and Guattari allude to Russell's well-known practice of description (the analytic version of writing *sous rapture*). This involves redescribing a phrase ("the present king of France," "the author of Waverly," "Pegasus") in such a way that one is able to maintain its meaningfulness while avoiding the appearance of unwelcome ontological commitments. The creation of problems (philosophy since Plato) is replaced by the translation of propositions into logical functions.

In Bergson's *Creative Mind*, it is preexisting problems (or debates) that are labeled false; the label true is reserved for the practice of creating new problems along with their definitive solutions.[42] For Bergson, the defining feature of most debates within philosophy is the fact that they ignore qualitative multiplicity or duration: "the radically new and unforeseeable," "the uninterrupted upsurge of novelty."[43] His new problems are designed to illuminate this process of creativity. The philosophical demonstration that creativity is real (and that the real *is* creativity, mobility, and change) takes the form of a creative act. When Deleuze borrows Bergson's distinction between true and false problems, he also amplifies this connection between philosophy and creativity.[44] Philosophy demonstrates the reality of genuine creativity and radical difference by producing the new – by producing difference.

In *What is Philosophy?*, this distinction between false and true problems takes the form of a distinction between the logician's questions and the philosopher's problem. The first invites solutions in the form of propositional answers. The second demands expression through the rhizomorphic production of concepts. How, Deleuze and Guattari ask, could a question such as "How can we talk about Pegasus without sounding like we believe in Pegasus?" ever be confused with the construction of a problem or plane of immanence?[45]

Deleuze and Guattari make a distinction between scientific functions and philosophical concepts; they characterize the former as discursive or propositional, the latter as nondiscursive or nonpropositional.[46] Austin famously argued that philosophy as epistemology conceals the many things that can be done with words (the plurality of illocutionary forces) by focusing solely upon the way they can be used to make statements representing states of affairs.[47] In their critique of logic, Deleuze and Guattari argue that at the height of its powers philosophy has nothing to do with manufacturing or assigning a truth-value to propositional representations. Scientific functions establish a plane of reference populated by states of affairs, and do so through a system of propositions. But according to Deleuze and Guattari, philosophy's concepts are self-referential.[48] To understand what this means, and just as important what it does not mean, requires we take a closer look at a whole range of conceptual personae: the entire cast of *What is Philosophy?* minus the phenomenologist. Only by observing the performance of the philosopher, scientist, artist, and historian will we be able to fully identify the figure of the logician.

4   The philosopher, the artist, the scientist, the historian, and the logician

The average postmodernism or post-structuralism includes a rejection of foundationalist conceptions of philosophy's relation to other practices. Consequently, part of the internal standard of these categories is a range of post-foundationalist answers to the question, "What is philosophy?" or "What could philosophy be other than first philosophy?" First answer: because philosophy is nothing but the twin senses of foundationalism, post-foundationalism is equivalent to post-philosophy. This is the theme of overcoming philosophy – the theme of moving toward a post-philosophical culture. Second answer: philosophy is not science's ground, so it should become a strand of scientific practice. This answer is more post-analytic (Quine) than postmodern or post-structural. Third answer: philosophy's vocation is the critique of self-evidence (philosophy is the art of demystification). When philosophy is associated with false universals (appeals to purportedly self-evident principles) this third answer becomes the first. The mission of thought is to critique self-evidence, and there is no greater target than the history of philosophy. Fourth answer: while philosophy judges nothing, it is the thought of everything. Here anti-foundationalism involves a return to the idea of philosophy as the queen of the sciences. Philosophy is dethroned, but it remains the practice of thinking about or reflecting on other practices. Fifth answer: philosophy should be understood as a form of poetry or literature.

In his 1967 introduction to the anthology *The Linguistic Turn*, Rorty provides just such a catalogue of options. Following his critique of the philosophy of language the author muses on the possible outcomes of analytic philosophy's "creeping obsolescence."[49] The possibilities are given as answers to the question "should we philosophize?"[50] One possibility is philosophy's dissolution: "We would come to look upon a post-philosophical culture as just as possible, and just as desirable, as a post-religious culture. We might come to see philosophy as a cultural disease which has been cured."[51] Another is philosophy's transformation into poetry or a poetry analogue: "philosophy would cease to be an argumentative discipline and grow closer to poetry."[52]

That Deleuze's writings are disclosed on the interior of "post-structuralism" and "postmodernism" is indicative of his opposition to first philosophy. Throughout his writings he hammers away at the idea philosophy should be privileged over scientific and artistic practices. That Deleuze's writings are disclosed on the periphery of the interior suggests his answer to the question, "What else could philosophy be?" departs from the range of answers constituting the categorical standard. This departure enables his answer to serve as a sign or medium of becoming.

The location of Deleuze's work relative to the standard should force one's attention to his critique of reflection (i.e. of the idea that philosophy is the practice of reflection). In the pages of *What Is Philosophy?* Deleuze and Guattari repeatedly state that mathematicians are perfectly capable of reflecting on mathematics, scientists are perfectly capable of reflecting on science, and artists are perfectly capable of reflecting on art.[53] In "What Is the Creative Act?" Deleuze declares "the filmmakers, the film critics, or those who love cinema" are perfectly capable of thinking about cinema.[54] These are challenges to the idea of philosophy as foundation, and to the belief that philosophy is some vague enterprise of thinking about thinking. The belief philosophy grounds other disciplines presupposes philosophy is the practice of reflecting on other disciplines. In reality, though, this way of conferring priority, or at the very least importance, on philosophy renders it superfluous. Far from other practices depending on philosophy, philosophy is made to parasitically depend on other practices (those upon which it reflects).

At the same time, Deleuze and Guattari's critique of reflection is a critique of the idea that philosophy is essentially criticism. Under the heading of reflection is placed both the notion of founding and the notion of upsetting apparent foundations. Distinguishing philosophy from both types of reflection, however, is not intended to signal its obsolescence. For Deleuze, reflective missions only appear to extend philosophy's strength. In reality they dilute it: "Treating philosophy as the power to 'think about' seems to be giving it a great deal, but in fact it takes everything away from it."[55]

For Deleuze, philosophy's nonsuperiority is also the nonsuperiority of science, art, and historiography. In place of vertical conceptions of philosophy's relation to nonphilosophy, or of philosophy's dissolution into either science or art, Deleuze advances a horizontal vision of three specific, independent practices. Philosophy remains an enterprise distinct from science, literature, and historiography but ceases to be a tribunal. Philosophy retains a unique vocation, but this vocation is neither criticism nor a free-floating "thinking about."

The reason Deleuze's horizontal vision is disclosed as peripheral is because the standard is one in which philosophical specificity is associated with foundationalism. Positive conceptions of philosophy are associated with foundationalism; distinguishing between philosophy and literature is associated with foundationalism. Similarly, distinct conceptions of philosophy, science, art, or history are associated with reductive visions of each and with the policing of intellectual borders (with a prohibition on interdisciplinarity). But Deleuze offers nonreductive views of each practice, promotes and describes their interaction, and produces texts that are the result of such interactions. For Deleuze, clear, specific definitions of the practices are prerequisites for describing these interactions, and they are catalysts for powerful interactions.

How, though, should philosophy, science, art, and history be distinguished from one another? Then there is the question of logic. Where does it fit into this grid of practices? In terms of Deleuze's theatre, we need to get to know the philosopher, scientist, artist, and historian. And we need to get to know the logician better. Discussing Leibniz's philosophy, Deleuze argues that philosophers often give two answers to the same question.[56] The first is accessible (or at least more accessible). The second is more demanding and profound. In *What Is Philosophy?* there is both an accessible account of the different practices, and a challenging, but more original, one. The latter is found in several opaque, provocative, and overlooked passages of the book.

The easy answer turns upon the familiar distinction between formalism and representation. Deleuze and Guattari associate both the scientist and the historian with propositions or the setting up of planes of reference. In contrast, the philosopher and the artist are described as creating nonpropositional surfaces. The historian would be distinguished from the natural scientist by the subject matter of their propositions (history versus the natural world). Similarly, the philosopher and the artist would be distinguished by the types of surfaces they create – what populates their surfaces. The philosopher creates a problem, the artist "blocks of sensation."

This definition of art cuts across the distinction between figurative and nonfigurative, form and content, by encouraging us to perceive works of art as expressions.[57] The definition is general enough that it cannot be confused with a proposal (i.e. it is not an argument for a particular kind of art or "anti-art"). At the same time, the concepts of sensation and expression are in no way intended to represent works of art as vehicles for the artist's inner life. If the aesthetic monument is an expression it is because it is an assemblage of percepts and affects on a material support. A percept is neither the artist's nor the spectator's point of view. Rather, it is a point of view preserved by the work (that exists as long as the material support). Key phrases within this aesthetics are "stands by itself" and "exists in itself."[58] A successful work of art exists independently of the artist and spectator. As with percepts, so with affects. A work's affect is irreducible to the artist's feelings (or affectations), as well as to the diverse range of feelings it may elicit in its viewer. Like the percept, it is preserved and stands by itself (provided, of course, it has a little material support). Success in parenting is described as creating children capable of living on their own. In *What Is Philosophy?* Deleuze and Guattari describe artistic success as a matter of constructing feelings and perspectives that can stand on their own. The sentiments of Ahab exist alongside of Melville's ocean and whale. They live together, on their own.

The figure of the logician would be the one that positioned scientific propositions as philosophy's subject matter. In particular, the logician would claim to legitimate scientific discourse by translating it into logical functions. The tremendous discord between this practice and the history of philosophy would be dealt with through the retroactive bifurcation of the latter. Passages in classical philosophical texts which could be construed as linguistic analysis become "true philosophy." The remainder are relegated to the category of art or poetry. Philosophy becomes a tribunal for distinguishing between science and pseudo-science, philosophy, and poetry.

Does the distinction between form and representation correspond to the distinction between creation and discovery? For Deleuze and Guattari the answer is clearly no. Science, history, philosophy, and art are all creative or constructive endeavors. One anti-foundationalist reaction to logical empiricism is the claim that philosophy's real affinity is to art rather than science; philosophy creates rather than discovers. In contrast, *What Is Philosophy?* challenges the idea that scientific propositions are simply read off of the world. There is "as much creation in science as there is in philosophy or the arts."[59] Within this philosophy of science, reference – in the sense of "planes of reference," "systems of coordinates," and "states of affairs" – is defined as a "functive." Science is regarded as referential, but the referent is understood as intrinsic to scientific theories or functions. What could this mean?

The point Deleuze and Guattari are making can be usefully compared to Quine's notion of theoretical underdetermination.[60] For Quine, a good scientific theory is one that fits empirical data. But this pairing up of theory and data cannot be understood as the latter causing or explaining the selection of a theory without remainder. This is because there can exist more than one tight-fitting propositional shirt. This gap between theory and data is why it makes sense to refer to scientific truths as human inventions. Similarly, in *What Is Philosophy?* states of affairs are described as functives or as products of scientific practice. Under the heading of "states of affairs," Deleuze and Guattari include the propositional content of scientific discourse. What about the labors of the historian? Just as the propositions of science cannot simply be read off of the world so we can think of historians as constructing, through a process of focus and selection, their own planes of reference or explanation. Functives or scientific propositions are underdetermined by the empirical reality; so are historical explanations.

As suggested earlier, this corresponds to one, accessible, not unfamiliar way of differentiating philosophy, art, science, logic, and history. Does it represent a deviation from the average? Sure. The distinction between construction and realism, creativity and re-presentation is dismantled. Nevertheless, the terms of the deviation are not unusual ones. We are familiar with the limitations of viewing a work of art as if it were a proposition. The anti-foundationalist tendency to associate philosophy with art reflects an awareness that philosophical systems are not simplistic propositional bodies. Finally, the phrase "construction" is commonplace in discussions of science and history even if it marks a site of contention.

Now, however, let us turn to the more demanding way of differentiating the practices. A key feature of Deleuze's writing is the existence of "thresholds of indiscernability" within the definition of philosophy. These are points at which his definition of philosophy becomes indistinguishable from his metaphysics. Here are a couple of examples. In *Difference and Repetition*, philosophical systems are defined as problems. But then being is defined in such a way that to be an entity (any entity) is to be a solution to a problem.[61] In *What Is Philosophy?* the authors carefully define the philosophical concept. A rigorous formalistic mode of interpreting philosophies is encouraged. But then the authors begin to refer to the conceptual side of bodies.[62] In both books, specific passages fold a definition of philosophy into a more general consideration of being. The question, "What is Philosophy?" is folded into the question "What is a being?" The answer to the latter takes the form of a distinction within the real, but not a distinction between entities or a distinction between this world and a transcendent principle. A being is the actualization of a problem or differential. Or, a being is the actualization of an incorporeal in a corporeal mixture.

This incorporation of metaphilosophy into metaphysics serves multiple functions. One is that it reminds us that philosophies belong to the world. For Deleuze a metaphilosophy untethered to metaphysics will in fact perpetuate the metaphysical idea of transcendence. An image structures the entire debate surrounding philosophy and re-presentation, science and re-presentation, and language and re-presentation. The image is one of two distinct objects in space. On the left, we have philosophy, language, and science. On the right, we have the world. Philosophy, science, and language are discussed and thought of *as if* they existed outside of the world: Does philosophy or language mirror the world? Does science construct or represent the real? One side says yes; the other says no. Both sides obscure the obvious: philosophy, science, art, historiography, logic, and linguistic acts exist within the world. The image is one of Marx's principal targets in the *Theses on Feuerbach*: the entire debate between idealism *and* classical materialism involves the belief that our principal relationship to the world is comparable to watching figures on a screen (are the figures representations of real objects, or are real objects nothing but figures?).[63] But this image is also a target of Spinoza's. For Spinoza the mind and body are two expressions of the same individual. Thus the discussion of the mind's activity is accompanied by one of philosophy's great accounts of our body and its encounters. That being said Spinoza's philosophy is an inclusive disjunctive synthesis. The extreme materialist is also the extreme idealist. For Spinoza, the dream of a comprehensive, definitive account of the world is a reality. But this comprehensive system does not transcend the world: it is part of it. Thought is one of Nature's attributes, and the idea of the whole of Nature is one of its infinite modes.

Like Spinoza, Deleuze's work suggests that a metaphilosophy and metaphysics have to identify the specific reality of philosophical systems ("what is this real thing we call a philosophy?"). By extension, differentiating philosophy from other practices requires an account of how the reality of philosophy is different from the reality of science, art, historiography, and logic. All the practices belong to the world; all the practices create things in the world; but the practices interact with the rest of the world in different ways. The scientist construct planes of reference or propositions depicting states of affairs or bodies. The historian constructs a plane of reference or propositions depicting states of affairs, "actual factors," or the "actual side" of an event.

The philosopher constructs concepts and some of these concepts depict "pure events," "becomings," or "inseparable variations." Another name Deleuze and Guattari give for the pure event, becoming, or insepara- ble variation is the "concept." This means that one class of philosophi- cal concepts depicts concepts. Far from being the comfortable idea of second-order concepts (a conception of what a concept is), we are deal- ing with an ontological commitment to extra-philosophical concepts within the world.

How is this differentiation of practices via their respective objects developed? Let us start with the distinction between philosophy and history. In *What Is Philosophy?* and the important essay "May 68 Did Not Take Place" Deleuze and Guattari characterize events as hav- ing two sides: the virtual side and the actual side.[64] The virtual side of the event is also identified as the "pure event." The historian's perspective or propositions represent an effort to explain historical phenomena, and these explanations circumscribe the phenomena within well-defined borders. An origin (simple or complex) and an end are assigned to the event. A "before the event" and "after the event" are identified. According to Deleuze and Guattari, the reduc- tion of the event to such an explanation represents an implicit meta- physical position. This is the idea that the whole is given – the entire content of the event can be found in the origin (antecedent condi- tions) or end (the result).

This account of the metaphysics (i.e. the unacknowledged metaphys- ics) of historical explanation is directly inspired by Bergson. In *The Creative Mind*, Bergson can be read as endorsing the historicist critique of the philosophical tradition. Philosophers promulgate the notion of timeless principles or constants, and they present them as the infra- structure of what happens in time. Change, mobility, and difference are positioned as secondary to permanence and identity. Instead of think- ing of change as something undergone by a substance (a permanent or relatively permanent entity), Bergson argues that change should be elevated to the position of substance. Change, novelty, or qualitative multiplicity is the infrastructure of the real: "it is change itself that is real…it is even substantial."[65]

At the same time, Bergson argues that historicism typically involves a denial of history or real time. In fact, Bergson could be seen as argu- ing that a Platonic image structures how the historian thinks of time. Like Plato, the historian explains what happens in time in terms of pre- existing principles. For Plato these principles are ideas; in historical expla- nation they are antecedent conditions, possibilities, and potentialities.

Retroactively, everything that occurs is depicted as the product of antecedent conditions, as the realization of preexisting possibilities, or as the fulfillment of preexisting potential.[66] The existence of duration – the reality of genuine novelty or radical change – is obscured by an image in which the whole is already given (the future is already contained in the present as the present was already contained in the past).

Like Bergson, Deleuze and Guattari *do claim* that historical episodes such as the Paris Commune, the 1917 Revolution, and May 68 possessed antecedent conditions: "the historical phenomena that we are invoking were accompanied by determinisms and causalities."[67] In this respect, historical explanation is a legitimate enterprise. However, in contrast to the implicit metaphysical claim of the historian (the whole is given), Deleuze and Guattari assert the existence of a virtual remainder. This remainder is a gap between these antecedent conditions and the massive, unpredictable, corporeal reorganization defining the episode (bodies execute general strikes, occupy factories, create autonomous universities, etc., etc.). Deleuze and Guattari describe revolutionary moments as "social mutations" – episodes possessing a dimension "irreducible to any social determinism, or to causal chains."[68]

Drawing upon *The Logic of Sense*, Deleuze and Guattari describe this reorganization of bodies as the actualization of an ideal event, incorporeal, or concept. This ideal event is not a transcendent cause of what the bodies are doing. Rather, it is a sense or meaning subsisting on the surface of the action. On the one hand, we have the actions bodies perform in revolutionary situations. On the other hand, there is the answer to the question "what is happening?" For Deleuze and Guattari, what happens in revolutionary situations is the actualization of the concept of revolution. This is equated with an enlarged sense of possibility:

> There were a lot of agitations, gesticulations, slogans, idiocies, illusions in 68, but this is not what counts. What counts is what amounted to a visionary phenomenon, as if a society suddenly saw what was intolerable in it and also saw the possibility for something else. It is a collective phenomenon in the form of "Give me the possible, or else I'll suffocate..."[69]

The emergence of radically different, nondocile bodies, along with a variety of new lived experiences, has as its meaning the belief in and demand for a different world.

A critical notion within Deleuze's metaphysics, however, is that this new sense of possibility can only be new if it is not the realization of a possible. In other words, the emergence of a new sense of possibility does not represent society realizing a possibility or realizing its potential: "The possible does not preexist, it is created by the event."[70]

Like Bergson, Deleuze consistently argued that the notion of realizing possibilities or realizing potential suggests that what appears in time already existed (as a possibility, as potential).[71] "It was possible, but not yet a reality;" "the potential was there; it just needed to be tapped into." This conflicts with the idea of radical novelty, and the actualization of the concept of revolution (the actualization of the sense of possibility) is deemed an instance of radical novelty.

To say a historical episode actualizes the concept or pure event of revolution is to say it precludes the reduction to antecedent conditions, antecedent possibilities, or preexisting potential. But Deleuze and Guattari also contest the idea that the virtual side of revolutionary situations can become outdated. There may be an "after the revolution" with regards to the actual side of the event but not with regards to the concept of revolution: "Even if the event is ancient, it can never be outdated."[72] Effects (in particular, the feeling that a dominant order is intolerable) can persist long after historical accounts have marked an event over or even a failure. Deleuze and Guattari, though, are making a more significant point. Just as new actualizations for philosophical concepts can be created, so new actualizations of the concept of revolution can and should be created.

In a frequently overlooked passage of *Difference and Repetition*, Deleuze reminds us that Marx was in no way advocating an analogical approach to history when he declared that "history repeats itself."[73] Marx was not indicating the existence of historical parallels or encouraging us to notice ways in which the present is like the past. Rather, Marx was describing the role identifications with the past have played in bourgeois revolutions – how action in the present has required construing that action as a repetition of the past: precisely when the living are engaged in "revolutionizing themselves and things" they "anxiously conjure up the spirits of the past to their service."[74] Marx links the tragic form of repetition with the creation of something new. In its comedic, farcical form, repetition serves to disguise the unremarkable, banal character of a present undertaking. As for the proletarian revolution, Marx argues it should be the first revolution that is free of repetition, free of ghosts: "Earlier revolutions required world-historical recollections ... the revolution of the nineteenth century must let the dead bury their dead."[75]

What Deleuze suggests is we consider repetition an essential rather than accidental characteristic of revolutionary situations. In every case the concept or pure event is actualized. In every case, bodies and lived experiences are reorganized in a manner that can only be understood as the creation of a new sense: a sense that the impossible is possible.[76] But Deleuze defines actualization as a process of differenciation.[77] Lines of actualization are characterized by nonresemblance. Actualizations do not resemble what they actualize (the pure event or incorporeal sense is distinct from the organization of bodies it subsists upon) and actualizations do not resemble one another. The idea that revolutionary situations are heterogeneous actualizations of a virtual concept requires us to think of the situations as linked *and* to think of each situation as unprecedented. Marx's discussion of repetition concerns the creation of difference through the use of the past (through identification with previous revolutions). We have seen how, for Deleuze, the creation of difference in philosophy involves mediums of becoming. The clearest instance of this is Deleuzian portraiture. Deleuze leaps into the past to leap forward. Perhaps, then, the repetition of the concept of revolution will involve the kind of leap into the past advocated by Benjamin ("a tiger's leap into the past").[78] Deleuze and Guattari associate historical explanation with the obfuscation of novelty. Benjamin associates historical explanation with narratives of progress predicated upon the expulsion of insurrections and failed revolutions; "official history" is highly selective and reflects the interests of the ruling-class. Deleuze and Guattari's notion of the concept of revolution, the notion of a virtual side to revolutionary situations, is a protest against resignation. The concept of revolution is advanced against post-68 platitudes such as "the revolution failed," "all revolutions fail," "revolutions are a thing of the past," "all revolutions lead necessarily to unbridled oppression and savagery." Benjamin separates eschatology (the notion of redemption) from teleology with the hope of making historical materialism the winner. For Deleuze and Guattari, we need to create difference or reactualize the pure event of revolution. For Benjamin, we need to make the "continuum of history explode" by inserting into our present "chips of Messianic" time. The revolutionary's responsibility is less to "future generations" than to the past. Forgotten failures must be recovered, brought into the present, and turned into the story of victory.

Deleuze and Guattari differentiate philosophy and history by distinguishing between the virtual and the actual, or between an incorporeal sense and its corporeal actualization. The absence of philosophy, the concealment of the virtual, or the reduction of history to the actual is associated with a specific political attitude – resignation. The distinction between philosophy and science is developed in a similar fashion.

The scientific perspective is associated with specific kinds of "states of affairs," while philosophy is associated with the virtual events these states of affairs actualize. For the authors a familiar way of looking at the world is in terms of distinct, self-enclosed entities; each entity is regarded as a kind of thing (i.e. as an instantiation of a species-concept or essence). To view an entity as a distinct, fully defined member of a natural kind is to view it as if it were a classical substance, as if it instantiated a classical essence: there are primary properties and there are secondary properties, there is the thing and what happens to the thing over time, there is the thing and how the thing changes, there is the thing and the processes in which the thing participates. The issue is less a matter of an overt commitment to the notion of substance and classical essences than a way of experiencing the world. Reiterating Bergson's depiction of natural perception and science as "a snapshot," the authors write: "In the case of science it is like a freeze-frame. It is a fantastic *slowing down*, and it is by slowing down that matter, as well as the scientific thought able to penetrate it with propositions, is actualized."[79]

Deleuze and Guattari declare philosophy to be concerned with the "the event, not the essence or thing."[80] As before, the distinction between states of affairs and events is developed in terms of a distinction between an arrangement of bodies and an incorporeal sense or concept. One class of philosophical concepts concern the concepts actualized by bodies: "The concept is an incorporeal, even though it is incarnated or effectuated in bodies."[81] Elsewhere, though, the distinction between states of affairs and events is described as the difference between an entity as a distinct, substantial or quasi-substantial thing and "inseparable variations."[82] The description of entities, or at least one side of entities, as "inseparable variations" should be read as two related claims. The first is the negative proposition that things cannot simply be regarded as well-defined, relatively self-identical things belonging to kinds, undergoing accidental modifications, and so on. To say that entities have a virtual side is to say that beneath the appearance of a principle of identity there resides difference. However, the second claim is this underlying difference is not devoid of order or composition. "Inseparable variation" evokes Bergson's notion of qualitative multiplicity. The elements of such a multiplicity (the moments of duration) are fused or interpenetrating rather than discrete, and the elements of such a multiplicity are heterogeneous. A qualitative multiplicity corresponds to the perpetual creation of novelty or difference. According to Deleuze the virtual is difference but not disorder. Difference is a differential structure comparable to a complex unfolding curve complete with singular or notable points (sharp changes of direction). But these "variations" are inseparable in that each singular point is connected to others via a series of ordinal points. Against the notion of substance and the dichotomy of identity or disorder, substance or disorder, Deleuze gives us the idea of difference as a determinate process. What does this mean as far as the distinction between science and philosophy?

Whether the distinction is that of bodies and incorporeal events or states of affairs and inseparable variations the message is the same. What science regards as things or quasi-substances, as representations or quasi-representations of essences, are dynamic processes. Within the scientific perspective, things undergo processes; an event is something happening to a thing. For the philosopher, entities are processes. Entities are events. Entities are happenings.

Does this mean the difference between philosophy and science corresponds to a distinction between being and appearance? When it comes to this question we should bear in mind the distinction between philosophy and history. Historical explanation does not receive the simple definition of misrepresentation or appearance. Part of revolutionary situations is their actual side. What does this mean? There are elements that are anything but unpredictable. And, the pure event of revolution does not occur in a vacuum. The pure event is distinct from its actualizations, but it exists solely within its actualizations. Similarly, Deleuze and Guattari write "No doubt, the event is not only made up from inseparable variations, it is itself inseparable from the state of affairs, bodies, and lived reality in which it is actualized or brought about."[83] With regard to scientific states of affairs, one must keep in mind that for Deleuze science is something that occurs within the world. The distinction between being and appearance, like the distinction between representation and misrepresentation, and even the distinction between realism and construction, represents an implicit, unacknowledged commitment to transcendence. If it makes sense to speak of things or substances as "appearances," it is also the case that such appearances belong to reality. Deleuze's appreciation for Marx's notion of commodity fetishism should come as no surprise.[84] Fetishism is not an accidental, erroneous belief but an objective appearance – an illusion that is part of the material world, and that can only be understood through an analysis of the material world. One should also recall in this context the influence of Bergson's and Spinoza's thought on Deleuze. In *Matter and Memory*, Bergson describes the experience of discrete things (which is to say the distinction between an entity and its environment) as a product of perception's pragmatic role.[85] The given is a function of the faculty of perception subtracting portions of the world (a continuous, series of interactions) in the interests of action ("There is a cup of coffee I could grab," "there is a train I could ride," etc.). Similarly, in the *Ethics*, Spinoza presents the experience of the physical world as divisible (i.e. composed of discrete, autonomous bodies) as a product of the imagination, where the imagination is linked to our body's interactions in the world.[86] In each case, the distinction between being and appearance or reality and appearance is replaced by a consideration of the place of appearance in the world, or of the real world basis for how the world ordinarily appears, or of perception as a way a certain entity (e.g. a person) relates to and interacts with the rest of the world.

Once we take this metaphysical turn in the definition of practices, a couple of pressing questions arise. Deleuze consistently describes philosophical systems as constructions. Philosophical concepts are not ready-made but must be invented. How, though, does the idea that concepts are constructed, cohere with the idea that some concepts have as their objects aspects of the real? The pure event is described as existing within its actualizations. For example, the event of revolution exists in its heterogeneous actualizations. The virtual tendencies actualized by an entity only exist within the actualizations. What the philosophical concept of a pure event embodies is the separation of the virtual from its actualizations. The pure event is extricated and inscribed in a philosophical system or act of thought: "The event is actualized or effectuated whenever it is inserted, willy-nilly, into a state of affairs; but it is *counter-effectuated* whenever it is abstracted from states of affairs so as to isolate its concept."[87] For Deleuze and Guattari a philosophical concept is defined by its internal and external consistency: the relations between its components, and its relations with other concepts.[88] The concept of a pure event is not the virtual as it was (a virtual actualized in bodies or states of affairs), but a new virtual. This is the virtual "rendered consistent." As a concept within the system ("a plane of consistency") the pure event is now defined through its relations with its fellow concepts.

Here Deleuze's metaphysics is designed to help us understand and talk about several concrete aspects of philosophy. A philosophical system is part of the world and it has a definite relationship to what is outside of it (i.e. the rest of the world). Articulating this relationship, however, is no easy matter. One thing is clear: the notion of representation is truly inadequate. The notion of representation suggests that a philosophical system is a passive picture or record of what is outside the system. But we read philosophies precisely because they display the power of thought. A philosophy is a complex act of thought, not a passive image. Moreover, these acts of thought are inspired by the philosopher's concrete encounters in the world (their encounters with signs). Our encounters with this philosophy, with these acts of thought, can in turn compel us to think. Last but not least, we recognize great philosophy as a powerful display of creativity, but not one that precludes a consideration of what is happening outside of the philosophy (i.e. the creation of thought is not the same thing as a flight of fancy).

Deleuze's notion of counter-effectuation or counter-actualization enables us to talk about philosophies as radically novel and as connected to the outside. The border separating the philosophy from the outside is porous rather than rigid. Philosophical creativity presupposes encounters with an outside (with signs), and philosophical creativity can take the form of an intervention. This circuit of encounter and intervention should be considered an alternative to representation. The concept of counter-actualization is precisely this circuit.

To illustrate this process of counter-actualization, let us return to Deleuze and Guattari's discussion of the concept of revolution. Initially, the concept of revolution is an abstract formula (the sense that the impossible is possible). This abstract formula exists within its heterogeneous actualizations (the concept of revolution is expressed in different ways in different situations). The authors encounter one of these actualizations (May 68). This encounter forces them to think through, to understand, the actualization. Thinking through the actualization, they arrive at the concept. But arriving at the concept is not the contemplation of the concept. The philosophers grasp the concept of revolution by simultaneously separating the concept from its actualizations and moving it into their philosophical system. But this re-territorialization embeds the concept in a web of conceptual relations. This concept of revolution can now, only be grasped, by considering its numerous connections to the other concepts in the system. The counter-actualization of a concept is not a re-presentation but a creation – the creation of a philosophical concept. The reterritorialization of the concept of revolution is the creation of the philosophical concept of revolution. This philosophical concept is then introduced to the world with the aim of defeating passivity and servitude. That is, the function of the philosophical concept of revolution is to inspire, in a world of servitude, new actualizations of the extra-philosophical concept of revolution.

With the notion of counter-actualization the idea of formalism reappears, but it is something along the lines of an aspect of the real that has been rendered formal. The counter-actualization of a concept is the production of a philosophical concept. This concept is "self-referential," in that "it is defined by its consistency" – by the relations comprising the philosophical system.[89] Moreover, our earlier distinction between the formalism of art and philosophy and the propositional or representational character of science and historiography reappears. The scientist and the historian both create propositions concerning states of affairs. Both practices are valuable, but both conceal the virtual. If the philosopher "counter-effectuates" the pure event, reinscribing it onto a plane of immanence, the artist free points of views and sentiments from their incarnation in the lived experience of empirical subjects. The percept is a point of view, the affect a sentiment that has been reinscribed on the material surface of the work of art. Philosophers are only successful if they successfully incorporate the event in a system of philosophical concepts. Artists are only successful if their work can stand on its own – if the percepts and affects exist independently of their own lived experience: "By means of the material, the aim of art is to wrest the percept from perceptions of objects and the states of a perceiving subject, to wrest the affect from affections as the transition from one state to another: to extract a bloc of sensations, a pure being of sensations."[90]

We now have distinct, positive definitions for the practices of philosophy, art, science, and history. A certain proximity but nonequivalence has been found in Deleuze and Guattari's figures of the philosopher and artist, and in their figures of the scientist and the historian. What about the conceptual persona of the logician? Above I described the way Deleuze defines the logician as the one who believes philosophy is a practice of reflection, in particular a practice of reflecting on scientific discourse – legitimating science by opposing it to "emotional," "poetic," or "pseudoscientific discourse." Deleuze contends this style of privileging philosophy has the reverse effect. In addition, Deleuze consistently challenged the idea that philosophical systems could be approached as propositional systems. The discipline of logic provides models of reasoning bearing little or no resemblance to the texts comprising the philosophical tradition. Corresponding to the threshold of indiscernability or metaphysical turn in their definition of the philosophical concept, Deleuze and Guattari add one more detail to the figure of the logician. The logician is one who is only able to think in terms of well-defined entities (i.e. they are incapable of thinking the virtual).

In his discussion of Leibniz's philosophy, Deleuze distinguishes between the logical and mathematical notions of singularity.[91] In logic the operative distinction is between the singular proposition and the general proposition (an individual possesses a particular property versus some entity or all entities possess a particular property). In contrast, the mathematical notions of singular and ordinal points enable us to think the individual entity as a dynamic structure. The incorporation of early calculus into *Difference and Repetition* is designed to challenge the reduction of thought to recognition (the location of entities within sets and subsets or species and subspecies).[92] *What Is Philosophy?* reinforces the association between the logic and the classification of entities.[93] As with every other practice the drama of logic unfolds within the world. And yes, logic, like philosophy, science, art, and historiography, is constructive. Logic creates logical functions. At the same time, Deleuze and Guattari position logic (at least when it is equated with philosophy and viewed as the ground of science) as a distraction. Logical functions get in the way of a genuine understanding of the discourse they claim to ground; they are little more than a caricature of philosophy's systematicity and rigor; and on a metaphysical-political level they reduce thought to the most prosaic act imaginable: placing an object in its appropriate box.[94]

I want to conclude this section with a quick summary of some of the essential points of the typology of practices – philosophy, science, art, and historiography. Deleuze defines and differentiates the practices by identifying what each creates. Each represents a specific form of creation within the world. Philosophy is defined as the construction of concepts on a plane of immanence, science as the construction of propositional functions on a plane of reference, art as the production of monuments or blocks of sensations. Philosophy's concepts are no more "ready-made" than art's percepts and affects.[95] Additionally, there is nothing idealistic about recognizing the way science constructs functions, and that such construction is a necessary condition for a reference being a reference, a state of affairs being a state of affairs:

> The idea that truth isn't something already out there we have to discover, but has to be created in every domain, is obvious in the sciences, for instance. Even in physics, there's no truth that doesn't presuppose a system of symbols, be they only coordinates.[96]

Similarly, each practice involves experimentation. Philosophy and art are as experiment-driven as science (of course such experiments are of a different nature). In addition to epistemological uncertainty ("I don't know if it is true") there is an experimental uncertainty of the form ("what will happen if"). Thus Deleuze states that "philosophy and science (like art ...) include an *I do not know* that has become positive and creative, the condition of creation itself."[97]

Finally, each practice is internally diverse. The definition of philosophy draws attention to a concrete heterogeneity in the form of incommensurable conceptual systems or planes of immanence. Artists work with different types of materials (words and syntax, sound, paint, etc.) and employ a plurality of methods in their construction of heterogeneous monuments. As with philosophy and art, the definition of science entails the production of "irreducible, heterogeneous systems of coordinates."[98]

If science, philosophy, and art share the properties of creativity, experimentation, and diversity, why does Deleuze insist upon differentiating them? There are three ways the differentiation of practices could turn into an unacceptable reduction. The first would be if any practice was defined as monolithic. The second would be if segregating the practices in definition, suggested or encouraged segregation in practice. The third would be if any one practice was granted priority over the others. In the strongest possible way, Deleuze's definitions circumvent these risks. The definitions are levers for introducing a strong sense of difference for each practice. Even as it justifies speaking of *a* history of philosophy, the idea of constructing a plane of immanence inserts a principle of incommensurability into our understanding of the philosophy of history. Disparate problems, planes, or conceptual systems cannot be understood as participants in a common discussion. Finally, as we have seen, Deleuze insists upon nonhierarchical differentiation. Philosophy can have a specific role without that role being that of epistemic tribunal.

Deleuze avoids the risks associated with differentiation, and he argues these risks are actually consequences of nondifferentiation. Any conflation of practices buries in vagueness concrete encounters between practices. The function of Deleuze's three definitions is to encourage and enable us to describe with precision the process of continual and reciprocal interaction. Deleuze's writings continually addressed literature and incorporated literary passages (even the occasional scientific term was appropriated for good measure). Likewise, an author such as Kathy Acker incorporated Deleuzian concepts and passages from Deleuzian texts into her novels.[99] Describing Deleuze as doing literature, Acker as doing philosophy, or Deleuze and Acker as practitioners of intertextuality tells us nothing. Philosophers' encounters with literary works compel them to create concepts. Acker encounters Deleuze's work, urgently lifts phrases from this work, and surrounds them with ones of her own. This reinscription or reterritorialization is an act of literary rather than philosophical creation.

5   The phenomenologist as hero; the phenomenologist as parasite

The final conceptual persona of *What Is Philosophy?* is the phenomenologist.

The phenomenologist and the logician are depicted as married, but it is an unhappy, antagonistic union. Each character confuses philosophical concepts with propositions (though not with the same propositions). Both figures separate philosophy from its creative power by defining philosophy in proximity to science. One argues philosophy grounds scientific discourse through a criterion of meaning; the other that philosophy identifies the pre-theoretical ground or precondition of scientific understanding. In each case, philosophical practice is parasitic upon a particular conception of science.

That Deleuze and Guattari challenge applied logic and phenomenology side by side is not a unique feature of their anti-foundationalism. Despite clear methodological differences between Russell's logic and Husserl's phenomenology, Rorty (in *Philosophy and the Mirror of Nature*) identifies the orientations as parallel efforts to transform philosophy into a rigorous, quasi-mathematical activity.[100] Additionally, Rorty uses these projects to elegantly delimit what he considers the principal challenge facing those who attempt to define philosophy as a specific practice.[101] If philosophy is defined as logic or, more generally, as a rigorous enterprise it will be "brushed aside" by science and mathematics. If philosophy goes in the other, "historicist" direction, it will be assimilated by literary criticism and the history of ideas. Part of Rorty's charm as a writer and thinker lies in his serene indifference to this tension. Deleuze's writings display a similar indifference, but for a different reason. Deleuze's image of philosophy is such that philosophy moves neither in the direction of logic nor historicism. Moreover, philosophy is and always has been rigorous. Philosophy possesses a rigor all its own: it is the urgent, painstaking construction of a problem or plane of immanence.

5.1   Counter-actualization and conceptual personae

At this point, though, the question of Deleuze's definition and assessment of phenomenology requires us to pause, and proceed with the utmost care. The picture I just presented could be construed as follows.

Deleuze asks the question "What is phenomenology?" That is, Deleuze poses the question of phenomenology's essence – the principle instantiated by the various writings within the phenomenological tradition. Deleuze then identifies this essence, where the identification includes an assessment: phenomenology is bad because of the way it associates philosophy with propositions and science. Deleuze's treatment of phenomenology is depicted as an exclusive use of the disjunctive synthesis; his actions as those of the professional rather than the schizo.

That the picture is erroneous, that Deleuze *is* scrambling coordinates, requires us to notice a truly unusual feature of Deleuze's writings. Deleuze does not produce a definition of phenomenology but two radically different definitions over the course of three texts. The account of phenomenology in *What is Philosophy?* should be placed alongside the one given in *Empiricism and Subjectivity*, as well as the one provided in the essay "Michel Tournier and the World without Others." The different definitions are at the same time the creation of conceptual personae. There is not one phenomenologist in Deleuze's theatre but two. The shift in definition is accompanied by an equally dramatic shift in evaluation. One conceptual persona is radical and heroic; the other conservative and parasitic.

As I will show in the next section, the same shift in definition, evaluation, and character is found when considering Deleuze's relationship to structuralism. Deleuze produced three readings or accounts of structuralism. These are contained in *Empiricism and Subjectivity*, "What is Structuralism?" and *Anti-Oedipus*. These three readings represent two dramatically different evaluations. And, through these three readings two dramatically different conceptual persona are conceived. One structuralist is radical and heroic; the other conservative and slavish. Furthermore, the phenomenological series and the structuralist series are isomorphic compositionally: first, a consideration of each orientation is incorporated into a portrait of Hume, then you have a portrait of the orientation (i.e. phenomenology and structuralism are each portrayed in the medium of Deleuze's philosophy), finally each orientation is subjected to extreme ridicule.

Understanding these two parallel series, and understanding what Deleuze is up to when he poses and answers a question such as "What is phenomenology?" or "What is structuralism?" requires we revisit the concept of counter-actualization. Once again, the concrete experience of Deleuze's writing requires the utilization of a Deleuzian concept.

For Deleuze, the essence of structuralism or phenomenology is not some principle that could be relayed through a standard dictionary style definition. The only essences are differential structures. The question "What is phenomenology?" is the question, "What assemblage of intellectual habits constitutes phenomenology's differential, and how is this assemblage actualized in radically different ways in the different writings of the phenomenological tradition?" Deleuze identifies the concept (the essence, differential, or problem) of phenomenology, and the concept of structuralism, through a consideration of their heterogeneous expressions.

At the same time the concept of phenomenology or structuralism one finds in Deleuze's writings is specific to his philosophical system. Each conceptual persona can only be understood through a consideration of its home. The characters are characters within the Deleuzian drama. The issue is that of theoretically capturing an absolutely concrete and basic experience of philosophical characters in general. We recognize the inspiration for the characters is the behavior of individuals existing outside of the system. At the same time, we recognize that the characters are concepts among other concepts in a philosophical system. The Socrates one encounters in Plato's dialogues did and did not exist outside these dialogues.

Deleuze's notion of counter-actualization suggests the following relationship between conceptual personae and persons. The philosopher identifies a structure of tendencies that is exhibited in diverse ways by various individuals in the world. Deleuze identifies the concept of phenomenology or the concept of structuralism. As an immanent cause, abstract machine, or virtual structure, the concept (the differential of tendencies) does not exist outside of its actualizations. The philosopher, however, can pull the concept out of the actualizations in an act of thought. This act of thought could be described as the philosopher forming a concept of the concept. What this means is that when the philosopher extricates the concept from its actualizations, he or she is simultaneously reinscribing the concept within their system. As a concept within their system, its specific identity will be a function of its new home (a function of its complex relations to all the other concepts in the philosophy). The concept of a concept is not a re-presentation. The initial concept is redefined as it moves from one territory (what goes on outside the philosophy) to another (the philosophy). The contemplation of a virtual structure or differential is simultaneously a practice. The practice is the creation of radically new conceptual personae.

But counter-actualization can include selection. A concept is a diverse array of tendencies; the philosopher's concept of that concept can emphasize some of these tendencies more than others. Radically different conceptual persona can be born from the same essence or concept of phenomenology. Thus the heroic phenomenologist and parasitic phenomenologist, the experimental structuralist (the structuralist that experiments on themselves), and the structuralist who is a "dog" in the palace of academia. Each persona belongs to Deleuze's philosophy. At the same, time each personae is engineered by incorporating tendencies or habits existing outside of the system within the system (in the form of a character). A philosopher's theatre is always inspired by how people live. A philosopher's theatre is a response to tendencies people live; a philosopher's theatre is always an attempt to influence the tendencies people live.

Therefore, when Deleuze asks a question such as "What is phenomenology?" or "What is structuralism?" no exclusive disjunctive synthesis is involved. Each question receives not one answer but two. And each answer is an act of counter-actualization; a display of creativity. Each pair of characters (or each series of readings) is an expression of Deleuze's problem or differential. Our task, then, is not that of figuring out Deleuze's position on phenomenology and structuralism. We have to see how Deleuze engineers new expressions of his problem through acts of counter-actualization.

5.2   The phenomenology series

A salient target of *Empiricism and Subjectivity* is interiority. Any act of knowing is a conscious act. "Interiority," though, involves an additional move. Consciousness is taken to be both subject (the knowing subject) and object (what is known): if consciousness is not the ultimate object of knowledge, it is nevertheless the case that knowledge is produced through an analysis of the contents of consciousness. Deleuze makes clear his opposition to this move:

> All serious writers agree on the impossibility of a psychology of the mind. This is why they criticize so meticulously every single identification between consciousness and knowledge.[102]

Hume's thought is positioned in opposition to any epistemology which suggests inner life is inherently systematic. Here Deleuze anticipates the way in which, following the publication of *Tristes Tropiques*, the development of structuralism would go hand in hand with a rejection of phenomenology, where "phenomenology" was treated as synonymous with interiority. Without question this is a dubious conflation, especially when one considers the phenomenologies of Heidegger, Merleau-Ponty, and Sartre. In his critique of Sartre, Lévi-Strauss assumes that the simple decision to speak of consciousness as an object of research carries with it Cartesianism (the belief that the mind is an insular container distinct from the world). In other words, despite phenomenology's overhaul of the traditional picture of consciousness, structuralism made it appear as simply the latest chapter in the story of philosophy as Cartesianism. Nevertheless, the influence of the structuralist caricature of phenomenology (especially Sartre's philosophy of existence) should not be underestimated. Deleuze's critique of interiority can be seen as part of this larger story – that of phenomenology's waning influence and structuralisms' ascendancy. Against a philosophy of the mind or science of consciousness concerned with disclosing mental contents or structures, and against the popular definition of empiricism (the reduction of the intelligible to the sensible), Deleuze describes how a knowing, acting, and speaking subject is constituted through the influence of extra-conscious principles.

The 1967 essay "Michel Tournier and the World without Others" (published as an appendix in both *Logic of Sense*, and in the original, French edition of Tournier's novel *Friday*) might seem like an odd choice for considering Deleuze's treatment of phenomenology. For the most part Deleuze adheres to the language of Tournier's novel *Friday* (in particular, the terminology contained in the journal of the protagonist Robinson). That being said, the novel itself contains several clear references to Husserl and Heidegger. Moreover, Tournier, in his memoir *The Windsong*, discusses the importance of Sartre's *Being and Nothingness* for himself and for Deleuze.

Deleuze thus follows Tournier's lead by directly addressing phenomenology in his commentary. Moreover, reading Deleuze's essay, it is clear the exposition of the novel is inseparable from a process whereby he engineers a philosophical concept – that of "the Other." The creation of this concept illustrates the notion of philosophy's becoming literature. As a becoming, this is not a matter of philosophy turning into literature. Rather, an encounter with literature compels the philosopher to produce a concept. Because he is engaged in portraiture, however, Deleuze presents this concept as if he were simply summarizing Tournier's novel.

My contention, though, is not simply that Deleuze mentions phenomenology, or creates a concept, but that his essay represents a novel formulation of phenomenology. In particular, the Tournier piece erases the earlier opposition between empiricism and phenomenology in favor of a general equivalence. Many a Deleuze scholar has gravitated toward "Michel Tournier and the World without Others," sensing the document to be not just an original piece of literary criticism, but an important component of Deleuze's philosophy.[103] The text, however, is commonly segregated from *What is Philosophy?*, *Instincts and Institutions*, and *Empiricism and Subjectivity*. Doing so obscures the precise role the essay plays in Deleuze's system.

By keeping in mind Deleuze's conception of the subject as a system of habits, we can see how he, in his piece on Tournier's novel, undoes his earlier distinction between empiricism and phenomenology. Furthermore, we can see how both treatments of phenomenology are expressions of a single problem. The different counter-actualizations of the concept of phenomenology unfold on a single plane.

While the notion of habit is tacit in Deleuze's discussion of *Friday's* narrative, it is explicitly referenced within the novel itself. In the course of conducting what he refers to as a philosophical investigation, the character of Robinson offers the following definition of the self:

> a fragile, complex framework of habits, responses, reflexes, preoc-
> cupations, dreams, and associations, formed and constantly trans-
> formed by perpetual contact with his fellows.[104]

Worth noting is the fact that Tournier helped Deleuze prepare the manuscript for *Empiricism and Subjectivity*. One could say Tournier folds Deleuze's conception of the subject into the novel which, in turn, cre-ates an opportunity for Deleuze to further develop not just this concept but the problem it expresses. A becoming philosophy within literature gives rise to a becoming literature within philosophy.

As suggested by the quote above, the notion of habit contained within *Friday*, and implicit in Deleuze's exposition of *Friday*, is significantly larger than the one in *Empiricism and Subjectivity*. Perhaps it is best to say that "Michel Tournier and the World without Others" participates in the process of extending the Humean notion of habit begun in Deleuze's books *Empiricism and Subjectivity* and *Instincts and Institutions*. There it will be remembered Deleuze presents Humean empiricism as first and foremost, a philosophy of practice. Empiricism's subject matter are social practices. If the term "habit" designates the customary, exter-nal relations constitutive of the understanding, it also designates what Deleuze calls "institutions." As developed in *Instincts and Institutions*, an institutional habit is a form of conduct or a specific organization of the body ("every institution imposes a series of models on our bodies") that cannot be explained as simply the expression or suppression of human nature (or instincts).[105]

The essay on Tournier's *Friday* extends the empiricist notion of habit further by folding into it some of the fruits of phenomenological description. Deleuze positions phenomenology as a reliable instrument for describing a certain set of perceptual habits. These habits are in turn identified as part of a more general, dominant habitual structure. In short, phenomenology is treated as a tool for making us aware of the dominant form of perception (just as Bergson's metaphysics includes an account of ordinary or natural perception). Within Deleuze's philosophical horizon, this awareness is linked to the more significant insight of how the language of essences, invariants, and bodies as organisms is no more than the description of deeply entrenched, contingent structures. The Deleuzian identification of structures opens up rather than forecloses the question of different organizations and new structures. Like Bergson's empiricist striving for a less natural, less human perception, the heroic phenomenologist does more than describe lived experience; they search for ways to alter it. Let us consider how this occurs in Deleuze's portrait of Tournier's novel.

First, Deleuze prepares the ground for the extraction of the central concept of his essay – the concept of the Other. This takes the form of a cursory overview of what is deemed the dominant system of thought and perception. In the course of this overview, Deleuze enlists well-known features of both empiricism and phenomenology. The novelty lies in the fact that the two are presented as useful instruments for describing one and the same system. Empiricism, especially the Humean variant, draws our attention to the typically smooth and regular transition between thoughts. One idea of sensation engenders another, or an impression of sensation engenders an idea of sensation. This is not because the terms are internally related, but because external, habitual relations have been established courtesy of the principles of association (Deleuze emphasizes the principles of contiguity and resemblance).

Deference is shown toward phenomenology – in particular, the figures of Husserl, Heidegger, and Sartre – because it provides a more adequate account of ordinary perception.[106] In particular, four results of phenomenological research are referenced in passing. Each represents an improvement upon modern philosophy's tendency to depict the field of experience as a sequence of deep-focus presentations or pictures the content of which is unconditioned by any spatial or temporal absence. First, phenomenology draws our attention to the fact that a perceptual field can possess a center and a periphery, a foreground and a background, and that a single perceptual moment can contain within itself different degrees of clarity and distinctness. Second, in

"The Phenomenology of Time-Consciousness" Husserl describes how the content of perception is irreducible to what is present in the present. Experience is conditioned by primary recollection (or retention) and primary anticipation (or protention). Our experience of the "present" is shaped by absence in the sense of what was present and what we anticipate will become present. Third, Heidegger and Sartre describe how the disclosure of the world is a function of our temporal, which is to say nonsubstantial, character. As thrown projections, we at each moment belong to the past and the future. Fourth, what is spatially present is constituted as a transcendent object; it is experienced as the profile of an object of which an indeterminate number of other, currently absent, profiles are possible.

I have already mentioned how this account of thought and perception – a peculiar hybrid of empiricism and phenomenology – is no more than an initial move Deleuze makes in formulating his concept of the Other. The next step involves locating within the experiential field something on the order of an ego. This is in turn linked to the accent Deleuze places on transitions within the field (i.e. his analysis focuses upon the emergence and disappearance of a form within experience). Given the detour through existential phenomenology, the reader should not expect the ego to conform to the Cartesian picture of self and world as separable compartments (interiority and exteriority), or even to the self of "reflective consciousness." Rather, "ego" merely refers to a minimal sense of separation of consciousness and object. The experience of an object is felt to be my experience, not the object's (i.e. the object's self-awareness).

The replacement of one form for another can be calm or violent, smooth or jagged. According to Deleuze, the experiential system described above is one in which the transition between forms is typically harmonious. The reason for this is that the new experience was in some sense anticipated. To experience a form as a profile of a transcendent object is to anticipate some of the other profiles that are possible. Our experience of the foreground involves a sense of the kind of distinct objects lying in the background. Our experience of what is present is conditioned by what we believe we would encounter were we to enter a building, turn our head, continue reading, and so on.

By "Other" Deleuze means neither ego nor object. Moreover, "Other" does not denote Sartre's circuit of objectifying-objectified gazes.[107] The Other is an *a priori* structure in that it is a necessary condition for the possibility of the above-described system of experience an essential characteristic of which is smooth transitions. Changes as far as experiential content are not typically shocking because most forms, prior to their presentation, belong to a background of expected or anticipated objects. This background of possibility (in the sense of possible objects of experience) is expressed within the present (in the sense that the content of experience is marked by what is absent but anticipated). Deleuze extracts "the Other" from this phenomenological picture by presenting it as a necessary condition for membership in the background of "possible worlds." To sense an object as possible for me is to posit it as actual for another. What I anticipate perceiving (if I turn my head, if I walk around a building, etc.) is what someone else is perceiving now, or, at the very least, might be perceiving now.

This concept of the other or alterity becomes clearer when we return to the issue of thought. As with perception, movement in the field of thought is typically continuous; our next thought will most likely not be experienced as an unexpected, violent intrusion. Unlike the encounter of a sign, we are not typically surprised by what we find ourselves thinking. For Deleuze, this is because the thought will conform to the sensed background of possibility; the thought will conform to what we sense others were already thinking. What we are about to think will be "the kind of thing people think." In this way, the concept of the Other subsumes a phenomenology of perception into a more general account of entrenched structures. The empiricist/phenomenological account of thought and perception paves the way for a similar account of the structure of desire and the body.

Changes in the structure of desire are typically smooth because the objects abandoned and assumed are "possible" objects of desire. We are not surprised to find ourselves presently desiring a particular object because it conforms to our sense of what people desire (i.e. it is the "kind of thing" people desire). Here Deleuze introduces the "classical" image of desire the most elegant formulation of which is provided in Plato's *Symposium*: desire is always a desire for something, and desire is always predicated upon an experience of lack. An object is only desired if it is felt to be lacked. In Deleuze's analysis of *Friday*, the reader can discern some of the themes of *Anti-Oedipus*, a book that completely overhauls this way of talking about desire. The Platonic and psychoanalytic conception of desire corresponds to the structure Deleuze and Guattari call "Oedipus" or "repression." In addition to being fueled by lack, the conventional structure of desire involves well-defined subjects (defined according to the exclusive disjunctions of male and female, adult and child, human and inhuman) selecting equally well-defined objects. By opposing Tournier's novel to the literature of interiority (or inner life),

Deleuze highlights the way that Robinson's discussion of the organization of lived experience (thought, perception, desire, sexuality) is simultaneously an analysis of the organization of the body. The journal kept
by Tournier's Robinson is an example of what, in *Anti-Oedipus,* goes by
the name of conjunctive synthesis; it is a representation or identification ("What is happening to me?" "This is what is happening to me")
produced alongside of a process of disordering and reordering.

With the concept of the Other, Deleuze has fused together the empiricist notion of transitions, a phenomenology of perception, and the
classical image of desire. Deleuze uses Tournier's novel to produce a
map of the typical subject or ordinary life: a map of our lives. Just as
important, Deleuze short-circuits any and all attempts to pass off this
complex physical-experiential structure as immutable. This requires
him to undo the distinction between synthetic *a priori* principles and
contingent systems of habits or institutions. Why, then, does Deleuze
refer to the Other as an *a priori*? The Other is not an object of experience, but what makes possible the harmonious transitions within
experience. The Other is *a priori* in the sense of being a condition for
specific, actual experiences; it is not *a priori* in the sense of being a universal and necessary condition for experience in general. Concrete lives
should be understood as exhibiting or instantiating a general structure,
but only on condition these structures are not regarded as some sort of
inflexible, inviolable nature. Phenomenology can serve as useful instruments of analysis, so long as the object of analysis is understood to be,
not immutable formations, but deeply entrenched habits. The implicit
Deleuzian position is that many of the techniques for identifying transcendental conditions, human nature, and essential dispositions can be
salvaged as devices for delimiting organizations that, while tenacious,
are neither necessary nor unbreakable.

A central distinction in *Empiricism and Subjectivity* is the one between
the notion of habit and a representational epistemology. This distinction is maintained in "Michel Tournier and the World without Others,"
but is secondary to the one Deleuze draws between strong habitual
organizations and their interruption, established institutions and their
destabilization. This interruption can take the form of a permanent
breakdown. One's feelings, perceptions, and desires can become nothing but the negation or inverse of a previous system. But an interruption
can also be temporary. There can be a restoration of the old. Or, a new
way thinking, perceiving, and desiring can be constructed. A parallel
shift occurs with the notion of institution. In *Empiricism and Subjectivity*
and *Instincts and Institutions*, the notion of institution is designed to

move thought away from appeals to human nature as well as negative conceptions of the social. With "Michel Tournier and the World without Others," this critical, antihumanist position is secondary to the distinction between an old institution and a new one. Because an institution is a particular way of organizing the body ("every institution imposes a series of models on our bodies") the distinction between old and new institutions anticipates one of the key notions of *Anti-Oedipus* and *A Thousand Plateaus*: desiring-production or the engineering of bodies without organs.[108]

As far as Deleuze's philosophy is concerned, Tournier's *Friday* is a key mediator in that it facilitates the formulation and reformulation of important Deleuzian themes concerning modes of organization: the contingency of structures (structures as habits or institutions), the undoing of structures, the distinction between restoration and innovation. Deleuze's characterization of Tournier's text as an "experimental and inductive novel" is far from arbitrary.[109] What Tournier "induces" is the ordinary composition of perception, desire, and sexuality. And he does so by imagining a set of material circumstances that would threaten this composition. As in Defoe's *Robinson Crusoe*, Tournier strands his protagonist on an island. In this milieu of solitude, the absence of others entails the gradual erosion of the Other along with the physical-experiential organization it makes possible. The process occurs in a series of stages. Initially the structure persists. Robinson's memory of his pre-wreck interactions, along with his belief that others may live on the island, assures that his presentations remain expressions of possible worlds. But time and the awareness of being isolated gradually takes its toll on the structure of the Other. As with Defoe's Robinson, Tournier's Robinson reacts by attempting to duplicate the world left behind. In *Friday*, these efforts include a rigid work schedule and memorable attempts at having the island function as a heterosexual object-choice. Eventually, under the strain of isolation, the structure collapses; each new presentation enters Robinson's consciousness like a violent intruder. The protagonist runs the risk of psychosis – the risk of a paralyzing, permanent breakdown.

As one might expect, Deleuze's interest in the novel lies precisely in the fact that its ending involves neither a recovery of the old organization nor the absence of organization. The character Friday joins Robinson, but instead of instantiating the Other, he serves as a mediator facilitating the production of a new organization. This new organization is a new "inhuman," or "elemental" sexuality; a new body (one no longer organized through the regimentation of time and the adoption of projects); a new experience of the island as "erect" or "straight" (the possibles are ironed out of presentations making the latter appear as flat, one-dimensional surfaces); and a new, egoless relationship between consciousness and object (Robinson experience his thoughts as the self-consciousness of the Island).

The perverse, divergent direction of Tournier's novel should be contrasted with two other narratives – Defoe's original telling of the story and Descartes' *Meditations*. As Deleuze points out, Defoe's Robinson reproduces or re-presents the political and economic order left behind (the ideological character and use of Defoe's novel is well-known). Similarly, Descartes' solitary interrogation of habitual judgment is performed with the aim of restoration. The narrator of the *Meditations* renders his old system of habitual beliefs durable through the construction of an epistemic foundation.

Deleuze refers to the alternative organization engineered by Tournier's Robinson as a "double" and as a "phantasm."[110] This language is best understood as a reiteration of Deleuze's treatment of Plato in *Difference and Repetition*, and in his most well-known essay "Plato and the Simulacrum." In both pieces, Platonism is defined as the hierarchical differentiation of particulars into true and false claimants. Instead of being the heart of Platonism, the doctrine of forms or essences is the means to this classification. One class of particulars is privileged as true through their classification as representations of original forms. Another class of particulars is disparaged as false by identifying them as simulacra. Simulacra only appear to be representations. In the *Republic*, Plato describes the danger of poetry, arguing that people confuse the moral code they suggest for justice (i.e. for the authentic representation of justice embodied in the philosophical life). What connection is there between this Platonism and the narratives of Defoe and Descartes? In each case what is privileged falls squarely within the order of representation. In Tournier's narrative, however, the final organization is a double in the sense of a phantasm or simulacrum. His protagonist reaches a unique state (i.e. one that does not re-present a preexisting mode of existence).

In her often-cited feminist analysis of Deleuze's essay, Alice Jardin attempts to uncover evidence of Tournier and Deleuze's phallocentrism. But her argument conflicts distinct stages of Robinson's transformation. Robinson's attempt to marry and copulate with the island has more to do with the old, indisputably phallocentric organization, than the one eventually produced. Jardin confuses Tournier's description of phallocentrism (and of Robinson's attempt to preserve it in isolation) as an endorsement. Similarly, Jardin points toward Deleuze's description of the transformation ("a generalized erection" or "straightening up" of the island), but without identifying what this language means. The vertical imagery is used to convey the collapse of the background of possible worlds (perception becomes a collision with flat, upright, one-dimensional surfaces), and the production of a sexual economy that is explicitly nonphallic. In fact, Robinson's sexuality has nothing in common with what most people would recognize as sexuality.

Another error to avoid concerns Deleuze's discussion and praise of solitude and solipsism. Obviously Deleuzian solipsism can be neither an inner journey nor an absence of encounters. Here one only need refer to the indispensable role played by the character of Friday. Friday is Robinson's sign or medium of becoming. This presupposes that Friday does not instantiate the Other. The encounter does not enable Robinson to preserve his old organization. Rather Friday is a reference point and external force that inspires and facilitates the construction of a genuinely novel organization of thought, perception, and desire. Deleuzian "solitude" or "solipsism" can only mean a flight from the "kinds of things" people say, think, and feel. Solitude can only mean a flight from generic forms of desiring and acting.

A final erroneous interpretation would take Deleuze's account of creativity to be one in which, through a simple quasi-consumerist choice, individuals reinvent their way of living. The word Deleuze uses to describe Robinson's situation is "catastrophe." Catastrophe, because the changes Robinson undergoes presuppose a radical change in his material circumstances. Catastrophe, because the structure that collapses is a set of deeply entrenched habits, its collapse represents the risk of psychosis, and the restructuring that occurs is not modeled on an artificial territory of capitalism. Robinson's reinvention is not the adoption of a billboard lifestyle. Deleuze's problem of the new is explicitly counterposed to the problem of being on the "cutting edge" of fashion, just as his definition of the concept is explicitly opposed to the advertiser's (the concept as marketing strategy).

For Deleuze, philosophical discourse contains distinct forms of comedic criticism: humor (overturning a law through over-conformity), black humor (the combining of radical, noncontradictory differences), and irony (presenting "noble," "original" principles as derivations of base origins).[111] The best way to understand the anti-phenomenological message of *What Is Philosophy?* is as an ironic, genealogical assault on the conservative tendencies within the phenomenological tradition. This critique is accomplished through a dual positioning of phenomenology. On the one hand, phenomenology is located within a larger history – the idea of philosophy as *doxa* or true opinion. On the other hand, phenomenology is located at the side of logic in a marriage that, while quarrelsome, is a marriage all the same. On Deleuze's plane of immanence, the conceptual personae of the logician and the phenomenologist live as an unhappy couple. As was the case with logic, phenomenological definitions of philosophy and of the concept are diagnosed as a diminishment of philosophy's power to create.

A central theme in Deleuze's account of the history of philosophy is the tension between immanence and transcendence. Recalling Spinoza's depiction of the pre-Socratics and drawing upon the research of French historian Jean-Pierre Vernant, Deleuze argues that philosophy began when Greek thought underwent a process of secularization.[112] The cause of nature's order was sought within nature itself rather than in a dramatic contest between supernatural agents. Vernant explains this cosmological shift, along with the emergence of the figure of the philosopher, as part of a broader, more sweeping alteration in the organization of social life. In short, the polis came to replace the palace. In Deleuze's account, emphasis is placed on the way the history of philosophy, from inception, displays both the movement toward immanent explanation described by Vernant, and a tendency to arrest this movement through positing transcendent principles:

> Greek philosophy still remains attached to that old Wisdom ready to unfold its transcendence again, although it now possesses only its friendship, its affection. Immanence is necessary, but it must be immanent to something transcendent, to ideality.[113]

The passage is useful for seeing why and how Deleuze tethers his arguments against transcendence and for immanence to a Spinoza/Nietzsche-inflected representation of philosophy's power: philosophy proceeds to its limit by avoiding the notion of transcendence.

This brings us to the relationship between opinion (*doxa*) and the history of philosophy. In *What Is Philosophy?* the discussion of opinion centers around this idea of philosophical immanence becoming an immanence to transcendence.[114] The narrow target of this section of the book is phenomenology, so we should expect phenomenology to be presented as a reiteration or quasi-reiteration of transcendence. But first, let us see how Deleuze and Guattari relate philosophy to *doxa*.

On the one hand, philosophy's connection to opinion places it on the side of immanence. The figure of the philosopher is contrasted with that of the sage. The latter is associated with the possession of wisdom (or at least the claim to possess wisdom). But in the above quote, the philosopher is defined as the friend or lover of wisdom. In this respect, the philosopher only possesses opinions. In addition to this negative definition of opinion – having an opinion is not having wisdom – Deleuze and Guattari provide a positive one. An opinion is described as a function comprised of a dual extraction or recognition. In concrete situations, one extracts a "perceptual quality" and a general "power of affection." This language is designed to accentuate a couple of features of opinions. Opinions have a content (they are a way of looking at things) and opinions are attributed to a subject (the one who holds an opinion). Moreover, both content and subject involve abstraction, and, for this reason, possess a degree of generality.[115] An opinion is formed in response to a particular situation (a "perceptive-affective lived situation"), but it is only an opinion if it exceeds this setting, if the one who holds it ends up exercising that opinion in other settings. If an individual regards the opinion as one he or she holds ("I see things this way"), it is also the case that the subject identified be a more general subject ("We see things this way" or "I am not alone in looking at things this way"). Deleuze and Guattari's illustration clearly reveals their wish to separate the philosophical concept from the structure of opinion: "many discussions can be expressed in this way: 'as a man, I consider all women to be unfaithful'; 'as a woman, I think men are liars.'"[116]

On the other hand, ancient philosophy exhibits the desire to elevate philosophy over mere opinion or arbitrary opinion. The figure of the philosopher is distinct not only from the sage but also from the sophist. How to legitimate the distinction between the philosopher and the charlatan? Unlike Deleuze who also employs this distinction, the Platonic justification involves an appeal to transcendent principles (this is how Plato secures the distinction between the philosophical life and the simulacrum of sophism). In *What Is Philosophy?* several brief allusions to Plato's *Symposium* serve to illustrate how philosophy becomes a practice of advancing criteria for dividing "proto-opinions" or true opinions from simple opinion.[117] The dialogue is well-chosen, for it illustrates philosophy's relationship to immanence as well.

Socrates' opening move is to challenge the belief that Eros is good, wise, beautiful, and immortal. Desire is the desire for and movement toward these properties and this presupposes lack rather than possession.[118] But if philosophy's movement (the philosopher as the lover) is based upon its distance from beauty, wisdom, and the good, it is also based on the nonarbitrary status of its opinions. A child of Poverty and Resourcefulness, Eros knows how to travel toward what it is missing. The road of philosophy has a determinate end, even if this end is unreachable.

> Platonist philosophers themselves had an extraordinary answer that, they thought, allowed them to select opinions. *It was necessary to choose the quality that was like the unfolding of the Beautiful in any lived situation,* and to take as generic subject Man inspired by the Good.[119]

In the case of the *Symposium*, this formulation of the "Platonic test" involves a complex set of relations between the path of *eros*, immortality, community, and beauty. Desire is the desire for immortality, but our finitude entails that the closest we can come to achieving immortality is to create things for which we will be remembered and praised. If the initial aim of philosophical desire (the journey of one "pregnant in the soul") is to create memorable thoughts, its ultimate result is a memorable life. The central idea in Plato's description is conveyed in the cryptic phrase "one can only give birth in something beautiful."[120] Creation occurs in the presence of beauty. What does this mean?[121] First, creation occurs in partnership with those who are beautiful (the physically beautiful followed by the spiritually beautiful). Second, the thoughts created within these beautiful relationships are themselves beautiful. Third, these beautiful thoughts are thoughts of beauty. The thoughts are formed through the recognition of the types of beauty particulars instantiate: the beauty of bodies, of souls, of art, of legal-political institutions. While this process culminates in the contemplation of absolute beauty, the *Symposium* is a great dialogue for seeing how this contemplation is inseparable from an existential transformation. For Plato, the lover is the one whose life gradually becomes a representation of absolute beauty. The *Symposium* is also a great dialogue for seeing why and how Deleuze privileges the simulacrum. The protagonist of Socrates' speech should be juxtaposed with the Deleuzian hero found in "Michel Tournier and the World without Others" (as well as "How Do We Recognize Structuralism?"). The Platonic jump to transcendence and formulation of proto-opinions is at the same time an answer to the question, "How does one think and live differently?" The lovers' creation of a unique, memorable life is a matter of making their life a representation. The Deleuzian protagonists shape their lives into simulacra. The creation of difference entails the absence of representation – the absence of an original or model.

When philosophy is conceived as *doxa*, philosophical concepts are advanced as foundational opinions. Philosophy assumes the form of an exclusive disjunctive synthesis. Rival groups engage in discussion and debate. Each group attempts to show that the opinions that define them as a group (or generic subject) are the ones that are true (i.e. are the ones that reflect the proper perceptual extraction or way of looking at things).

Under the heading of the "triumph of opinion," Deleuze and Guattari pull together a variety of tendencies: the image of philosophy as a tribunal (the practice of assigning opinions truth-values), the penchant for claims of transcendence (the identification of proto-opinions), the image of philosophy as an arena in which opinions are discussed, communicated, or debated. In a loose, even improvisational manner, these themes are hooked onto two others: orthodoxy and marketing. *Doxa* may be the simultaneous recognition of a perceptual quality and generic subject, but when qualities and subjects congeal and solidify, it turns into the demand that recognition conform to the judgments of a preexisting group or majority: "The essence of opinion is a will to majority and already speaks in the name of a majority."[122]

If defining philosophy in terms of opinion reduces the concept to the recognition of a quality and a generic subject, and orthodoxy reduces the concept to the expression of preexisting subjects, marketing reduces the concept to the packaging of commodities and purchasing groups. The perceptions of *doxa* become clichés, while the generic subjects become "labels" or groups that are little more than artificial territories of the marketplace. In essays such as "Michel Tournier and the World without Others," and "How Do We Recognize Structuralism?" Deleuze links creativity to the discovery that structures of thought, perception, and behavior are violable. The declaration that capitalism reduces the concept to marketing strategies, along with the more thorough examination of capitalism's cynical production of beliefs and groups contained in *Anti-Oedipus*, represents an indispensable corollary. Any serious discussion of creating alternative forms of existence has to include an examination of how the marketplace offers us fashion, prefabricated lifestyles, and cut-rate phrases of self-empowerment as an art of living. Deleuze recognizes these forces to be a far more powerful agent of representation (or the return of the same) than Platonism, the history of philosophy, or the history of metaphysics.

The attempt to elevate philosophical opinions over mere opinions is linked to the belief that academic discussions are similarly elevated. Deleuze offers an ironic challenge to this belief. In one of the more humorous passages of *What Is Philosophy?* the nature of opinion is illustrated as follows: some cheese is brought to the table, an individual extracts a pure quality (they "recognize" that cheese in general is foul), the individual identifies a general power (the group of cheese haters) along with a rival (those who love cheese). Then, in the name of the generic subject, the individual insults the rival.[123] Through this parody of academic discourse, Deleuze inserts a wedge between, on the one hand, philosophy and, on the other hand, the search for true opinions, the formulation of criteria for measuring the truth of opinions, the communication of true opinions, and the debate over which generic subject's opinions are true:

> Ours is the age of communication, but every noble soul flees and crawls far away whenever a little discussion, a colloquium, or a simple conversation is suggested. In every conversation the fate of philosophy is always at stake, and many philosophical discussions do not as such go beyond discussions of cheese, including the insults and the confrontation of worldviews.[124]

It may seem that with this discussion of immanence and transcendence, doxa and orthodoxy, proto-opinions and debate, we have traveled far away from the figure of the phenomenologist. But it is within this rhizome that the conceptual persona resides. This decentered network of concepts and relations is the character's neighborhood on Deleuze's plane of immanence. The phenomenologist's concepts are not presented as simple documentations of experience, but as representations of a general underlying, pre-theoretical structure of experience. This is reflected in the fact the generic subject to whom these experiences are attributed is deemed to be more or less universal. The notion of "lived experience" is an attempt to illuminate "being-in-the-world." The philosophical creation of concepts becomes a search for foundational opinions. The notion of "lived experience" plays a role comparable to the Platonic "forgotten homeland," in that its employment is used to confer priority upon one class of opinions, propositions, or representations over another (those that represent a more or less immutable structure). In particular, phenomenological propositions are opposed to scientific propositions. The distinction between true and false opinions is reconfigured as a distinction between the original and the derivative, the concrete and the abstract, the pre-theoretical and the theoretical.

As previously mentioned, Deleuze creates the conceptual personae of the logician and phenomenologist as a couple. The first character orients philosophy in the direction of science. The philosophical concept is defined as a logical function. The second character protests that scientific theory has a concrete, pre-theoretical background. The philosophical concept is segregated from scientific discourse by becoming the representation of science's remainder. For Deleuze this is analogous to "the rhinoceros and the bird that lives on its parasites."[125]

According to Deleuze, the most prosaic thought imaginable lies behind the celebrated rigor of the logical function: "this is a chair, while that is a desk." Similarly, in the name of identifying pre-theoretical, background conditions ordinary perception (*a* structure of perception) can be passed off as perception in general. In contrast, it should now be clear why an absolutely indispensable component of Deleuze's writings is the way they reference and incorporate fictional and nonfictional texts detailing extreme, aberrant experiences, just as it is an indispensable component of Deleuze's writings that measures are taken to avoid romanticizing such experiences (i.e. Deleuze refuses to present them as good in the sense of risk-free).

6   The structuralist as hero; the structuralist as palace dog

Earlier I quoted Foucault declaring he and Deleuze "never do structural analyses" and "are absolutely not structuralists." But Deleuze is too much the schizo, his recording apparatus too peculiar and inclusive, for us to expect his relationship to structuralism to be as straightforward as Foucault suggests. In this respect, the question, "was Deleuze a structuralist?" is a bad one. Unless, that is, we avoid seeking a yes or no answer, and instead use the question to illuminate the peculiarities of Deleuze's recording apparatus (the coordinates he uses to situate his work), and his production, through counter-actualization, of conceptual personae.

Reading 1953's *Empiricism and Subjectivity*, we discover Deleuze was among the first philosophers to appreciate and express reservations concerning incipient structuralism (this two years before Lévi-Strauss' breakthrough work *Le Triste Tropique*).[126] During the structuralist adventure "empiricism" denoted an epistemology that reduced the intelligible to the sensible (i.e. "empiricism" meant the belief that knowledge is a collection of sensory facts). Deleuze argues, however, that Hume's focus is not unrelated, atomistic facts but the formation of relations irreducible to observable facts. This process is described as one in which the mind or imagination – a collection of unrelated contents – is organized into a system of habits by external principles (the passions and princi-ples of association). With the accent squarely on relations irreducible to consciousness and on the constitution of the subject, Deleuze anoints Hume the unacknowledged forbearer of "human science!"[127] Deleuze's portrayal of Hume as a proto-structuralist inoculates the latter's phi-losophy from structuralist attacks, and it cuts off at the pass what would become *the* structuralist representation of the philosophical tradition. Within *Le Triste Tropique*, Lévi-Strauss follows Freud in equating philos-ophy with interiority: the belief that the ultimate objects of knowledge are contained immediately and inherently within consciousness.[128]

Three decades later, 1973 finds Deleuze penning the entry on structuralism for Francoise Châtelet's encyclopedia of philosophy. The opening paragraph of "How Do We Recognize Structuralism?" dates the essay a few years earlier (*"This Is 1967"*). Between these two dates, Deleuze would meet Guattari (1969) and the two would write *Anti-Oedipus* (published in 1972). Whatever the date of "How do we Recognize Structuralism?" one thing is clear; it is a most unusual ency-clopedia article.[129] The essay begins innocently enough. The basic structuralist act is defined as equating structure with language, fol-lowed by the discovery of languages in new, unexpected places. This notion of structure or language is described as the introduction of a third element – the symbolic. Deleuze presents this notion as an act of thought circumventing the old distinction between the imaginary and real. The goal is no longer that of describing how imagination's opposite, the intellect, represents the real; or how the imagination is able to grasp a higher, nonintellectual reality; or how the demands and prohibitions of the real lead to imaginary forms of gratification. Deleuze links the notion of the symbolic to the idea that sense is a function of nonsense (signs are a function of elements that are inher-ently meaningless), and he uses this fact to explain the structuralist penchant for the metaphor of the game as well as the specific way in which structuralism is a form of antihumanism (there is no conscious agency at the center of a structure).

At this point in the article, the familiar lexicon of structuralism begins to gradually be supplanted with language from Deleuze's ontology (*Difference and Repetition*) and theory of desire (*Anti-Oedipus*). Repetition and difference: Deleuze constructs structuralism's doppelganger. He creates a portrait or likeness of structuralism in another medium (this other medium being his philosophy). Deleuze takes structuralism from behind and creates a child that the structuralist would want to disown but could not.

For some, this last metaphor suggests a strong parallel between Deleuzian portraiture and Derridean deconstruction. But such a comparison renders the term "deconstruction" vague and conceals precisely what makes each mode of reading noteworthy. In fact, the essay "How Do We Recognize Structuralism?" is a perfect text for highlighting the nondeconstructive character of portraiture because we can compare it with Derrida's treatment of the same material.

In his classic essay *Structure, Sign, and Play in the Human Sciences*, Derrida positions Lévi-Strauss's work in relation to logocentrism. For Lévi-Strauss the representation of myth's structure is itself a permutation of that structure. In other words, the subject that knows the structure of myth is at the same time instantiating the structure of myth. On the one hand, this reconfiguration of epistemology represents a challenge to the logocentric notion of objectivity. On the other hand, Lévi-Strauss's concern that structuralism be perceived as scientific, not to mention his subsequent, quasi-Hegelian allusions to structures teleologically realizing themselves in the mind of the structuralist, reinforces logocentrism. The rhythm of Derrida's text is established by a rigorous movement between the general notion of logocentrism and specific passages of Lévi-Strauss's writing. This movement is internally divided by the fact that some passages are represented as stabilizers, others as destabilizers of logocentrism.

Structure, Sign, and Play in the Human Sciences is fairly representative of one of Derrida's major compositional styles. The identical rhythm and divided movement is found in his treatment of the thought of Saussure (*Of Grammatology*), Heidegger ("The Ends of Man"), Austin ("Signature, Event, Context"), and Foucault ("Cogito and the History of Madness"). For our purposes, what is important is that no reader could possibly mistake Derrida's text with that of "How Do We Recognize Structuralism?" On a strictly material level, no passage from Derrida's text could ever be confused with a passage from Deleuze's or vice versa. Why is this? At no point does Deleuze identify a flaw with structuralism. As discussed earlier, this is an essential feature of Deleuzian portraiture. Also characteristic is the fact that the one criticism Deleuze does make is directed toward critics of structuralism: "Books against structuralism...are strictly without importance; they cannot prevent structuralism from exerting a productivity which is that of our era."[130]

As already mentioned, in-between this concluding sentiment and the early passages, a strictly implicit, undeclared translation into Deleuzian metaphysics occurs. Following Saussure, the standard structuralist line is that language as *langue* is the union of two planes – a plane of signifiers and a plane of concepts. The identity (or value) of the elements of each plane along with the identity of the conventional but durable connections between the planes are held to be a function of difference. In place of this terminology, Deleuze describes the structure as a differential or distribution of singularities (the notion of differentiation in *Difference and Repetition*). Additionally, he avoids the tendency to describe the difference of structuralism as one of opposition or negation. A conventional definition of structuralism would include the distinction between *langue* and *parole*, between a system of signs and the different utterances it makes possible, between a structure and its concrete permutations. In Deleuze's portrait, the structure is defined as a "virtual multiplicity." Rewriting the distinction between *langue* and *parole*, Deleuze characterizes the structure as nonactual, while arguing for the need to distinguish the category of the virtual from that of the possible. The multiplicity is virtual rather than possible because it possesses "a reality proper to it." And, it is virtual because it differenciates itself through heterogeneous actualizations. Deleuze argues that the actualization of the virtual is not the realization of a possibility ("what was possible is now real"), the instantiation of a self-identical essence, the representation of a preexisting principle, or even the realization of potential.

From being a term opposed to the real (the signified is not the referent) the symbolic becomes a theory of the real. On the one hand, the real has an actual side comprised of well-defined individuals and exclusive disjunctions. On the other hand, there is a virtual side comprised of pure difference. The transformation of linguistics into metaphysics is completed when Deleuze, instead of invoking the largely epistemological theme of the "death of the subject," offers a redefinition of the subject: "neither personal nor universal, it is without an identity, made of nonpersonal individuations and pre-individual singularities."[131] Then, in a move illustrating Deleuze's tethering of metaphysics to questions of practice, the future of structuralism is presented as one in which the identification of structures will be regarded as a means rather than an end. The ultimate objective is not epistemological, but a practice of experimentation. Deleuze describes a "structuralist hero" who through "creative force" allows a "new structure not to pursue adventures that again are analogous to those of the old structure."[132]

Having shown the compositional and normative difference between deconstruction and portraiture let us return to the question of Deleuze's response to structuralism. As mentioned in the previous section, a structuralism series runs parallel to the phenomenological series in Deleuze's writing. When it comes to situating Deleuze in relationship to structuralism, sections from *Anti-Oedipus* must be placed alongside of *Empiricism and Subjectivity* and "How Do We Recognize Structuralism?" Deleuze's complete "response" to structuralism is made up of an interpretation of structuralism as a successor to philosophical empiricism, an equally unorthodox portrait of structuralism drawn in medium of metaphysics, and a critique without reserve.

Recalling *Empiricism and Subjectivity*, *Anti-Oedipus* includes a critique of treating social practices and artifacts as permutations of an innate mental system. Such a model of explanation conceals the social as a site of institutions or concrete strategies. The more dramatic critique of structuralism, however, is found in the authors' discussion of structuralism's critique of the signified or privileging of the signifier. Like the ferocious parody of phenomenology, this critique of structuralism should be understood as a genealogical deflation of the pretensions of structuralism and semiotics. The structuralist orientation is described as the product of a fundamental shift in the order of inscription or representation.[133] Within the earlier "territorial machine" speech and graphism are two heterogeneous elements conjoined when a third visual element (an eye) jumps between the two in a "system of cruelty." Body parts are assigned a place in a community's cycle of debt by being cut, tattooed, severed, and so on. A designated authority sees this inscription and hears in the voice of the recipient that the pain is sufficient. The genealogical break occurs when writing is aligned with or flattened onto a speech from "up high." What does this involve? For Deleuze and Guattari, the law does not originate as a form of protection against despotism but as the representation and dissemination of the despot's absent voice. The basis for the notion of interpretation (the idea that inscriptions or utterances are envelopes for determinate signifieds) is an obsession with the despot. The despot's functionaries spread his word; the subjects attentively consider the meaning of his declarations ("what am I being told to do?").

But the obsession with the despot is also the basis for its inverse, the transgression of the despot. The "despotic signifier" is the flood of critiques directed toward the classical notion of interpretation: the signified is in reality a signifier, meaning is indeterminate, no signified saturates the identity of a signifier, the reader contributes to the meaning of a text, and so on. Recalling Sartre's characterization of anticommunists as dogs, Deleuze and Guattari link the classical notion of interpretation *and* its inverse (the valorization of the signifier) to inaction and passivity:

> The imperialism of the signifier does not take us beyond the question, "What does it mean?" it is content to bar the question in advance,

to render all answers insufficient by relegating them to the status of a simple signified. It challenges exegesis in the name of recitation, pure textuality, and superior "scientificity" (*scientificité*). Like the young palace dogs too quick to drink the verse water, and who never tire of crying: The signifier, you have not reached the signifier, you are still at the level of the signifieds![134]

By now it should be clear that evaluation plays a strictly secondary role within Deleuze's philosophy. What a mistake to read any of Deleuze's responses to structuralism as a cluster of static ideas coming before the Deleuzian tribunal. On a related note, the different evaluations should not be approached from within a developmental perspective. The change should not be understood as Deleuze changing his mind ("but then Deleuze realized structuralism was bad"). The change of value is superficial relative to more striking, features of the interpretations. Together they affirm experimentation, condemn resignation. With *Empiricism and Subjectivity*, structuralism is linked to the thought of Hume; the idea of structure becomes the idea of a structure composed of habits. "What is Structuralism?" introduces the persona of a heroic structuralist who embodies the break up of an old structure, the production of a new one. *Anti-Oedipus* gives us the persona of the structuralist lapdog, the one who confuses criticism of the signified with radical thought.

7   Philosophy's encounter with literature

Crucial to understanding Deleuze's thought is to see how the lines dividing philosophy, art, and historicism, while rigid in certain respects, are at the same time highly flexible. The practices continually converge, and being able to identify such moments with precision is a major reason for distinguishing between the practices. The strength and flexibility of the distinctions, along with the multiple critical and positive reasons for each are summarized in the following remarks:

> [W]e really have to see philosophy, art, and science as separate melodic lines in constant interplay with one another... What we have to recognize is that the interplay between the different lines isn't a matter of one monitoring or reflecting another. A discipline that set out to follow a creative movement coming from outside would relinquish any creative role. You'll get nowhere by latching onto some parallel movement, you have to make a move yourself.[135]

Deleuze describes two ways the practices can converge. On the one hand, he analyzes the way autonomous lines of development can engender moments of resonance.[136] Parallel formations can arise in philosophy and science, science and art, and so on. On the other hand, the practices can influence one another. Artists and scientists can encounter one another's work. Artists encounter philosophical and scientific signs that compel them to create new percepts and affects. Scientists encounter artistic and philosophical signs that compel them to create science. Philosophers encounter and re-territorialize aggregates of percepts and affects as philosophical concepts. To claim artists incorporate philosophy into their work without understanding it misses the point. To argue that Deleuze and Guattari's discussion of roots, trees, and rhizomes displays a lack of proficiency in the area of botanical research would be truly bizarre.

The theme of Deleuze and literature is a useful vantage point from which to survey philosophy's interaction with literature. Though relevant to the study of literature, Deleuze's philosophy is not a form or method of literary criticism.[137] The more philosophy is conflated with literary criticism, the more philosophy and literature are regarded as simply two genres of writing, the less relevant Deleuze's work will seem.

Continually re-territorializing aspects of literature, Deleuze upsets attempts to police the border dividing philosophy and literature. At the same time, each of Deleuze's reterritorializations is a rigorous display of philosophical creativity. Such concrete relations between philosophy and literature are concealed by vague celebrations of interdisciplinarity or intertextuality.

7.1   Literary genre and the book of life

The section from *A Thousand Plateaus* entitled "1874, Three Novellas or 'What Happened?'" begins with a typology of literary genres designed to highlight differences between novels and tales.[138] Here, as in so many other places, Deleuze and Guattari display their fondness for the linguistic categories of Louis Hjelmslev (plane of expression, plane of content, form and matter of expression, form and matter of content). While there is no uniform application of these categories in their writings, each use represents an attempt to circumvent a two-term, signifier-signified analysis. In the case of literary texts, the desire is to move past a simple explication of meaning ("the text means...") as well as second-order discussions of indeterminate meaning.[139] "Expression," is defined as the appearance of the temporal present. In the case of the novella, "expression" refers to the way the past is structured as a secret (the "form" of expression), and the way this past, regardless of the nature or even existence of an actual secret (the "matter" of expression), defines the present. In the case of the tale, the present leans heavily into a future possessing the form of discovery. This difference in the novella's and tale's plane of expression ("What happened?" versus "What is going to happen?") is linked to differences on their respective planes of content. "Content" designates the organization of the characters' thoughts and bodies. The novella is populated by mental and physical postures comparable to reactions, the tale by attitudes and positions comparable to "unfoldings."

Although interesting, this typology merely sets the stage for the invention of a neighborhood of concepts. Were this not the case, philosophical thought would, implicitly, be serving as an instrument of reflection. Deleuze and Guattari state that the novella deals in a striking way with a "universal matter." This subject matter is the way the lives of individuals and groups are comprised of lines:

> For we are made of lines. We are not only referring to lines of writing. Lines of writing conjugate with other lines, life lines, lines of luck or misfortune, lines productive of the variation of the line of writing itself, lines that are *between the lines* of writing.[140]

Accompanying this definition is the problem or task the authors refer to as "cartography." The problem of the new becomes the task of discerning the multiple lines that together form a concrete life.

This approach to the issue of subjectivity nicely illustrates Deleuze's modus operandi; one particularly visible in his work with Guattari. The typology of literary genres, more importantly the typology of lines, is an explicit exercise in abstraction. Inspired by Spinoza's conception of the individual life as a mixture of passivity and activity; Bergson's conception of the individual subject as a mixture of two, radically different forms of multiplicity; and Sartre's conception of the group as a mixture of seriality and the group-in-fusion, Deleuze endorses a specific form of abstraction, and a specific way of understanding the relationship between the abstract and the concrete. Qualitatively different principles are abstracted out of a concrete being. Thus, instead of disclosing a principle of unity beneath difference, Deleuzian abstraction discloses the difference within an individual unity. A useful analogue is the attempt to discern through taste the disparate ingredients that went into a pie. But if a pie is naturally understood to be a product of different ingredients, the concrete phenomena Deleuze and Guattari analyze (a life, a group, etc.) are easily mistaken for simple, homogeneous phenomena. While a pie's ingredients initially exist independently of one another, the different principles abstracted from the concrete only exist within concrete mixtures. "Abstract machines" are called "abstract" precisely because they are immanent rather than transcendent causes. Without the qualifier "abstract" we might be tempted to regard the machines as transcendent principles existing independently of their actualizations. While there is no aspect of Deleuze and Guattari's social theory free of a normative, political impulse, individual principles are not presented as good or bad.[141] The description of different "living lines" includes an account of the dangers inherent to each.

The jarring transition between the consideration of literary forms and the problem of lines is due to the absence of the standard argumentative bridge. If the analysis of lines reflects an alternative conception of subjectivity, Deleuze and Guattari do not identify those positions to which the alternative is an alternative. Nevertheless, a careful reading of their theory enables us to identify these positions. The definition of the subject as a set of entangled lines should be contrasted with the following: the belief a life is an instantiation or realization of a traditional essence or nature; the belief we are traditional substances rather than temporal structures; the belief we are at bottom nothing but thrown projections or facticity and transcendence; the claim an individual life is nothing but an instantiation of traditions; the idea one can define a life without discussing issues of class, race, gender, and sexuality; the idea a life can be considered nothing more than a nexus of these intersecting categories. Under the pretext of analyzing the novella, Deleuze overhauls our way of talking about and thinking about subjectivity.

Several features of our lives or of a life are folded into the first category of line – molar lines or rigid segments. Well defined, culturally inherited projects constitute rigid lines, as do the ways social roles condition the purposeful and predictable movement of our bodies through space (e.g. from job to school to home). Molar lines include aspects of a life typically referred to as the social location or subject position of an individual. But in addition to the categories of class, race, and gender, Deleuze and Guattari include as molar lines a host of distinctions that operate as exclusive disjunctions. Individuals are recognized as, and recognize themselves as, human rather than non-human, young or old, employee or boss, student or instructor, and so on.

The second type of line – molecular lines – are referred to as "quanta of deterritorialization" or as "flows and particles" falling outside of the molar lines. What could this be other than some vague, unclassifiable set of leftovers? The answer lies in the fact that lines are characterized as inscriptions on the body-without-organs. We have already seen how Deleuze's distinction between established institutions and new institutions, or established corporeal organizations and alternative corporeal organizations, represents an antihumanist challenge to the notion of body as organism (i.e. to the idea that the body is reducible to a single, natural form). A quanta of deterritorialization will be an organization of the body that surpasses one or more of society's exclusive molar territories. Individuals can "not act their age," a group of student-activists can "forget" they are in a classroom; women can act in ways that violate one or more of the components of the dominant conception of gender.

The difference between molecular lines and the third type of line – lines of flight – is described as the difference between quanta of deterritorialization and absolute deterritorialization. Even lives composed primarily of rigid segments, lives that are far from experiments in living, can involve corporeal articulations exceeding molar identifications. When humans play with their pets or adults play with children their bodies constitute a temporary becoming-animal or becoming-child. As with Robinson's relationship to Friday in Tournier's novel, a mediator (or "medium of becoming") facilitates a temporary reassembly of the body discontinuous to molar lines. A line of flight represents a more radical and consequential break with molar territories. When Deleuze and Guattari speak of "flight" or "escape," as they often do, these are opposed to flights of fancy.[142] A line of flight involves putting the social to flight. Hence, illustrations of the third type of line are drawn from the realm of politics, in particular the prison letters of George Jackson: "I may be running but I'm looking for a gun as I go." At this point, it becomes clear that, for Deleuze and Guattari, the divided quality of lives now applies to the life of a society. In fact the notion of lines invites a retheorization of the individual and the social. For Spinoza every individual is a compound formation; consequently, communities can be considered individuals of a higher order of complexity.[143] For Deleuze and Guattari, no individual society is self-identical in the sense of being saturated by its dominant relations or molar territories:

Lines of flight, for their part, never consist in running away from the world but rather in causing runoffs, as when you drill a hole in a pipe; there is no social system that does not leak from all directions, even if it makes its segments increasingly rigid in order to seal the lines of flight.[144]

Understanding the social body requires we recognize that, like any body – like any individual – it is a mixture of coexisting norms and alternatives.

7.2   The literature of capitalism

The claim lives combine molar territories and molecular deterritorializations is strongly related to the implementation and discussion of literature in *Anti-Oedipus* and *Dialogues*. With perhaps the sole exception of *A Thousand Plateaus*, *Anti-Oedipus* involves a greater appropriation of literature (in the sense of direct fold-ins) than any other philosophical text. The words of Henry Miller, D.H. Lawrence, William S. Burroughs, Jack Kerouac, Antonin Artaud, Samuel Beckett are used to propel forward a positive alternative to the classical definition of schizophrenia (schizophrenia as a flight from the real in the form of autism or dissociation). At the same time, this positive definition is a conception of desire as nonOedipal, immediately social, and lack-free.

Earlier I described how, in Deleuze's thought, "Anglo-American literature" and "American fiction" are terms of privilege. More often than not both are opposed to "French literature." Philosophical and literary currents are brought together in the conceptual persona of the Anglo-American thinker. In *Anti-Oedipus*, English and American fiction is privileged for the way it conveys the dual, ambiguous character of capitalism. On the one hand, following Marx, Deleuze and Guattari argue that, as a quantitative calculus, capitalism is ungoverned by qualities in the sense of beliefs and values. As a critical force, capitalism puts philosophical skepticism to shame. At the same time, in order to realize surplus value, ensure resignation, and reproduce docile bodies, capitalism utilizes and encourages countless residual territories of belief (and any belief is fine so long as it contributes to displacing capitalism's internal limits). The literature of American writers such as Miller, Lawrence, and Kerouac embody not only the disruption of molar lines, the dislocation of a well-defined ego, an overthrow of preexisting values but also the movement of re-territorialization – the reinscription of a life on capitalism's artificial territories:

The case of Jack Kerouac, the artist possessing the soberest of means who took revolutionary "flight," but who later finds himself immersed in dreams of a Great America, and then in search of his Breton ancestors of the superior race. Isn't the destiny of American literature that of crossing limits and frontiers, causing deterritorialized flows of desire to circulate, but also making these flows transport fascisizing, moralizing, Puritan, and familialist territories?[145]

In this respect the privilege Deleuze affords "American literature" is linked to its failures as well as its accomplishments: American literature as inspiration, American literature as capital's cultural logic.

7.3   Two more portraits: Whitman and Proust as philosophers

In *Dialogues* (the section entitled "On the Superiority of Anglo-American Literature") and the essay "Whitman," the privileging of Anglo-American writing is explained by its usefulness for re-envisioning the nature of philosophical thought.[146] Each piece argues for a parallel or point of resonance between English-language fiction and empiricism. As mentioned earlier, Deleuze associates French literature with a focus on interiority, and a belief in internal relations or organic concepts of systematicity. Whitman's work, though, with its strings of fragmentary percepts undercuts organic conceptions of unity. In so doing, it contributes to an understanding of relations as external (a move that, for Deleuze, is indispensable to undoing the classical distinction between the One and the Many).

Lest we turn the distinction between Anglo-American and French literature into an absolute, Deleuze's reiterates his theory of relations or unity using Proust's *In Search of Lost Time*.[147] One scene in particular is useful for driving home the position that a relation always means an act of relating and that, as an activity, a relation can never be explained simply by referencing the content of the terms related. The narrator, struck by the way the sunrise turns a particular portion of the sky "a glowing pink," engages in an act of unification despite being on a separate train:

> I spent my time running from one window to the other to reassemble, to collect on a single canvas the intermittent, antipodean fragments of my fine, scarlet, ever-changing morning, and to obtain a comprehensive view and a continuous picture.[148]

In *Proust and Signs*, we also find Deleuze adopting literature as a mediator for the production of a new vision of philosophical apprenticeship.[149] What does Deleuze take to be the classic vision of apprenticeship? This is the idea that through the simple decision to follow a method, individuals begin to think philosophically and continue to do so until they have successfully generated a body of objective representations or necessary truths. The person undergoing a philosophical apprenticeship does so in full awareness they are spending their time doing philosophy. Deleuze uses *In Search of Lost Time* to mount a remarkable challenge to this picture.

Deleuze's reading emphasizes Proust's theory of the faculties in which the results of voluntary exercises of memory, observation, the intellect, and the imagination are distinguished from the results of involuntary ones. The spontaneous instances implicit in the idea of method are criticized as unreliable, capable of generating nothing but weak abstractions. Only when the faculties are triggered by an Outside, coerced by external pressures, are they capable of yielding substantive products. Proust writes

> As for the truths which the intellectual faculty – even that of the greatest minds – gathers in the open, the truths that lie in its path in full daylight...they have no depth because no depths had to be traversed in order to reach them.[150]

The taste of a madeleine, the feel of uneven cobblestones, the image of trees, the sound of proper names and musical phrases all force themselves upon the narrator as mysteries to be solved. These are the "signs" in the title *Proust and Signs*. The solution of these mysteries does not take the form of contemplating a content, or disclosing a secret through rules of discovery. The solution is creation in the sense of the act of writing. In a clever play on philosophical modalities, Proust demotes the necessary truths of philosophy to the category of the "merely possible," while classifying the truths of art as necessary – necessary because contingent. Only chance encounters and pressing questions yield necessity. Only an encounter, a violence that could just as well not have occurred can lead to literature that had to be written. For Deleuze, thought disconnected from the outside only yields possible books (books free of urgency).

Related to this critique of unconstrained thought and the reworking of the distinction between contingency and necessity is the moving account Deleuze gives of philosophical pedagogy. Proust's narrator complains his time for writing is being continually squandered and lost as a result of other responsibilities and pursuits. He complains he is continually being taken away from his vocation, unaware this time lost will be regained by becoming the subject of his literary project. Similarly, Deleuze argues philosophy occurs, not through lessons or in classes packaged as philosophical, but through experiences whose philosophical import is initially unrecognizable:

> This is why, when we think we are wasting out time, whether out of snobbery or the dissipation of love, we are often pursuing an obscure apprenticeship until the final revelation of a truth of "lost time." We never know how someone learns; but whatever the way, it is always by the intermediary of signs, by wasting time, and not by the assimilation of some objective content.[151]

Several features of Deleuze's portrait of Proust coalesce in a scene near the end of *In Search of Lost Time*. The scene represents the culmination of the narrator's literary apprenticeship. Fittingly it occurs during a "non-literary" affair. In the middle of a musical piece, in the time between being led into a sitting room and summoned into a party already in progress, the narrator identifies the inadequacies of voluntary memory, deciphers the meaning behind the peculiar affect accompanying involuntary reminiscence, and most importantly, learns his life has been a vocation. Time wasted on activities other than writing has been, in reality, the apprenticeship of a man of letters. For Deleuze, however, this moment does not represent the underlying identity of the Proust narrative. In fact, Deleuze highlights the striking degree to which *In Search of Lost Time* is nonorganic, resembling a collection of multiple books belonging to multiple genres. The unity of Proust's novel is in fact only a moment of unification (one repeated in Deleuze's account of the novel as a story of apprenticeship). This unity is not the narrative's hidden structure, but a scene within it: a scene among other scenes, a part among parts.

7.4 Deleuze as philosophy's Dashiell Hammett

This tactic of positioning literary texts as mediators for the formulation of a positive, unorthodox image of philosophical thought can also be seen in Deleuze's remarks on the detective novel. In *Difference and Repetition* Deleuze declares philosophy should converge with this literary genre (i.e. assume a parallel form):

> A book should be in part a very particular species of detective novel. By detective novel we mean that concepts, with their zone of presence, should intervene to resolve local problems.[152]

This passage is commonly cited within Deleuze scholarship. At the same time, the reference is typically the beginning and end of the discussion of Deleuze and the detective novel. This is regrettable because Deleuze made additional comments about the genre, and because these comments complement the metaphilosophical project undertaken in *Proust and Signs*.

In *A Thousand Plateaus*, the detective novel is defined as a hybrid genre.[153] For an author to participate in the genre is for him or her to actualize in one and the same text the abstract machine of the novella and the abstract machine of the tale. As far as the plane of expression is concerned, the present is structured by the form of the secret and the form of discovery. The question "what happened?" is inseparable from questions such as "Will the detective be able to discover what happened?", "What will happen to the detective in the course of trying to discover what happened?", "Will the criminal responsible for what happened be able to elude capture?" A rhythm is established between two appearances of the present. There are moments in which the present leans into the past, moments in which the present leans into the future. The former is when the focus is on the crime, the latter when the focus is on the trials of the detective. With regards to the plane of content, the characters' minds and bodies reflect this rhythm, oscillating between being responses (postures) and developments (positions).

References to Deleuze's analogy between philosophy and the detective novel consistently ignore his qualifier "a very particular species." This suggests the existence of more than one species. As such, it may be an allusion to Deleuze's essay from two years earlier, "The Philosophy of Crime Novels."[154] Ostensibly a celebration of Marcel Duhamel's legendary *La Série Noire*, the piece turns upon a distinction between the old detective novel and the new. As always, Deleuze's typology is composed of abstract principles. "New detective novels" often contain the old in varying degrees.[155]

Fans of the genre will recognize this distinction as the one between mysteries and crime fiction. From the standpoint of the forms of expression and content, one could say that the organization of the mystery is one in which the question "What happened?" dominates (regardless of what happened or whether anything in fact did happen) while in crime fiction the question "What is going to happen?" dominates. More importantly, as was the case with the typology of literary forms discussed earlier, the distinction between old and new serves a decidedly philosophical purpose.

Deleuze describes the classical form of the detective novel as philosophical in nature: "the idea of truth in the classic detective novel was entirely philosophical."[156] Detective novelists actively assimilated philosophical components for literary aims. The model detective is a genius who employs the method of deduction (in the sense of intuition), the method of induction (in the sense of an interpretation of signs), or both. These efforts invariably climax in a scene where the results of the detective's mental powers are disclosed before a public that includes the reader. The form of the secret leads to the disclosure of the secret's determinate matter. An exact account of what happened is delivered.

Crime fiction or the "new detective novel" is not organized as a teleological progression to the truth. The anecdote about Chandler and the "mystery" portion of his novel *The Big Sleep* is significant in this regard. The fact the author never answers the question of who perpetrated the original murder, an indeterminacy passed on to Howard Hawks's cinematic adaptation, is rightly recognized as inconsequential. In the language of *What Is Philosophy?* the lack of an answer has no bearing on the novel's and the film's ability to "stand on its own."

What replaces the atmosphere of truth? Deleuze's answer is a "compensation of error" free of "self-sufficiency."[157] Neither intuitions nor the recognition and organization of clues propel the narrative forward; rather, it is the numerous errors and blunders committed by each group. I take Deleuze's claim that the chain of errors lacks self-sufficiency to mean its elements are heterogeneous. The errors come from different quarters, and an individual error is not necessarily an effect of an antecedent one. "Compensation" can be interpreted as the actions of the protagonist. The detective is the one who inserts himself/herself into the constellation of errors and proceeds to engender effects. Each act is a dangerous experiment ("What will happen?") rather than an attempt to answer a preexisting question:

> With *La Série Noire*, we've become accustomed to the sort of cop who dives right in, come what may, regardless of the errors he may commit, but confident that something will emerge.[158]

This figure should remind one of the "structuralist hero" in "How Do We Recognize Structuralism?" as well as the portrait of Tournier's Robinson in "Michel Tournier and the World without Others." The persona of the philosopher has many friends: the structuralist who undergoes a restructuring, the phenomenologist whose perception is altered, the detective who experiments rather than solves.

Deleuze develops his distinction between the old and new form of the detective novel into two theories of the social. In the former, the crime represents a clear violation of a social contract. The power necessary to restore this contract has to be at least as strong as the power responsible for the transgression. The master detective squares up against his "metaphysical reflection" the master criminal. Against this world of absolute inverses, in crime fiction the spheres of legality and illegality, the police and the criminal world, interpenetrate to varying degrees. As historian Mike Davis has pointed out, James Ellroy's novels set in 1950s' Los Angeles are on a "different plane" and "depending on one's viewpoint" are either the "culmination of the genre, or its *reductio ad absurdem*."[159] If we accept Deleuze's classification, the plane in question is that of the new form of the novel, while the ubiquity of corruption (the complete absence of any traditional moral center or outside) means we are dealing with something close to a non-mixture. In Deleuzian terms, Ellroy's *LA Quartet* comes close to actualizing the abstract machine of crime fiction independently of the abstract machine of the mystery.

Ironically, the new form is close to the original inspiration for the early instances of the old form – the memoirs of Francois Eugène Vidocq. The story of Vidocq's career change – from petty criminal to police investigator – does not read as an ascent from the gutter, but as the smoothest of transitions.[160] Investigations involve not mental effort, but the utilization of underworld connections. Deleuze underlines the departure crime fiction represents from the metaphysics of truth: "Police work no more resembles scientific inquiry than a telephone call from an informant, interpolice relations, or mechanisms of torture resemble metaphysics."[161]

Deleuze describes the theory of the social on display in the noir universe as both "a new realism" and a vision of "society at the height of its power of falsehood."[162] The reproduction of the social order involves the rhetorical deployment of the language of social contract theory (the false) and the interpenetration of legal and criminal spheres:

> A society indeed reflects itself to itself in its police and its criminals, even while it protects itself...by means of a fundamental deep complicity between them.[163]

This second use of the detective novel clearly anticipates portions of Foucault's *Discipline and Punish*, in particular the sections "Generalized Punishment" and "Illegalities and Delinquency."[164] In the first, Foucault details the emergence of social contract interpretations of crime and punishment. In the second, he describes the historical indistinguishability of the worlds of crime and law enforcement and identifies the function of the prison to be the production of delinquency (a class of crimes and criminals used to extend surveillance throughout the social body).[165]

Although not referenced by Deleuze, the novel *Red Harvest* by Dashiell Hammett represents the template for many volumes of Duhamel's *La Série Noire* (Hammett was in Duhamel's estimation the "greatest writer who ever lived"), and contains all of the genre elements pertinent to Deleuze's metaphilosophical and social-theoretical uses.[166] The novel contains a mystery. Who killed the son of the town's former boss? But the role this original crime plays within the narrative is strictly incidental (it accounts for the operative's presence in the town). This is why adaptations of the novel have either placed this mystery off to the side (the Coen Brothers' *Miller's Crossing*) or eliminated it altogether (Kurosawa's *Yojimbo* and Leone's *Fistful of Dollars*).

The real focus of the novel is the space of Personville or "Poisonville." The model for "Poisonville" was Butte Montana where Hammett, while in the employ of the Pinkertons, was sent to break the miner's strike against Anaconda. While there he was asked to murder Wobbly organizer and martyr Frank Little. *Red Harvest* is populated by several equally corrupt figures (the chief of police, a loan-shark, a gambler, and a smuggler) who, in the wake of a strike they collectively smashed, vie for control.

The protagonist's principal aim is not solving the mystery but altering the social fabric ("cleaning-up," "busting-open," "ventilating," or "harvesting"). Along with survival, this project is incompatible with the observance of preexisting rules ("anybody that brings any ethics to Poisonville is going to get them all rusty").[167] The key is to figure out the combination (the precarious arrangement of forces Deleuze calls a "chain of errors"), to place oneself in the middle, and to manipulate (to "play em like cards").[168] This uncertain negotiation of forces (a matter of "juggling death and destruction") resembles not a method of inquiry, but a risky experiment: "Plans are alright... And sometimes, just stirring things up is all right – if you're tough enough to survive."[169]

7.5   Philosophy is not poetry; poetry is not philosophy

Three salient uses of literature have been discussed: the development of an alternative conception of subjectivity (or, more generally, of a life), an analysis of the capitalist social machine, and the formulation of an unorthodox image of thought. As pointed out earlier, Deleuze's approach to literature should not be considered a method of literary criticism unless by literary criticism one means the maxim "philosophers, let literature aid you in the invention of new problems and concepts." Given this objective, it should come as no surprise that Deleuze's engagement with literature is dramatically different from readings that, while called philosophical, turn entirely on the clichés of common sense ("what everybody thinks"). Nothing could be further from a Deleuzian approach than recent philosophical interpretations of Proust based upon such insights as "literature often does a better, more nuanced job of describing emotional life than philosophy," or "those passages in Proust that advocate isolation and withdrawal are erroneous because relationships with others are important." Similarly, Deleuze is profoundly sensitive to how the notion of life as an experiment can be confused with the platitudes of self-realization cooked up by advertising firms.

Deleuze's use of literature also displays a critical feature of his anti-foundationalism. If philosophy is not granted priority over literature, neither is it conflated with literature. Within a Deleuzian orientation, we can discern the risks posed by such a conflation. First and foremost, the waning of philosophy's specific type of creativity – the invention of problems and concepts. Additionally, I have described Deleuze's concern with a particular style of policing the borders between practices. For Deleuze, the charge that authors of detective novels misunderstood the philosophical methods of deduction and induction miss the point (the point being the specific problems and aims of literature). Likewise, the charge that Deleuze fails to adequately represent Proust's *In Search of Lost Time* misses the point (the point being philosophy's distinct vocation).

One final concern over conflating philosophy and literature can be extracted from Deleuze's thought (though Deleuze himself does not raise this concern). Philosophy does not have the best track record when it comes to describing or identifying the nature of literature, in particular poetry. To be precise, philosophers have displayed a penchant for negative definitions of poetry. In the case of Plato, poetry (in the sense of the epic poetry of Homer and Hesiod) was defined as a simulacrum or nonrepresentation of virtue.[170] For an entirely different set of historical and intellectual reasons, logical empiricism used the term "poetry" to describe counterfeit science, counterfeit philosophy, and pseudo-propositions. In short "poetry" was every discourse construed as devoid of cognitive meaning. Needless to say, an anti-foundationalist equating of philosophy and poetry no longer employs the adjective "poetic" as a pejorative. Nevertheless, negativity still reigns supreme. Philosophy is poetry means philosophical texts are not authoritative representations. Philosophy is like poetry in that poetic texts are not exercises in foundationalism. Deleuze, however, provides a series of positive, necessarily general, and necessarily inclusive definitions for art as a whole (assemblages in which percepts and affects stand alone) and for literature (a minor language, a stammering or language within language).[171] This along with his positive definition of philosophy expresses one of the basic commitments of Deleuze's style of anti-foundationalism. Philosophy and poetry are often defined in an entirely negative manner. Philosophy and poetry deserve better.

8   Why does the hero loath discussion? The abstract machine of philosophical discourse

Over the course of the preceding pages, it should have become clear that Deleuze does not have *a way* of writing. He engages in multiple forms of commentary. Each form is highly specific, and each form violates conventions governing the way commentators express their proximity or distance from a subject. Deleuzian portraiture asserts neither proximity nor distance. Instead, all evidence of separation between the author and model is erased. Deleuzian multiplication (on display in *Difference and Repetition, Logic of Sense, Dialogues, Anti-Oedipus*, and *A Thousand Plateaus*) increases the number of voices. At no point does the reader experience the text as a single, unmediated voice. Deleuzian genealogy or irony amplifies critique. The relationship between author and target is never one of diametrical opposition (this is a salient feature of a genealogical critique), and the distance between author and target is stretched beyond the parameters of polite debate. The position expressed by such a critique could be considered explicit indifference. The author identifies a target but avoids having it become an organizing principle for his thought.

When it comes to the assessment accompanying portraiture and critique we have seen how this is simply epiphenomenal. As in his description of the Schizo or desiring-production, Deleuze "scrambles all the codes, 'and never' invokes the same genealogy."[172] At the end of the day Deleuze is not interested in taking a stand on phenomenology or structuralism, unless by taking a stand you mean privileging certain actualizations of the concepts of phenomenology or structuralism over others. Deleuze's compositional styles, do, however represent a decisive position on the practices of discussion and debate. They are evaluations of these practices. At the same time, these evaluations take the form of philosophical concepts. Tendencies actualized within the space of academia are counter-actualized; they are reinscribed within Deleuze's system through the creation of particular concepts. Therefore, any discussion of Deleuze's critique of discussion and debate must begin by indentifying the philosophical concepts of discussion and debate (i.e. the concepts of discussion and debate as they exist on Deleuze's plane of immanence).

8.1   Discussion and debate as Deleuzian concepts

One reason for foregrounding this aspect of Deleuze's style and taste (i.e. how he engages in commentary) is that it can help explain two of his pervasive, negative definitions of philosophy. Deleuze repeatedly distinguishes philosophy from discussion and debate. This is to say that Deleuze's hero – the conceptual persona of the philosopher – exhibits a strong aversion to discussion and debate. Here is a relevant passage:

> Philosophy has a horror of discussions. It always has something else to do. Debate is unbearable to it, but not because it is too sure of itself. On the contrary, it is its uncertainties that take it down other, more solitary paths.[173]

Along with his disparagement of communication, Deleuze's attacks on discussion and debate remain unexplained and undeveloped in Deleuze scholarship. That their significance is far from self-evident follows directly from the fact Deleuze's writings are not composed as monologues. They are not presented as a first person report or as the expression of a hermetically sealed inner life. Granted, Deleuze advances a notion of solitude or solipsism. But he does this through Tournier's fiction, and he does this with Claire Parnet in a book entitled *Dialogues*. Little surprise then that Deleuze describes philosophy's solitary path as "absolute" and "populous."[174]

The analysis of Deleuze's modes of commentary enables us to recognize that discussion and debate are specific concepts. As such, they are defined by their "endoconsistency" and "exoconsistency." That is, they are defined through their internal components as well as through their relationship to other concepts on Deleuze's plane of composition. With regards to exoconsistency, the most important thing to recognize is that discussion and debate are terms within specific conceptual pairs. Discussion should be opposed to portraiture, becoming, or encounter.

In fact, Deleuze has even contrasted discussions with conversations: "Conversation is something else entirely. We need conversation."[175] Deleuze does not discuss Hume or Foucault; he constructs a portrait of them. Deleuze does not discuss things with Guattari; he undergoes a becoming or has an encounter with Guattari. Debate should be opposed to Deleuze's style of criticism. Deleuze does not debate psychoanalysis, structuralism, or phenomenology so much as craft a tactical, deflationary genealogy of them.

The term "discussion" is inadequate for portraiture because it suggests an author speaking in the first person about a philosophy attributed to another. Along with "communication," "discussion" is an inadequate characterization of becomings for it too suggests two well-defined terms, along with a clear attribution of content to one or the other. In an illustration of the notion of becoming, what begins as a well-defined exchange (the initial pages of *Dialogues* are comprised of two distinct, signed statements) becomes a fierce, unmanageable, and nonattributable proliferation of concepts. As noted by the books translators: "In the other chapters the halves are unsigned and it is no longer possible to extricate the individual contributions."[176]

As for the term "debate," it is inadequate for Deleuzian critique because it suggests a shared topic or question operating as a point of disagreement. What is a useful analogue, however, is the act of opting out of a debate. One form this can take is when a participant interrogates rather than answers the questions posed to him or her. The question is called into question. The question is attacked as an ill formed, obstacle to thought. In *Empiricism and Subjectivity*, Deleuze contends there is no "critique of solutions, there are only critiques of problems."[177] *Bergsonism* begins with the imperative to "apply the test of the true and false to problems themselves."[178] Finally, in *Dialogues*, Deleuze writes "If you aren't allowed to invent your questions...if people 'pose' them to you, you haven't much to say."[179] Together these passages suggest debate is associated with competing answers to shared problems or the reinforcement of preexisting problems. Deleuzian critique, however, is associated with the displacement of preexisting problems. At the same time, Deleuzian critique should not be considered the pronouncement of a final verdict. As we have seen with structuralism and phenomenology, an orientation subjected to ridicule can also be transformed through repetition or portraiture into an experimental praxis.

Deleuze's metaphilosophy affords us two additional connotations of discussion and debate. Each was touched upon in the pages above.

The concepts of discussion and debate should be opposed to Deleuze's notion of problem and plane of immanence. For Deleuze, positioning philosophies on a common plane (e.g. reducing two philosophies to competing sides of a debate as if they were two sides of the same coin), conceals the singularity of each: "Sometimes philosophy is turned into the idea of a perpetual discussion ... Nothing is less exact."[180] In *What Is Philosophy?* Deleuze and Guattari incorporate the notions of discussion and debate into their critique of the idea of philosophy as *doxa*. The public battle between generic subjects over competing perspectives is presented as a failure to carry immanence to its limit. To debate is to confuse philosophical concepts with transcendent or quasi-transcendent opinions.

8.2   How do the concepts operate within Deleuze's system?

Earlier I described the specific character of conceptual oppositions within Deleuze's philosophy (especially in his work with Guattari). Each term possesses normative ambiguity in the form of specific, existential risks. Additionally, I noted that each term is or belongs to what Deleuze refers to as an "abstract machine." Abstract machines are immanent causes. Abstract principles are derived from and exist solely within the concrete, and concrete individuals tend to be actualizations of multiple, qualitatively different abstract principles.

Could the distinctions between discussion and conversation, debate and becoming, be such abstractions? Could the aim of these concepts be that of illuminating the heterogeneous, mixed character of concrete, discursive units? That this is the case is made clear in a section from *A Thousand Plateaus* explored earlier: "Three Novellas, or 'What Happened?'" While Deleuze and Guattari stress that the lines of writing comprising our lives are not primarily lines of writing (or speech), each type is partially defined in relation to discourse. The three types of lines can be and usually are actualized together within one and the same concrete mixture. By extension, individual verbal or written exchanges are or can be combinations of the heterogeneous principles of discussion and solitude, debate and becomings. These principles are represented as a "whole subconversation within conversation."[181] This phrase highlights the manner in which Deleuzian abstraction is an attempt to locate difference within what seems simple or uniform.

Molar lines are taken to include endless, highly regimented linguistic interactions ("there are many words and conversations, questions and answers, interminable explanations").[182] Molecular lines are associated with silence. This silence, though, does not preclude locutions ("conversation is full of long silences").[183] More precisely, molecular lines are connected to freedom from speech – an escape from the obligation to talk. Of course this suggests the linguistic acts of molar lines involve an element of coercion (a point that will be developed below). Finally, one form of social leak – one way the social can take flight – consists of sending "the major language racing." In "conversation" with Claire Parnet and Antoine Dulaure, Deleuze succinctly refers to these three moments – the obligation to speak, freedom from this obligation, and the creation of a minor language (a language within language):

> We're riddled with pointless talk, insane quantities of words and images. Stupidity's never blind or mute. So it's not a problem of getting people to express themselves, but of providing little gaps of solitude and silence in which they might eventually find something to say.[184]

The fact Deleuze's remarks on discussion and debate are part of a conceptual opposition has gone unnoticed. Similarly, no attention has been devoted to the fact this opposition is a component of his and Guattari's more general approach to language. Precisely because it is consistent with the rest of Deleuze's philosophy, this approach to language has some peculiar features: the analysis of language is subsumed within a broader consideration of how life is structured (i.e. how bodies, perceptions, and thoughts are and could be organized); locutions are related to social obligations rather than speaking-subjects; and there is a refusal to posit (for the sake of scientific inquiry) language as a homogeneous object.

8.3   There is no language, only an abstract machine

The distinction between the abstract and the concrete is ubiquitous in the area of linguistics. However, the distinction is not the same as the one found in Deleuze's thought. Deleuze's aim is not that of abstracting from the concrete an object comprised of universals or constants – an object that would then be differentiated from the concrete as an object of science is differentiated from extra-scientific dimensions, or as conditions of possibility are differentiated from the empirical or actual. Rather, Deleuze's goal is an analysis of the concrete, one sensitive to its perpetually heterogeneous constitution, one determined to identify the ratio of qualitative difference as it fluctuates from situation to situation.

The most thorough application of this model to language use is found in the section of *A Thousand Plateaus* entitled "November 20,

1923: Postulates of Linguistics." From the standpoint of criticism, the chapter represents a refusal to take the linguistic turn. This turn, not to be confused with the one constituting the analytic tradition, was the horizon within which much of the thought characterized as structuralist unfolds. Summarily put, this horizon consists of isolating language as an object of scientific analysis and of treating such an analysis as the key to unlocking the character of the social. In her account of the history of language and linguistics, Kristeva provides an elegant account of the relationship between this formula and the decentering of the individual subject associated with antihumanism: "Considering man as language and putting language in the place of man constitutes the demystifying gesture par excellence."[185] "Postulates of Linguistics" can be read as a rejoinder to this assertion. The question posed by Deleuze and Guattari is whether linguistics substitutes for the so-called cult of man a cult of language. Perhaps the ascension of linguistics brings with it new forms of mystification.

The "postulates of linguistics" represent what, according to Deleuze and Guattari, is the definition of language within linguistics. In this respect their position can be described as the rejection of the very idea of language. Hence their statement, "there is no language in itself."[186] What are these postulates of linguistics? What, according to Deleuze and Guattari, is the notion of "language in itself?" For simplicity's sake, I will condense the postulates into two basic categories. The first category involves defining language in terms of its function. Deleuze and Guattari associate linguistics with the belief language is first and foremost an instrument of communication. The second category concerns how the object of linguistics is delimited. On the one hand, linguistics acknowledges that language is a heterogeneous reality; language varies over time and place, even within a particular time and place. On the other hand, the linguist, in the name of science, aims to extract from this reality a homogeneous system. The reasoning here is that scientific inquiry presupposes a determinate, relatively stable object.

From Saussure on, linguists begin by carefully delimiting the interior and exterior of their domain – the science of language.[187] This inside can be construed narrowly (e.g. the synchronic representation of an individual natural language as a differential system of signs, as a specific metaphoric-metonymic axis, as a group of phonemes, or as a set of syntactical rules); it can also be incredibly general (e.g. a grammar understood to be a condition for any possible natural language). The outside varies accordingly, from *paroles* (actual acts of signification) to actual natural languages. What does not change is that the interior – the object posited as language – is a homogeneous system of universals and constants. By extension, use and practice, variation and circumstance, history and the social are all posited as extrinsic to language as a scientific object. As Deleuze and Guattari put it, "Pragmatics (dealing with the circumstances of language use, with events and acts) was for a long time considered the 'rubbish dump' of linguistics."[188]

This idea of language determines the theorization of slang or dialect. In relation to language as a homogeneous system, the heterogeneity embodied in so-called slang or in a dialect can only be interpreted as a set of accidental properties, as a set of extrinsic deviations, or as a language in its own right. When the performance of an individual speaking-subject evidences heterogeneity, it can only be interpreted as a movement between proper and anomalous uses of a language, or as a movement between languages. The fact the speaking-subject has been jettisoned to the exterior leads it to be represented in the most generic way imaginable: one hypothetical individual chooses to speak to another hypothetical individual. Language – a system of universals or constants – represents this act's instrument and condition of possibility. The visual representation of the individual act of speech (the "speech circuit") in Saussure's *Course in General Linguistics* brings together the two categories of "postulates." The decision to use language is characterized as "an individual act of the will."[189] What is willed is the communication of information (represented by two heads with curved lines and arrows traveling between them). This requires a shared faculty or homogeneous structure (represented by the terminal points of the curves).[190]

First and foremost the redefinition of language provided in *A Thousand Plateaus* involves repositioning the elements traditionally construed as exterior to a scientific consideration of language. To begin with this means that for Deleuze and Guattari, any adequate, systematic account of language must be a theory of actual locutions. Similarly, such an account must include within itself the variability of context (what Deleuze, informed by Stoicism and Spinoza, will describe as different corporeal mixtures). The "outside" must be located on the inside of language, or, what amounts to the same thing, language must be regarded as entirely within the outside. For Deleuze and Guattari, language is nothing but an activity in the world.

Similarly, the heterogeneity deemed slang or dialect is no longer considered exterior to a language (e.g. as a separate language). For Deleuze and Guattari, the only justification for representing the production of heterogeneous locutions as a movement from one insular system to another is the initial decision to theorize language as closed and homogeneous: "Is it not the abstract distinction between the two systems that proves arbitrary and insufficient?"[191] Against this decision (the notion of "language in itself"), the authors advance a conception of language as inherently plural – a "throng of dialects, patois, slangs, and specialized languages."[192] A single person, in the course of the day can move between highly different lexicons, syntaxes, and phonemes:

> He successively speaks as "father to son" and as a boss; to his lover, he speaks an infantilized language; while sleeping he is plunged into an oniric discourse, then abruptly returns to a professional language when the telephone rings.[193]

This is not a denial of regularity, but the claim that regularity demands explanation. For example, the way a boss speaks to his employee cannot be understood as an instantiation of a context-independent structure. Even treating such utterances as a peculiar context-specific instantiation of a context-independent structure only makes sense if language has been defined in advance as a context-independent set of principles or relations.

Deleuze and Guattari's theory of language is in reality the theory of an abstract machine one component of which is equivalent to the production of locutions. As should be expected by now, their critique of the abstractions of linguistics is not a critique of abstraction per se. For Deleuze there is abstraction that elides the concrete, and abstraction that facilitates an understanding of the concrete. Similarly, there is abstraction that moves in the direction of homogeneity and universality, and abstraction that discloses structures to be pseudo-universals and pseudo-constants. This is the gist of the authors' remark that the problem with linguistics is that it is not "abstract enough."[194] To be sufficiently abstract, constants (i.e. regularity in the area of actual locutions) must be understood as nothing more than a set of particular, regular actualizations. To be sufficiently abstract, the idea of language must be replaced with a conceptual machine that helps us analyze the actualizations occurring in concrete settings. In short, what Deleuze and Guattari attempt to pull off is an account of language that is simultaneously the most abstract and the most concrete.

The abstract machine presented in "Postulates of Linguistics" is comprised of a horizontal and vertical axis.[195] The horizontal axis is defined through the perpetual interaction of segments of content (or machinic assemblages) and segments of expression (or collective assemblages of enunciation). As for the vertical axis, it is defined as variables possessing a territorial side along with "edges of deterritorialization." At first, the terminology here can be confusing and off-putting. Fortunately, the basic features of and rationale for this "tetravalent" abstract machine have already been laid out. The horizontal axis short-circuits any discussion of language that is not, at one and the same time, a discussion of the social field. If "expression" or "assemblages of enunciation" denotes sense, "content" or "machinic assemblages" refers to the arrangement and interactions of bodies. In the idiom of Stoicism, you have a mixture of bodies and you have what is said of this mixture (the incorporeal *lekton*) by way of another body (the physical utterance or inscription). To choose one of Deleuze's preferred examples, you have the interaction of bodies in the courtroom, and you have what is said of the body of the defendant, most notably the final verdict.

Before turning to the vertical axis, I need to explain one of the principal concepts within Deleuze and Guattari's account of language: "order-words." The two go so far as to define the order-word as the basic unit of language.[196] In terms of the abstract machine, this means the concept of order-word pulls together the two axes. The concept demolishes the vague representation of *paroles*, and it accounts for why Deleuze and Guattari refer not to "speaking-subjects" but to collective assemblages of enunciation. At the same time, the notion of order-word invites us to differentiate types of collective assemblages, with the types corresponding to the two sides of the abstract machine's vertical axis. Of course this means that, ultimately, the concept of order-word is designed to illuminate the ratio of one collective assemblage to another – the ratio of territories to deterritorializing movements – within one and the same individual or group subject.

The introduction of the concept of order-word includes an endorsement of Austin's notion of illocutionary force as well as a critique of attempts to collapse the illocutionary into the performative. In Austin's *How to Do Things with Words*, the illocutionary appears following the collapse of the distinction between performative and constative utterances (or between saying and doing).[197] Along with the categories of the locutionary and perlocutionary, the illocutionary preserves the central insights surrounding performativity. There are actions internal to utterances such that executing the utterance entails executing the act, and philosophers err when they fail to recognize that language can do many things besides relay propositions or truth claims. At the same time, the illocutionary generalizes these insights and in so doing paves the way for pragmatics. The objective is no longer one of isolating a class of statements that perform actions, but of recognizing all utterances as forms of doing (the categories of locutionary, illocutionary, and perlocutionary can be used to identify the many actions one is performing with a particular utterance).

Positioning Austin's work as the doorway to pragmatics requires Deleuze and Guattari to deflect attempts to contain it within the parameters set by the "postulates of linguistics." One such attempt consists of treating every instance of illocutionary force as an explicit or disguised performative, while in turn analyzing performatives as a special category of propositional utterances. "Close the door" is considered equivalent to "I am ordering you to close the door," which is held to be a self-verifying truth-claim. Deleuze and Guattari describe this move as one in which the performative is granted priority over the illocutionary, then "walled in through specific 'syntactic and semantic' characteristics."[198] To privilege, as Deleuze and Guattari do, the illocutionary over the performative is to reject every attempt at reducing the function of linguistic acts to the transmission of truth claims or representations. More generally, it is to reject the idea that language is above all else a vehicle permitting the communication of information.

Pragmatics requires deflection of one other approach to illocutionary force. The distinction between *langue* and *parole* can return if the objective of analysis surrounding illocution is taken to be the identification of the conditions that must be satisfied for a hypothetical utterance to possess a particular force. The focus returns to possible rather actual acts. The answer to the question "who speaks?" is once again the generic speaking-subject (person A decides to make a verbal promise to person B). This can be seen in John Searle's taxonomy which matches up types of force with their condition of possibility (a project he explicitly compares to Saussure's notion of *langue)*, and in his definition of the speech act as an act of communication grounded in the transparent intentions of the speaker.[199] Deleuze and Guattari argue for a pragmatics that is also a politics of language. Such an approach would combine a commitment to analyzing the acts internal to actual locutions with the recognition these acts are not adequately explained in terms of the simple intentions of a speaker/writer to perform them.

At first glance the claim that "order-words" are the basic unit of language appears to be nothing more than a straightforward substitution. Deleuze and Guattari appear to want issuing commands to be considered the principal illocutionary force. "Philosophical discussions of language have privileged making propositions; they should have recognized that the principal thing done with language is make commands."

This is, in fact, the standard reading of this section of *A Thousand Plateaus*. The authors do, in fact, describe linguistic acts as conveying only that amount of information needed for the audience to know what is expected of them behaviorally. In other words, even when linguistic acts do convey information, this is merely a means for "commanding life."[200]

> We see this in police and government announcements, which often have little plausibility or truthfulness, but say very clearly what should be observed and retained. The indifference to any kind of credibility exhibited by these announcements often verges on provocation. This is proof that the issue lies elsewhere.[201]

But if the notion of order-words represented nothing more than the claim one illocutionary force is more prevalent than another, it would preserve the superficial representation of parole associated with linguistics. Individuals would simply be depicted as producing commands rather than propositions. But for Deleuze and Guattari, there is no speaking-subject or individual enunciation, only collective assemblages of enunciation. Furthermore, upon close reading we discover that for the authors, the "order" in order-words applies as much to the speaker as to the addressee.

A pragmatic and political approach to language highlights the way the production of locutions is related to the obligation to produce specific locutions within determinate environments: "Order-words do not concern commands only, but every act that is linked to statements by a 'social obligation'."[202] The act of speaking is never the arbitrary act of an abstract individual. Typically, it is the fulfillment of a social imperative to say certain things in a particular fashion. The act of speaking typically reflects a dominant mode of organizing the body. In this way the topic of "order-words" leads directly to the idea of discourse as essentially indirect and redundant. When it comes to explaining the production of actual locutions in actual situations, the most important point of reference is what individuals are supposed to say, what they are expected to say given their place within an organization of bodies (boss, employee, teacher, student, judge, etc.). In other words, understanding a locution requires the identification of a machinic assemblage and the collective assemblage of enunciation.

At this point, bringing the vertical axis into the picture is crucial. If a salient theme of Deleuzian ontology is how bodies are structured as organisms (i.e. as docile organizations), another is how this structuring fails to saturate their present and future identity. Not only are there established institutions but also departures from these institutions (departures of varying consequence). Bodies can be and are disassembled and reassembled in ways representing innovation rather than the fulfillment of social imperatives. Once again, Deleuze envisions the social in a nontotalizing fashion. There are not only territories, but also leaks (areas where the social is put to flight). Language is a site evidencing both of these characteristics, hence, the two segments of the vertical axis: major and minor. A "major language" is a linguistic act fulfilling and conveying the obligation to speak, write, and more generally, behave in a "socially respectable" manner. A "minor language" is a linguistic act demonstrating our ability to speak and write differently. The notion of the major and minor sides of language corresponds to the notion of bodies without organs and bodies as organisms.

We are now in a better position to discern the shape of Deleuze's and Guattari's pragmatics. Instead of equating language with a closed system, or identifying the conditions for possible utterances, there is a concerted effort to determine what exactly is happening – what is being done – by way of actual locutions. Answering this question requires an analysis of the act's place within a specific arrangement of bodies. At the same time, what has to be determined is the proportion of territorialization to deterritorialization within this specific organization of bodies and words.

8.4   The major side of philosophical discourse

The three Deleuzian pejoratives of "communication," "debate," and "discussion" should be situated in relationship to this theory of language. That is, they should be understood in relation to the abstract machine of locutions, bodies, territories, and lines of flight. Earlier "communication" meant commensurability – the shared parameters enabling us to say two well-defined persons are speaking of the same thing. "Discussion" and "debate" referred to this form of interaction with the latter obviously introducing connotations of each party challenging the other's positions on a common subject. Additionally, "communication" is associated with the abstract representation of the concrete production of linguistic acts: an individual speaking-subject decides to transmit information to an equally generic recipient and accomplishes this through organized sound or inscription. According to Deleuze, communicative conceptions of language, like communicative conceptions of philosophy, are inexact.

When the linguistic acts under consideration are philosophical (in the general sense of referencing philosophy), "discussion" and "debate" correspond to the major, territorial side of the vertical axis. "Communication" in the narrower sense (the principle of commensurability) similarly refers to the territorialization of philosophical thought. As noted earlier, these three terms need to be recognized as elements within a series of conceptual pairs. Their opposed terms – event, encounter, solitude, becoming, conversation – correspond to the minor, deterritorialized side of the vertical axis. As abstract principles, the concepts operate as components of language's abstract machine and, thus, can be used to identify the qualitative difference within philosophical discourse. Deleuze's protests against communication, against discussion, and against debate can appear casual if strident, extemporaneous if frequent. In reality, they are the rigorous extension of his theoretical principles to interactions within academic philosophy. This extension invites us to ask the following sorts of questions of particular interactions: To what extent is the circulation of words a discussion; to what extent is it an encounter? Where, within a particular territorialized interaction, do we see philosophical becomings? Would the complete absence of discussion (e.g. routine exposition) pose a threat to the potential for conversation?

Because Deleuze's definition of philosophy places it squarely on the minor side of the vertical axis, gauging the ratio of major to minor acts is equivalent to measuring the presence of philosophy. In a truly classic, Platonic gesture, the critique of communication, debate, and discussion becomes the question of determining the degree to which discourse packaged as philosophical is in fact philosophical. Deleuze's critique must be read in light of the defining ethical impulse of his philosophy – encouraging genuine creativity while identifying its obstacles and risks. In particular, one must keep in mind the metaphilosophical formulation of this problem, the view that philosophy's strength lies in the creation and systematic articulation of new problems. Doing so enables us to identify the major and minor sides, the territories and becomings, of what is commonly thought of as philosophical discourse.

When the topic is philosophical tradition, Deleuze associates debate and discussion with an imposition of commensurability obfuscating the heart and singularity of juxtaposed theories. At the same time, Deleuze's language of interpretive disclosure or concealment is inseparable from his conviction that invention in philosophy is bound up with the selection of mediators. Here the three pejoratives designate diluted forms of mediation. An implicit conviction within Deleuzian thought is that the explicit, rhetorical distance between a commentary and its subject is an index of its degree of creativity. Most commentators explicitly distance themselves from their subjects (e.g. by criticizing their subjects), but this distance is rarely genuine difference (philosophical creativity). Such gestures should be contrasted with Deleuze's notions of portraiture and repetition where the absence of rhetorical distance goes hand in hand with tremendous novelty: there is divergence in relation to the past (the reactualization of the philosophy is akin to a doppelganger), and there is divergence in relation to the contemporary intellectual landscape.

Deleuze summarily expresses his critique of discussion and debate by declaring they always arrive too early or too late.[203] What would it mean to engage with a philosophical text on time? Answering this question requires us to again move between two registers we are accustomed to keep apart. On the one hand, there is the language of interpretive fidelity. On the other hand, there is the language of creativity. To be "on time" would require a clear understanding of the problem the text expresses, and it would require using the text to facilitate the creation of new thought. An early arrival involves the production of description and criticism without any recognition of the text's defining problem and it represents a failure to actualize the texts (a failure to use them as mediators for the creation of difference). By "late," Deleuze means superfluous, and from a Deleuzian perspective the vast majority of verbal and written exchanges surrounding theory are as just that. Once the parameters of an earlier philosophy have been recognized, the Deleuzian question is whether to take up that problem anew or move onto something else.

The exception to this rule would be an orientation that severely impeded thinking differently. In such a case, "debate" would signify a critique that is too timid or too respectful of its target, or a view of creativity that is too timid, too respectful of its obstacles. In other words, "debate" is a concept Deleuze formulates in order to challenge the reduction of philosophy to critique. Such a reduction occurs whenever creativity is absent, or is subsumed under critique (e.g. the idea of conducting a critique in a creative manner). This is precisely what Deleuze is criticizing in the following passages from "How Do We Recognize Structuralism?" *Dialogues*, and *What Is Philosophy?* In the first passage Deleuze is responding to critiques of structuralism (in the pages immediately preceding the comment, structuralism was redefined as an experimental praxis):

No book *against* anything ever has any importance; all that counts are books *for* something, and that know how to produce it.[204]

The second strikes a more personal note; Deleuze is referring to challenges to his own philosophy:

> Every time someone puts an objection to me, I want to say, "Okay, Okay, let's go on to something else." Objections have never contributed anything.[205]

The third and final passage highlights the extent to which "debate" belongs to a conceptual pair, and how the underlying basis for the opposition is the problem of creating difference. From a Deleuzian perspective, positive and negative appraisals of a philosophy can appear as roughly equivalent when neither enacts new parameters of thought:

> Those who criticize without creating, those who are content to defend the vanished concept without being able to give it the forces it needs to return to life, are the plague of philosophy.[206]

Criticisms that are nothing but criticism, summaries that are nothing but summaries, should not be confused with the immodest project of producing, a new, heterogeneous actualization of a philosophical problem or concept.

8.5 One more battle: the philosopher versus the academic

The account of philosophical discourse's major and minor side is incomplete so long as the vertical axis is discussed independently of the horizontal. This would suggest that the linguistic acts comprising this discourse have a simple origin: independent of any context (any determinate arrangement of bodies), a generic, individual speaking-subject chooses to speak or write, and deems the content of their words philosophical. The horizontal axis precludes this scenario. The content of a linguistic act is a collective assemblage of enunciation, one existing in relation to a precise expression or machinic assemblage. In the case of territorial locutions, the assemblage of enunciation operates like a school of thought. The linguistic acts produced are essentially redundant reproductions of preexisting coordinates or orthodoxy.

Deleuze's concepts of discussion and debate are descriptions of the major or territorial side of philosophical discourse. This area of conceptual convergence encourages us to pose the question of what concepts, if any, corresponds to the collective assemblages of enunciation and machinic assemblages associated with the major side of philosophy. Deleuze answers this question in the following passage:

> Academics' lives are seldom interesting. They travel of course, but they travel by hot air, by taking part in things like conferences and discussions, by talking, endlessly talking.[207]

Just as Platonic narratives are contests between the philosopher and the sophist (or the philosopher and the poet), so Deleuze's plane of immanence is the stage for a contest between the philosopher and the academic. Deleuze's remarks on academic life, no less than his remarks on discussion and debate, need to be seen as delimiting specific concepts within his system. Within Deleuze's metaphilosophy, the vertical axis is comparable to the Platonic distinction between genuine and counterfeit philosophy, while the horizontal axis is comparable to the Platonic distinction between the philosopher and the professional educator.

In *Proust and Signs*, the metaphilosophical critique of the idea of method is at the same time a critique of orthodox notions of pedagogy. Similarly, on multiple occasions Deleuze reflects on the philosophical limitations and possibilities of courses "on philosophy."[208] That Deleuze himself worked within a university environment serves to highlight the way "academic" or "academia," along with "philosopher" designate specific concepts. In other words, they are abstract principles denoting tendencies that can exist together in a heterogeneous mixture. One and the same site can exhibit both. Deleuze's reactivation of classical conceptual personae in tandem with his critique of discussion are perhaps most useful for precisely those employed as philosophers. Essential, well-formed questions within Deleuze's philosophical orientation include "How can we be philosophers rather than academics?" "How can we do philosophy within academia?" "Where, within a particular academic environment, can we find philosophy happening?"

The horizontal axis brings into play additional connotations of "discussion" and "debate" found within Deleuze's writing. If the concept of discussion refers to nonproductive, commensurable exchanges, it refers as well to certain nonproductive forms of incommensurability. What is ostensibly an exchange of ideas can in reality be a proliferation of monologues. Unlike encounters, and like the earlier model of discussion, there is no displacement of well-defined egos. The components of the collective assemblage of enunciation correspond to the generic subjects associated with the circulation of opinions. At the same time, the discussion involves a sterile, unacknowledged diversity. Not only is philosophical innovation nowhere present, one is tempted to say this form of "communication" is one in which not even communication is taking place. On more than one occasion, Deleuze describes discussions as pseudo-exchanges where the "participants only seem to be talking about the same thing." "Very quickly you have no idea what is being discussed."[209] Lest this incommensurability be confused with the difference enacted by the creative act, Deleuze points out that such discussions are "an exercise in narcissism where everyone takes turns showing off."[210]

The connection between major philosophy and the discursive environment of professional philosophy gives us an additional sense of "debate". "Debate" refers not only to the privileging of criticism over construction but also to the proliferation of fraudulent criticisms. Earlier, I referred to Deleuze's contention that commentary on philosophies is typically premature. That is, it stems from a failure to recognize the parameters of theories – parameters that are a function of the singular problems of different philosophers. Bringing in the horizontal axis ensures we see Deleuze as describing the organization of discourse within the concrete settings or machinic assemblages of professional philosophy. This is how we should understand Deleuze's persistent association of debate or academic criticism with deliberate misunderstanding or "malicious stupidity."[211] For Deleuze, the potential of a philosophy exceeds both its original context and any finite set of readings. There is no limit to the number of ways a philosophical text can be read or used. The identity of the text is not entirely given; rather, it is open to the future. At the same time, the territorial side of philosophical discourse is characterized by the systematic, organized production of blatant misreadings. Because their pragmatics concerns the imposition of particular organizations on bodies and language, as well as challenges to these organizations, Deleuze and Guattari describe it as a politics of language. Similarly, Deleuze has alluded to the politics of misinterpretation.[212]

Deleuze first links academic criticism to blatant, sterile misinterpretation in *Empiricism and Subjectivity*. Enumerating the familiar charges leveled against Humean empiricism (the reduction of experience to atomistic impressions, the reduction of the intelligible to the sensible, etc.) he writes, "most of the objections raised against the great philosophers are empty," adding "the reader should not be surprised to find in the text itself the literal refutation of all these objections – despite the fact that objections come after the text."[213] These words anticipate a remarkable passage near the end *Anti-Oedipus*. The authors provide a laundry list of objections they expect to be raised against their work: they romanticize schizophrenia, conflate the schizophrenic and the revolutionary, and improperly marginalize the theme of class. Of course any reader who reaches this paragraph, and who has been earnestly trying to understand the text, would be inoculated against these misinterpretations. While *Anti-Oedipus* makes for a difficult read, the authors are quite good at anticipating and correcting misunderstandings along the way. Over and over they remind the reader that "schizophrenia" is a philosophical concept, one linked to a politicized reinterpretation of the diagnostic category but, at the same time, carefully differentiated from clinical schizophrenics. Both schizophrenia and schizophrenics are clearly distinguished from revolutionary movements.[214] Similarly, they anticipate, for good reason, that using the language of desire and desire's repression will evoke the notion of desire as a preexisting inner, lack-driven substance. But *Anti-Oedipus* systematically and directly dismantles this notion precisely because the authors recognize it to be a genuine obstacle for a new conception of desire and repression. Therefore, the authors' anticipation of future reproaches (of the objections that "will come after the text") is less about further clarification, then about connecting the political analysis of *Anti-Oedipus* (in particular, the positive definition of repression or "Oedipus") to the practice of reading. While less consequential than other practices, reading has its entrenched forms and its alternatives, its major and its minor sides. Deleuze and Guattari do not defend themselves against specious charges as much as take a stand against the territorialization of reading the charges reflect: "This would be a bad reading, and we don't know which is better, a bad reading or no reading at all."[215]

Part III
Affirming Philosophy

In discussions surrounding philosophical texts, the word "system" or "systematic" serves as a caveat, be it tacit or overt. One is cautioned against mistaking a part – a single passage, book, idea, or position – for the entirety of a philosophy. The text in question is positioned as a piece of some larger, "systematic" enterprise. As much as any philosopher Deleuze has heightened our awareness of the numerous types of system and images of system-building within the history of philosophy. In particular, Deleuze has made us aware of the fact that not every "plane of composition," not every instance of philosophical rigor, and not every relation of part to whole can be captured by the more familiar metaphors of the philosophical imagination: the organism (where each part plays a specific, fully determined role within an overall structure), the tree (the root and the body or the trunk and its branches), the building (with its foundation and vertically successive floors). *If only* philosophers had the decency of conforming to these metaphors. *If only* reading philosophy were as simple as following discrete premises on their linear path to a conclusion. *If only* understanding a philosophy were as easy as an elevator ride: stop on each floor until you reach the top or descend until you reach the ground.

A philosophy is not encountered as an immobile, passive picture. To read a philosophical work is to come into contact with a beautiful and intimidating display of the power of thought. Not an image but an action. And these acts of thought we call philosophies are comprised of innumerable movements: movements within movements, movements between movements. The familiar, ready-made concepts of system are not up to the task of thinking through, or talking about this kind of organization. Deleuze's concrete, firsthand experiences of reading and writing philosophy compelled him to create new metaphilosophical concepts: philosophies are less organisms than "bodies without organs," less trees than "rhizomes," less buildings than the heterogeneous actualizations of a differential. Should the word "systematic" still be used as a note of caution ("remember this is just one aspect of something larger)? Absolutely, the less organic a philosophical system, the more we need to bear in mind its systematicity. Defining a concept will require studying it in its diverse habitats. Identifying its contours will require traveling along multiple pathways.

An awareness of these challenges is indispensable when it comes to considering Deleuze's philosophy. Gradually, there has been recognition of Deleuze's endorsement of systematic philosophy. But this recognition is not always accompanied by sensitivity to the systematic character of Deleuze's project. The receptions of Deleuzian thought have suffered from a kind of unintentional metonymy. Consistently, the part has passed for the whole, or been passed off as the whole. The dominant, initial reception within professional philosophy reduced Deleuze's philosophy to those passages that seemed compatible with the themes of anti-foundationalism or deconstruction. Deleuze's project was positioned as one more challenge to the history of philosophy as foundationalism or logocentrism – one more critique of tropes deemed responsible for making certain texts "philosophical." Of course those who bothered to read Deleuze's books (any of his books) understood the extreme limitations of this characterization. Deleuze's work showed up, not as an instantiation of anti-philosophy, but as a sign. That is, it was disclosed as strange, as unclassifiable. Like Socrates, Deleuze's philosophy is experienced as *atopos*.[1]

Reacting against the shortcomings of this early reception, more recent interpretations have stressed the importance of Deleuze's metaphysics. Increasingly, the name "Deleuze" is associated, not with the theme of anti-philosophy, but with ideas such as the reality of the virtual (the delineation of the real in terms of the distinction between actual and virtual), and difference as different/ciation (differentiation plus differenciation).[2] Worth noting is the fact *this* reception is connected to the nascent trend of finding parallels between Bergson's philosophy and recent developments in the area of mathematics and natural science (in particular, the formation of the so-called sciences of complexity).[3] The accent is squarely placed on Deleuze's portrait of Bergson's thought.[4]

Without question, the idea of Deleuze the metaphysician is a vast improvement over the idea of Deleuze as anti-philosopher. At the same time, one should recognize the risk inherent in this new approach to

Deleuze's work. The focus on Deleuze's metaphysics could turn into myopia. The part could be perceived as the whole. After all, if Deleuze has a metaphysics he also has a metaphilosophy. More importantly, the abstract assemblage of tendencies that is Deleuze's problem exists within diverse expressions. Furthermore, the term "metaphysics" can be somewhat misleading. To show why we need to consider the way Deleuze situates his work in relation to Platonism.

One of his better known statements is "The task of modern philosophy has been defined: to overturn Platonism."[5] Often quoted, the significance of the passage seems easily translated into postmodern parlance. The task of modern philosophy is to reject universals, essences, foundations, and so on. But what is Deleuze's next statement? "That this overturning should conserve many Platonic characteristics is not only inevitable but desirable." No word can perfectly capture the complex relationship between Deleuzian thought and Platonism. "Portraiture" would highlight the extent to which the relationship turns upon Deleuze's own formulation of Platonism, but it would lose the sense of "overturning." Deleuzian portraiture (on display in his books on Hume, Spinoza, Bergson, Nietzsche, and Foucault) engenders strictly positive surfaces (surfaces devoid of critical annotations). In addition to being unwieldy "overturning/preservation" seems to suggest two distinct operations (as if Deleuze rejects some elements of Platonism, then chooses among the leftovers). Instead, each overturning includes preservation; preservation always incorporates an overturning. In *Difference and Repetition*, this procedure is reflected in Deleuze's ambiguous use of Plato's metaphor of the "cave." At times he uses it in a manner consonant with Plato (the cave is the site of our bondage).[6] In other passages, the metaphor is reversed (we need to escape into the cave).[7] Since the idea of "Deleuze overturning Platonism" has proven to be an obstacle for grasping his unique project, I propose we consider his work a "redirection of Platonism." Needless to say, this redirection will turn upon Deleuze's own interpretation of Platonism.[8]

In Deleuze's account of Platonism, the heart of Platonism is not the distinction between the forms and their representations, or between the universals and particulars. Rather, it is the practice of hierarchically differentiating particulars into representations and simulacra. The doctrine of forms is there to legitimate and cement this division into place. For example, the overall thrust of the *Republic* is the distinction between authentically just lives or social arrangements and the fraudulent, albeit seductive, depictions of morality provided by epic poetry. In short, Deleuze, in his reading of Plato's dialogues, asks us to consider the normative horizon of the commitment to universals. The fact Deleuzian thought is the "redirection" of Platonism means Deleuze's own onto-logical, ethical, aesthetic, and political commitments are interlocked. Deleuze declares "politics precedes being."[9] His aim is to "put metaphys-ics in motion," "to make it act."[10] The only Deleuzian metaphysics is an ethico-political metaphysics. The new penchant for defining Deleuzian thought in terms of his distinction between the actual and the virtual is the symptomatic equivalent of defining Platonism as the contempla-tion of abstract universals. What then is the Deleuzian equivalent of Plato's division of particulars? What division or hierarchical differen-tiation does Deleuze's "reality of the virtual" support? What kind of pedagogy, apprenticeship, and battles is the Deleuzian hero supposed to conduct? This is the question of Deleuze's theatre of operations, the subject of Part II.

Is there anything inherently wrong about treating or applying notions from Deleuze's metaphysical register independently of the rest of his philosophy? No. After all Deleuze's philosophy is itself forged out of a process of deterritorialization and reterritorialization (i.e. Deleuze lifted concepts from diverse sources and reinscribed them upon his own "plane of immanence"). Deterritorializing the Deleuzian virtual, however, (including reducing it to Bergson's philosophy) does cause considerable difficulties when it comes to understanding Deleuze's philosophy. And acknowledging this fact is no violation of the Deleuzian spirit. His body of work displays more than high veloc-ity, conceptual reinscriptions (*Capitalism and Schizophrenia*). There are also slow, sustained expositions of the systems of other theorists (e.g. his books and lectures on Hume, Bergson, Nietzsche, Spinoza, Leibniz, and Foucault).

All this raises the question of how to approach Deleuze's philosophy in a way that does not do a disservice to its systematic character. Part I was an examination of Deleuze's affirmation of systematic philosophy, his meditation on systematicity, and the type of system his philoso-phy embodies. Deleuze's system is a problem: an abstract assemblage of heterogeneous tendencies actualized in multiple concrete ways. The identity of Deleuze's system consists of the different expressions of an immanent differential. Part I concluded with an account of the five intellectual tendencies comprising this differential: the tendency to think in terms of incommensurability, to think of critique as subor-dinate to production, to rethinking identity and difference, to think of the social as a site of invention, and to think of the body as a site of organization and reorganization.

Part II was an overview of Deleuze's theatre: the characters populating his philosophical system. These characters are the product of acts of counter-actualization. Deleuze encounters actualizations of abstract tendencies in the world; he separates these abstract tendencies from their actualizations through the creation of new conceptual personae. The drama staged between the personae is an intervention in the world, an attempt to get us to actualize certain tendencies rather than others, or to increase the proportion of certain tendencies relative to others.

Here in Part III, we will be examining Deleuze's metaphilosophical and metaphysical registers in greater detail. Through metaphilosophy, through metaphysics, through the creation of concepts, and through the creation of new expressions of his problem, Deleuze affirms philosophy. That is, the principal way Deleuze affirms philosophy is by doing philosophy. On occasion, though, the affirmation of philosophy takes the form of a declaration. Deleuze states that he is a philosopher. And he laughs at another differential. This is the theme of the end of philosophy, an abstract formula actualized in diverse ways across the field of intellectual life.

1 Philosophy's demise has been greatly exaggerated

An interviewer once asked Derrida whether he considered his work literature rather than philosophy. Derrida replied: "my texts belong neither to the philosophical register nor to the literary register."[11] Referring to *A Thousand Plateaus*, Catherine Clement asked Deleuze whether he considered the book literature. Deleuze's response to this query was "It's just plain old philosophy."[12] Appreciating the significant, nonarbitrary nature of these two replies requires some understanding of a shared intellectual context. Deleuze's unqualified identification with "philosophy" should be placed alongside of his remark "I've never been worried about going beyond metaphysics or any death of philosophy;" his characterization of the debate over philosophy's end as "trying" and as "tiresome, idle chatter;" and his contention that philosophy will only die "choking with laughter."[13] In this way, Deleuze's affirmation of philosophy represents a specific, concrete attitude toward the theme of the end of philosophy. This attitude could be described as stated indifference or mocking indifference. Hearing noise outside philosophy's factory, Deleuze goes over to a window. A crowd has assembled, a banner unfurled. It reads "philosophy is over." He thinks, "I'm not worried," then returns to the task at hand: the task of manufacturing concepts.

1.1   The abstract machine of the end of philosophy

What exactly is Deleuze distancing himself from when he distances himself from the notion of the end of philosophy? With what is he identifying when he affirms philosophy? What does this twin-gesture tell us about the structure of Deleuze's ethico-political metaphysics and metaphilosophy? Part of the difficulty in answering this question stems from the fact that the slogan "the end of philosophy" has been in circulation in France since the 1930s. During this time its significance has fluctuated. Like most slogans within the history of ideas (even those crafted to pull together and describe events after the fact) it is both a compromise formation (it is composed of disparate, even antagonistic, elements), and it has a life and efficacy of its own (it can circulate in an ambient manner, coloring its various components and inspiring new ones).

With regards to its extension in France, the "end of philosophy" is built around a series of original reactivations and reformulations of German thought. There was, for example, Kojève's Hegelian inspired conception of philosophy's completion in an unsurpassable, complete description of the real – a thought that "exhausts all the possibilities of thought."[14] The completion/termination of history (i.e. the end of negativity or historically significant change) makes possible a full account of spatio-temporal reality. Since nothing more is going to happen, we are in a position to describe history in its entirety. A thought that "exhausts all the possibilities of thought" renders clarification or commentary the only authentic, post-historical, post-philosophical intellectual task. In sharp contrast to the silly neoconservative appropriations of his thesis, Kojève's account is laced with sanguinary flourishes, not to mention a humorous indecision over the time and place of history's and philosophy's burial.[15] These qualities combined with the provocative nature of his theses helps explain the appeal of Kojève's thought to his original audience. It also helps explain this audience's unorthodox style of disseminating Kojève's lessons. Consider, for example, Raymond Queneau's comedic novel *The Sunday of Life* or Georges Bataille's tortured reflections on "unemployed negativity" – (his own, and that of economic systems).[16]

Kojève's Hegel echoes in the pronounced tendency within French theory to announce and debate the existence of numerous ends. "The end of the book," "the end of the cinema," and "the end of the intellectual" are all themes that have followed in the wake of the idea of philosophy's and history's end. Paradoxically, Kojève's discourse anticipates as well critiques of foundationalism – of closed, unsurpassable explanations. For if Kojève's work is a totalizing discourse, it is one defined by the belief that the age of totalizing discourse known as the history of philosophy is over. The bridge between these two senses of end (the end as completion versus the end of this idea of completion) is the work of Maurice Blanchot. In *The Infinite Conversation*, Blanchot describes how the termination of history and philosophy entails a questioning without reserve (thought without repose).[17]

These traces of Kojève's thesis, though, should not make us lose sight of the fact that the abstract theme of the end of philosophy is actualized in diverse ways. Distinct from Kojève's end is the announcement associated with structuralism. Following in the footsteps of Freud, Lévi-Strauss uses the term "philosophy" to denote a historically tenacious error. While knowing presupposes consciousness (i.e. to know is to be aware of knowing), the philosopher mistakenly assumes the object of knowledge *is* consciousness. At the very least, the philosopher believes a correlate or representation of the object of knowledge belongs naturally to consciousness (i.e. a conscious representation of the object exists prior to methodical investigation): "...for too long now philosophy has succeeded in locking the social sciences inside a closed circle by not allowing them to envisage any other object of study for consciousness than consciousness itself."[18] Overcoming this error – revealing to consciousness "an object other than itself" – requires breaking with philosophy and enacting a social science inspired by Marx and Freud: "... the social sciences have taken over from philosophy."[19]

At times Lévi-Strauss's desire to "dissolve man" or the subject ("the major preoccupation of the whole of Western philosophy") leads him to represent the act of knowing itself as a manifestation of the object of knowledge.[20] That is, the chronologically final permutation of the structure is the representation of the structure in the mind and writing of the structuralist: "The structure of the myth, having been revealed to itself, brings to a close the series of its possible developments."[21]

In *For Marx*, Althusser describes how the "great, subtle temptation" of the "end of philosophy" proved irresistible for French Marxists as well. More specifically, the ambiguity within the notion of philosophy's end (the end as fulfillment versus the end as suppression) combined with Marx's own ambiguous use of "philosophy" served to determine competing accounts of the relationship between, on the one hand, philosophy and, on the other hand, Marxist theory and practice.[22] In what he labels the "militant interpretation," revolutionary practice was considered the realization of philosophy's objectives. Of course "philosophy" here refers to philosophy reconstructed along materialist lines. Materialist, in that the end of such a philosophy is social transformation rather than accurate representation; materialist, in that theoretical production alone is deemed an insufficient means to this end. In the "positivist" interpretation, "philosophy" signified the ideological obfuscation of origins and interests. The philosophical tradition was presented as an epistemological obstacle the evasion of which was a precondition for a scientific rather than pseudoscientific understanding of the social.

1.2   The concept of philosophy's closure

The singular position of Derrida within the debate over the possibility and meaning of a post-philosophical culture lies in the peculiar way he challenges both conceptions of the end. Deconstruction (especially in those texts in which Derrida uses and carefully defines the term) can be usefully considered an attempt to delimit philosophy's impossibility. Philosophy is impossible in that its internal agenda (self-evidence or explanatory closure) is one that cannot be met. The critic's responsibility is to challenge or "desediment" each and every appearance of self-evidence – to point out how philosophy never arrives at its end. This criticism, however, is not presented as a criticism of philosophy from the outside. Against Lévi-Strauss's notion of overcoming philosophy, Derrida argues that a critique of philosophy can never be delivered in a language purified of philosophical assumptions. Derrida brings together his reservations about each conception of the end in the notion "closure." The notion of philosophy's closure is presented as an alternative to the idea of philosophy's end. The notion marks philosophy's limits. Theoretical texts are not what they appear to be or what their authors present them as being; they are not transparent vehicles for definitive representations. Closure is also the idea that this limit cannot be overcome (because the notion of the end is itself philosophical): "... one does not leave the epoch whose closure one can outline."[23]

The notion of closure reflects the fact that while Derrida distances himself from the theme of the end of philosophy, he takes the theme very seriously. Opposition to the notion of end determines the rhythm and language of a Derridean text. On the one hand, there is the movement between the notion of philosophy as metaphysics and its instantiation in a particular historical document. On the other hand, there is the confession of guilt. The message of writing "under erasure," with all its scare quotes and qualifications, is the inability to break out of the prison-house of philosophy.

1.3   Deleuze's laugh

Deleuze laughs at this abstract machine of philosophy's end, which is to say he laughs at all of the machine's diverse, concrete expressions: the notion of closure as well as end. Even though this laugh is a spare part of Deleuze's system, it is connected to some of this system's most philosophical features. The laugh is a philosophical laugh: a stance engendering precise effects and substitutions.

The notion of the end of philosophy is just one example of the intellectual and commercial penchant for declaring ends. Therefore, Deleuze's laugh is connected to his slogan of "the middle." In the introduction, I presented the "middle" as a slogan that ripples across the surface of Deleuze's system. The prevalence of this expression is directly connected to the relative lack of birth announcements and obituaries in Deleuze's writings.[24] Lest we think of this substitution of middle for origin, middle for end, as a secondary feature Deleuze's system, we should recognize its appearance on the metaphysical register. There the obsession with origins and ends is linked to the category of the actual; the middle is linked to the category of the virtual. Historical occurrences have two sides.[25] One side, the actual, lends itself to being temporally circumscribed and explained in terms of antecedent conditions ("here's when it began and why," "here's when and how it came to an end"). The other side, the virtual, resists identification as well as historical explanation. Deleuze and Guattari's basic message is that all of the noise surrounding a phenomenon beginning or coming to an end engenders myopia. What is missed? What is the middle that goes unperceived? Perhaps that other, more profound and consequential phenomena exist: "Underneath the large noisy events lie the small events of silence."[26] Perhaps it is that events can persist long after the academic, commercial, and media fanfare subsides. Perhaps what is missed is Walter Benjamin's insight that the genuine event can always be reactualized (i.e. inserted into the present), and that, for the historical materialist the reactualization of certain events is a responsibility.[27]

A second effect of Deleuze's laughter is best seen through the juxtaposition of Kojéve's notion of the end of philosophy and Derrida's conception of philosophy as logocentrism. Remember, the former positioned Hegel's *Phenomenology* as "surpassing all possibilities of thought" and his own lecture as post-philosophical clarification (a matter of filling in the details). In contrast, Derrida's signature move is that of tracking down and contesting claims of explanatory closure, especially those found in theoretical texts. The juxtaposition gives us a clear sense of one set of parameters defining the debate surrounding the idea of the end of philosophy. On the one hand, we have foundational claims. On the other hand, we have anti-foundationalism. What does it mean to "not worry" about the end of philosophy in this sense? Deleuzian thought involves both the repudiation of foundationalism, and, just as important, is more than anti-foundationalism. Deleuze's laughter is a refusal to be blackmailed by the average postmodernist: either engage in the critique of foundationalism, an enterprise of demystification without end, or be guilty of foundationalism. This impasse conforms to some of Deleuze's specific targets. One is the set of paralogisms constitutive of Oedipus (the target of *Anti-Oedipus*). Another is the position of reactive nihilism (one of the targets of *Nietzsche and Philosophy*). If negative nihilism (or foundationalism) devalues life through the positing of higher values, reactive nihilism (or anti-foundationalism as an end-in-itself) devalues life by reducing it to the denial of higher values.[28]

As with the second, the third effect of Deleuze's laugh is best grasped through a juxtaposition: the structuralist overcoming of philosophy with the Derridean closure of philosophy. In both cases, philosophy is characterized as a reoccurring error (the belief that the object of knowledge is consciousness, the belief in pure presence or self-identity). But the two positions are different answers to the question, "can philosophy be surmounted?". The notion of "closure" is presented as a challenge to the possibility of overcoming philosophy: the best, most self-conscious, critique of philosophy is one that recognizes philosophy's inescapability.

One obvious site of incommensurability between this thematic and Deleuze's writings is the connotation of "philosophy." For Deleuze, philosophy is not a surmountable or an insurmountable obstacle to thought; it is the vocation of thought. In place of the idea of philosophy's end or closure, Deleuze returns again and again to the idea of an apprenticeship into philosophy. This philosophical apprenticeship (or "pedagogy of the concept") is filled with contingent, unintentional encounters (the subject of Deleuze's *Proust and Signs*). Study of the history of philosophy is an indispensable component of this process:

> I think that it is very difficult to do philosophy if you do not have a kind of terminological certainty. Never tell yourself that you can do without it, but also never tell yourself that it is difficult to acquire. It is exactly the same as scales on the piano. If you do not know rather precisely the rigour of concepts, that is, the sense of major notions, then it is very difficult.[29]

However, for Deleuze the history of philosophy is frequently unable to function as a scale. Tradition functions as Oedipus ("How can you talk about this subject without referring to Hegel?" "First you must read

Aristotle."); it is packaged as a test ("Please answer the following questions concerning Nietzsche's *Zarathustra*").

> The history of philosophy can only be created by philosophers, yet alas, it has fallen into the hands of philosophy professors, and that's not good because they have turned philosophy into examination material and not material for study, for scales.[30]

We can grasp this nonprofessorial pedagogy of the concept by considering Deleuze's penchant for referencing activities such as swimming, surfing, and tennis. Learning how to swim is not a matter of forming correct representations, but a matter of developing a specific kind of encounter between your body and another. Learning to swim is physical education (i.e. a matter of the body reorganizing itself): one must learn how to "conjugate the distinctive points" of one's body within the ever-changing body of the ocean.[31] Similarly, the body of the successful tennis player is one that, through a grueling process of trial, error, and frustration, is able to make it past an obstacle. The successful player requires the creation of a body that can serve the ball differently: "the history of sports runs through these inventors, each of whom amounts to something unforeseen, a new syntax, a transformation."[32]

The sport of philosophy is not a contest of lingo. One must learn to think; one must learn how to organize *and* reorganize one's thoughts. An encounter is comparable to slamming into a wall. Getting through this the wall requires smashing and rebuilding your skull: "it's by banging your head on the wall that you find a way through."[33] Philosophical apprenticeship requires familiarity with a medium, and it requires working on that medium in order to create thought anew. The medium – the ocean in which we learn to swim – is philosophy's history. Those who genuinely encounter a philosophy are painfully aware of being nonswimmers. They know they have been thrown into the middle of the ocean. They know it is sink or swim.

For Deleuze thought truly has to be created, forced into existence. The structuralist end and deconstructionist closure both turn upon the idea that "philosophy" and the "history of philosophy" are daily occurrences. In the former, philosophy is the pervasive belief that, while we can be opaque to others (hidden to others), we are transparent to ourselves. In the latter, the very act of speaking – the use of a noun, the use of the word "is" – is philosophical. With each thought and utterance we are doing the history of philosophy (i.e. stuck within the history of philosophy). Deleuze depicts philosophy as an extraordinary occurrence, an interruption of the everyday. Philosophy, including the Platonic dialectic, has little or nothing to do with prosaic questions of the form "What is x?": "The question 'What is X?' animates only the so-called aporetic dialogues, those in which the very form of the question gives rise to contradiction."[34] Philosophy has little to do with common acts of recognition ("that is a chair"). Rather, it finds its experiential models "among stranger and more compromising adventures."[35] The discussion of intoxication and alcoholism, schizophrenia as process and clinical schizophrenia, existential breakthroughs and breakdowns, is in this regard an essential component of Deleuze's system. Artaud's horror at the way bodies are structured replaces Descartes' "I hear a noise," "I see the wax."

Deleuze's laugh does not preclude a robust critique of the history of philosophy. It does, however, require that this critique not be packaged as a critique of philosophy as such. Passages of Deleuze's work appear commensurable to other critiques of philosophy: the Heidegerrian critique of philosophy as forgetfulness (the forgetting of the distinction between being and beings, disclosure and entities); the Derridean critique of philosophy as logocentrism; Hélene Cixous's, Genevieve Lloyd's, Andrea Nye's, and Elizabeth Spelman's critique of philosophy as phal-logocentrism; Richard Rorty's critique of philosophy as first philosophy.[36] In fact, the Deleuzian critique anticipates, contains, and exceeds many of the points made in these interpretations of the history of philosophy. As Foucault pointed out, "Instead of denouncing the fundamental omission that is thought to have inaugurated Western culture, Deleuze, with the patient of a Nietzschean genealogist, points to the variety of small impurities and paltry compromises."[37]

Foucault's words – "impurities," "paltry compromises" – are well chosen. In place of the idea of philosophy as obstacle, Deleuze gives us the idea of obstacles to philosophy. Playing off of Deleuzian metaphysics we can say that the history of philosophy is a mixture of different directions, different tendencies. But the heart of philosophy is not these different directions (as if the essence of philosophy were to be found between the tendencies). Rather, philosophy is one of the two tendencies, the one that deserves the name "philosophy," but also "difference," "desire," and "creativity." The other tendency *is* contained within the history of philosophy. The history of philosophy is a differential structure. But as a set of "compromises," or "impurities" this other tendency is the separation of philosophy from its power to act. The living history of philosophy is filled with moments of vitality and sickness. Today, philosophy's health requires we increase the proportion of the first tendency relative to the second.

In *Proust and Signs*, Deleuze locates a challenge to philosophy within the writings of Proust. The "philosophical bearing of Proust's work" is that it "vies with philosophy."[38] But just a few pages later this challenge becomes a philosophical challenge: "It may be that Proust's critique of philosophy is eminently philosophical."[39] The Proustian image of thought is not an alternative to philosophy, but an alternative conception of philosophy. The actualization of one of philosophy's tendencies is contested through the actualization of the other. In *Difference and Repetition*, the "dogmatic image of thought" is found throughout the history of philosophy: it is "the subjective presupposition of philosophy as a whole."[40] But the fragments and combinations constituting this dogmatic image are not philosophy as such. Rather, they are a "hindrance to philosophy;" they are philosophy's "fetters."[41] In *What Is Philosophy?* Deleuze and Guattari emphasize the intractable quality of certain illusions (transcendence, universals, the eternal, and communication). At the same time, these illusions are not the plane of philosophy, but illusions surrounding the plane; they are not thought but "thought's mirages."[42]

Needless to say, construing the target of critique as the shackles of philosophy requires Deleuze to provide us with a positive definition of philosophy. In other words, Deleuze has to show how what he calls philosophy *is* a deep tendency within the differential structure of philosophy's history. A central feature of the "philosophical direction" or "philosophical tendency" within the history of philosophy is immanence. For Spinoza, philosophy began with the notion of an immanent cause.[43] The Pre-Socratic explanation for nature's order is the *arché* rather than transcendent gods (a principle that is within nature). His own notion of immanent cause is presented as a new actualization of this tendency. Similarly, Deleuze accepts the findings of historian Jean-Pierre Vernant.[44] Pre-Socratic thought substituted the figure of the philosopher (the friend of wisdom) for that of the sage (the one who possesses wisdom), a movement of immanence (or secularization) for that of transcendence.[45] In *What Is Philosophy?* Platonism is depicted as the early dilution of philosophy's relationship to immanence. At times, Deleuze like Plato uses the cave to symbolize the necessity of an escape: we "remain imprisoned by the same cave or ideas of the times which we only flatter ourselves with having 'rediscovered'."[46] But what needs to be overcome includes the Platonic division of the real into two worlds. Platonic ascent has been replaced by a Spinoza-Nietzsche mediated descent. Transcendence has been replaced by immanence. Thus, "the thinker of the eternal return ... refuses to be drawn out of the cave, finding instead another cave, always another in which to hide."[47] The Platonic distinction between genuine and counterfeit, representation and simulacrum, philosophy and convention, becomes in Deleuze, the distinction between the active and reactive forces within the history of philosophy; a distinction between the creative force of philosophy and the forces of diminishment.

Granted philosophy's origin may lie with immanence. But Deleuze's own account suggests that much of the history of philosophy is a restriction of immanence. This represents a problem when it comes to equating immanence with the "philosophical" side of the history of philosophy. Moreover, the Deleuzian middle requires that his definition of philosophy not lean heavily on the "way things were at the beginning." Deleuze's next move – the identification of a second positive feature of "philosophy" – is a critical one.

Structuralist and deconstructionist critiques do not tell us what philosophical systems are, only what they are not: Descartes advances his system as apodictic knowledge, it isn't; Plato claims to offer an authoritative definition of justice; he doesn't. Part of Deleuze's importance resides in the fact that he offers us a positive vision of the history of philosophy. For Deleuze, the history of philosophy is not a series of flawed answers but a process of articulating new problems via the creation of concepts. As much as Nietzsche's writings, Plato's or Descartes' involves the construction of a conceptual system (or plane of immanence). A system that moves away from immanence, that advocates the notion of transcendence, is still a display of philosophical creativity (the production of concepts). For Deleuze, systems actualizing the nonphilosophical tendency, systems that exemplify the nonphilosophical side of the history of philosophy, are at the same time philosophical. They also actualize the philosophical tendency within the history of philosophy. As such they are concrete mixtures of the two tendencies.

Every concept, every plane of immanence, embodies philosophical creativity. But some represent a compromise. Some concepts are presented in a way that conceals the very fact they are creations rather than discoveries. They simultaneously express and obfuscate philosophy's creative vocation. They simultaneously inspire and thwart future creative acts. As for Deleuze, his laugh is connected to a merciless campaign against compromise. Deleuze's critique of the history of philosophy is equivalent to the twofold process of selection he finds in Nietzsche's concept of the eternal return.[48] To enact the eternal return is to contribute to the nonreturn of timid, average, or academic modes of thought; to enact the eternal return is to contribute to the nonreturn of the dogmatic image of thought that shackles philosophy. Deleuze's philosophy engineers such an eternal return: he increases the ratio of the philosophical tendency relative to the nonphilosophical tendency. This occurs through the separate practices of production (more of the philosophical tendency) and critique (kill the nonphilosophical tendency).

2   The first metaphilosophical question: what is a philosophy?

Deleuze's metaphilosophical register is comprised of two relatively distinct neighborhoods. Within Deleuzian thought, the metaphilosophical question "What is Philosophy?" is in fact two questions. The question "What is philosophy?" is the question "What is a philosophy?" ("What is the nature of a philosophical system?). Additionally, the question "What is philosophy?" is the question "What does it mean to think?" Deleuze's answer to the first question represents his way of looking at the history of philosophy; his answer to the second represents his image of thought. Both of these metaphilosophical neighborhoods contain important critical moments. But, the affirmation of philosophy demands we keep our eye on what Deleuze builds. Deleuze may perform critique in a creative manner but the creativity of Deleuzian thought is irreducible to criticism. Similarly, the concepts he produces may possess critical import, but their effects exceed those of opposition.

2.1   Philosophical history

In *Empiricism and Subjectivity*, Deleuze first poses the question, "What is a theory?"[49] Immediately preceding this question he considers the goal of reconstructing a theory's origin (identifying its psychological and/ or sociohistorical context). His assessment of this project is straightforward and critical: it leads to the imposition of fictitious, highly general, psychological types or notions such as *Zeitgeist* or cultural milieu. Additionally, the goal fosters the view that philosophies belong to the past: the past contains the whole of their identity. For Deleuze, it is no coincidence that a common way of criticizing a philosophy is by referencing the author's psychology: "what a philosopher *says* is offered as if it were what he *does* or as what he *wants*."[50] What better way of keeping Platonism dormant than presenting it as a thing of the past, presenting this past as a set of beliefs held by Plato, and presenting these beliefs as patently false: "Poor Plato, if only he had seen what we do; the belief in the world of forms cannot be justified."

What Is Philosophy? involves a slight reworking of this distinction between the correct and incorrect way of approaching philosophy. There concepts *are* described as having an origin (they are "dated" as well as "signed"). The identification or reconstruction of this origin, however, is not the province of philosophy. There is, however, a philosophical correlate of historical reconstruction. This involves tracing the philosophical history of a concept. This history is the movement of a concept not only within a system but also between systems. The deterritorialization and reterritorialization of a concept occurs within and between philosophies: "we say that every concept always has a *history*, even though this history zigzags, though it passes, if need be, through other problems or onto different planes."[51] Each reterritorialization is not a re-presentation but the creation of a new line of thought. The reterritorialization of a concept in a new system is the expression of that system's problem.[52] There is no narrative closure in the philosophical story of a philosophical concept. If philosophical concepts are "dated," they are also "eternal." If they are formed through a process of cut and paste, components of them can always be creatively recut, repasted. In contrast to the logic of fashion and the idea of the end of philosophy, Deleuze insists philosophies never go out of date.

2.2   The incommensurability *and* interpenetration of problems

What is the history of philosophy? There is a short, accessible way of formulating Deleuze's answer; the history of philosophy is a series of incommensurable problems. What, though, is the exact notion of commensurability being challenged? In *Anti-Oedipus*, it appears as Kant's "exclusive disjunctive syllogism." Kant presented this "syllogism" as a nonmetaphysical definition of god (god as creator): you arrive at the identity of a thing by taking a part of the real and subtracting the rest (i.e. x is what it is because it is not everything else).[53] From the Bergson and Nietzsche studies to *Difference and Repetition*, this manner of thinking identity and difference goes by many names: difference as negativity, opposition, or contradiction. The term "contradiction" does not refer to the logical principle of noncontradiction: x and not x. Rather, "contradiction" is the principle responsible for what individual things are: what x *is*, is not not x. A things identity is a function of the fact that it is not every other thing.[54]

A central feature of Bergson's metaphysics is that the real should not be reduced to how we typically perceive and talk about it.[55] Bergson links reflection and language use to the notion of quantitative multiplicity.

When we talk about something we use words that are also used to talk about other things. To describe something is to immediately position it as a discrete member of a kind. But the real includes duration or qualitative multiplicity. This form of difference cannot be named, it can only be suggested. We all have the experience of it – moments in our life in which we think, feel, and act differently – but it is invariably distorted when we try to capture it in words or in an act of reflection. Similarly, Deleuze argues true identity should not be confused with how we reflect on or describe it. The typical way of capturing the identity of an entity is to locate it within a kind, to oppose it to the other members of the kind, and oppose it to the members of other kinds ("that is a cat meaning not a dog, a human, a table, etc."). Identity is thus a function of difference where difference is construed as opposition. For Deleuze, the notion of opposition, negation, or contradiction distorts real difference: "It is not difference which presupposes opposition but opposition which presupposes difference, and far from resolving difference by tracing it back to a foundation, opposition betrays and distorts it."[56]

This critique of determination through opposition is a constant of Deleuze's metaphilosophy. Deleuze argues that an individual philosophy is too distinct, too positive to be understood as "not another philosophy." Thus we are encouraged to regard as highly suspect any portrayal of philosophies as inverses or opposites. The difference between two philosophies cannot be captured as diametrically opposed answers to a particular question. More generally, the difference between two philosophies cannot be captured as different answers to the same question. Like Bergson, Deleuze endorses the "power of negation" displayed in Platonic dialogues such as the *Phaedrus* and the *Philebus*.[57] At first it appears as if Socrates is going to provide a different answer to an inherited question. But in the middle of articulating this answer he is interrupted (by his daimon, by a recollection). What follows is the invention and solution of a new question. Thus, in *Empiricism and Subjectivity*, Deleuze argues that a theory is an "elaborately developed question, and nothing else."[58]

Philosophies are thus incommensurable in that they are different questions rather than different answers to the same question. The difference between philosophy A and philosophy B is too great for the identity of A to be captured as not B (e.g. Hume's philosophy *is* more than a rejection of certain Cartesian tenets). Complicating this picture, however, is the fact Deleuze considers the history of philosophy to be comprised of different directions or tendencies. Engendering incommensurability or radical novelty belongs to the active or philosophical side of this history, while conversation, debate, and critical annotation constitute the academic or moderate side. The extreme side involves the production of a difference irreducible to opposition. This difference is a philosophical system. But for Deleuze, philosophy's power to act is continually being separated from what it can do. In the language of *Nietzsche and Philosophy*, philosophy is increasingly defined by a negative will-to-power (by an overall becoming-reactive of philosophical forces). The reactive side (conversation, debate, and "maliciously stupid" objections) increasingly shape our vision of the nature of philosophy.[59] The association between philosophy and incommensurability is descriptive: the philosophical side of the history of philosophy consists of the production of new problems. But it is also normative: "Don't debate, create." "Don't converse, create difference."

Complicating the simple assertion of incommensurability even further is the fact that Deleuze does not regard philosophical systems as hermetically sealed expressions of the inner-life of an author. Philosophers are influenced by other philosophers. Moreover, philosophers borrow the concepts of other philosophers. Here the principle of incommensurability is the alternative to representation. The concept of univocity moves from Scotus' system to Spinoza's system, from Spinoza's system to Deleuze's system. But this repetition of the concept is not a repetition of the same. The reterritorialization or counter-actualization of a concept is a new act of thought; the concept can only be grasped through a consideration of its new home. For Deleuze philosophies can influence one another. The question is how to understand this influence. For Deleuze interpreting two philosophies as a conversation (an exchange of words around a common topic), as a debate (different answers to the same question), or in terms of representation (sterile borrowings) is comparable to ignoring the existence of novelty and creativity within the history of philosophy. These images of difference are, at best, ways of capturing the nonphilosophical tendency within the history of philosophy. Similarly, negative definitions of a philosophical system or concept will never enable you to grasp its reality as a positive act of thought.

2.3   A problem *is* difference

In Deleuze's metaphilosophy there is the difference between philosophies, and there is the difference within a philosophy. The latter is not a difference resting upon a simple principle of identity; rather, the identity of a philosophy is itself composed of difference. To say philosophy is the practice of producing problems helps us think of the history of philosophy as a history of radical novelty and creativity. In fact, this is the principal reason Deleuze calls philosophies problems. Deleuze does not call philosophies problems because they are what are commonly thought of as problems. The complex movements of thought characterizing philosophies bear little resemblance to the act of posing a question. The familiar concept of "problem" conveys a sense of incommensurability. An adequate definition of philosophy, however, requires the construction of a new conception of problem.

Deleuze's most detailed account of philosophical problems is found in *Difference and Repetition*. There the notion of problem also goes by the names of Idea, complex theme, and sense. In Deleuze's reworking of the Platonic notion of Idea, philosophical systems are themselves Ideas, but not all Ideas are philosophical systems. Philosophies are problems, but not all problems are philosophies.

Deleuze's allusion to Plato is mediated by Kant's endorsement and reworking of Plato's notion of Idea in the Transcendental Dialectic: "Kant never ceased to remind us that Ideas are essentially 'problematic.' Conversely, problems are Ideas."[60] Central to Kant's appropriation of Idea is his distinction between an Idea's legitimate and illegitimate, regulative and nonregulative, immanent and metaphysical uses. Just as Plato differentiates the Idea from the particular, the intelligible from the apparent, so the Kantian Idea is defined by the fact it surpasses experience. There is no empirical instantiation for (no experience of) the idea of autonomy or morality, the idea of universal history, the idea of a soul, the idea of Nature as a totality.[61] Failure to recognize this engenders the fraudulent problems, not to mention solutions, Kant refers to as "metaphysics."

For Plato, of course, the nonempirical status of Ideas in no way compromises their reality or their importance for knowledge. In the *Phaedo*, the existence of universals is presented as a necessary condition for knowledge and rational discourse.[62] In the *Republic*, the idea of justice makes possible the evaluation of particular lives and social forms. Similarly, for Kant Ideas as "problematics" are prerequisites for knowledge and morality. An Idea is used in a regulative or immanent fashion when it operates as a horizon or unobtainable goal orienting thought. The idea of freedom enables us to consider the moral worth of particular acts; the idea of a totality lifts empirical science and the practice of history above the level of episodic observation. As Deleuze puts it, the Kantian Idea or problem is "a unitary and systematic field which orients and subsumes the researches or investigations in such a manner that the answers, in turn, form precisely cases of solution."[63] Because they are regulative principles, however, the Idea is not canceled out by these cases of solution. You cannot solve a problematic because there is no experience conforming to the Idea.

Kant's contention is that regulative Ideas enable us to avoid metaphysics and the reduction of understanding to scattered observations. Deleuze's contention is that attacking system-building (i.e. the production of Ideas or problematics) creates an impasse: "people can't imagine doing any serious work except on a very restricted and specific little series."[64] What, however, does it mean for Deleuze to consider the elaboration of a theory, or the articulation of a theory's implications, the solution to a problem? Deleuze's answer assumes the form of a paradox: the problem transcends and is immanent to its solutions. This proposal demands we ask how the transcendence-immanence of the problem does not belie philosophy's movement toward immanence? How is this transcendence-immanence not a matter of "immanence becoming immanent to something transcendent?"

The problem transcends its solutions in the sense of being distinct from them. How is it distinct? First, contrary to Plato, the relationship between Idea and solution is one of absolute nonresemblance: "the problem is extra-propositional... it differs in kind from every proposition."[65] But here we need to be careful. If the difference between being "extra-propositional" and "propositional" was simply a matter of two distinct illocutionary forces (posing a question versus making a claim), the difference would be one of degree rather than kind. In other words, when Deleuze says the problem is "extra-propositional" he means it is not the simple, self-identical content of an interrogative sentence. "Propositional" includes the meanings of utterances or inscriptions without propositional content in the traditional sense. For these reasons, the distinction between propositional and extra-propositional is best looked at as a distinction between the textual and extratextual.

Žižek finds in Deleuze's problem/solution distinction an echo of the belief books have a letter and a spirit (the "letter of the word" versus the "spirit of the word").[66] But the notion of a spirit of the text has connotations of self-identity (the idea of one, correct reading) and, presumably, the spirit of the word is believed to reside in the mind of the author. For Deleuze, the content of the Idea is a differential; the Idea is comparable to a complex, unfolding curve comprised of singular points and ordinary points, sharp bends and smooth, linear progressions.[67] Additionally, philosophical systems, no less than works of art, stand on their own independently of the author (this is part of what Deleuze means by their "self-referential" character).[68] Where, then, does the problem reside? Here is where the immanent side of transcendent-immanent comes into play. While different in kind from the solution, the problem is a strictly immanent principle: "A problem does not exist, apart from its solutions. Far from disappearing in this overlay, however, it insists and persists in these solutions. A problem is determined at the same time as it is solved, but its determination is not the same as its solution."[69]

Notice Deleuze's use of the singular and plural – one problem, multiple solutions. This passage also draws attention to the persistence of the problem in the solution. A problem transcends or is distinct from its solution, in that, like the Kantian Idea, it is not canceled out by the solution. We can say the problem is unsolvable, or every solution is a partial solution, or the problem permits an indeterminate number of solutions. For example, the only way to grasp Deleuze's own problem is by traveling through its heterogeneous solutions or expressions. That a problem admits any number of solutions means that the whole of the problem is not given in the past or present. New actualizations for a philosophy or one of its concepts can always be engineered: "If one can still be a Platonist, Cartesian, or Kantian today, it is because one is justified in thinking that their concepts can be reactivated."[70] If nonresemblance or nonidentity governs the relationship between the problem and each of its solutions, it is also the principle governing the relationship between solutions. The reactivation or repetition of a philosophical system has a precise relation to the original texts. The new actualization is the original text's doppelganger, portrait, or bastard child: maximum fidelity, maximum divergence.

In *What Is Philosophy?* the distinction between a problem and its solutions appears as the distinction between a plane of immanence and a network of conceptual multiplicities. The distinct but inseparable character of the philosophical Idea is reiterated. The plane is the abstract machine to the concrete assemblages that are concepts; the plane is the breath that animates a skeletal frame. "Concepts are like multiple waves, rising and falling, but the plane of immanence is the single wave that rolls them up and unrolls them."[71] In this passage the meaning of "immanence" is twofold. The plane is immanent because, while distinct from the concepts, it is inseparable from the concepts. In contrast to *Difference and Repetition*, the difference in kind between the problem and its conceptual articulation is no longer described as the problem being transcendent (in the sense of "transcendent-immanent"). "Immanence" also refers to philosophy's vocation of immanence. Granted, some philosophical systems include within themselves a division of the real into two worlds. But within Deleuze's metaphilosophy these philosophies are also planes of immanence. Even if they were originally presented as representations of transcendent principles, the philosophies are in reality concepts – concepts that were produced rather than discovered.

A striking feature of *What Is Philosophy?* is the incredible proliferation and elaboration of positive, metaphilosophical concepts. In addition to "plane of immanence" and "concept," there is "component," "neighborhood," "endoconsistency," "exoconsistency," "threshold of indiscernability," "movable bridge," and "conceptual persona."[72] This conceptual toolbox makes possible a thoroughly dynamic, and nonreductive description of philosophical systems.

The concept is neither static nor simple. Nevertheless, it is a rigorous composition. The term "endoconsistency" or "internal consistency" is used to capture how the concept pulls together, arranges, and rearranges components into distinct neighborhoods. Neighborhoods do not include every conceptual component, and some neighborhoods include "zones of indiscernability" in which two or more components become indistinguishable. As for a concept's "exoconsistency," it consists of the relations established between it and the other concepts within the system. Since *Empiricism and Subjectivity*, Deleuze has described how systems can be constituted through the organization of disparate elements. Organization or systematicity does not require internal relations, only relations. Whether we are dealing with concepts or with the components of a concept, the content of one term does not explain the movement between that term and another. Nevertheless, there is movement, consistency, or composition. Similarly, for Deleuze, organization does not presuppose a static, linear chain of elements. Components are arranged at varying degrees of distance and proximity into various combinations, while the bridges between the concepts are thoroughly mobile.

For Deleuze a plane of immanence is not expressed only in intraconceptual and interconceptual relations. Philosophical systems also possess a theatre of operations comprised of a cast of conceptual personae or characters: there is Plato's philosopher, sophist, and poet; Descartes' courageous narrator ("I am now doubting x") and the narrator's timid interlocutor ("but you couldn't possibly doubt y"); Derrida's logocentric philosopher and his or her critic. This notion of conceptual persona is clearly informed by the complex typology within Nietzsche's writings. As Deleuze explains "A type is a reality which is simultaneously biological, psychical, historical, social and political."[73] Nietzsche evaluates propositions and value judgments as symptoms or perspectives of such types. The question "what is ... ?" or "is it true?" is replaced with "which type is capable of uttering such a thing?" "which one is capable of such an evaluation?"[74] In Nietzsche's writings, we encounter the Judaic priest and the Christian priest, the slave and the master, Zarathustra and Zarathustra's ass.

As discussed in Part II, Deleuze's concept of counter-actualization accounts for the originality of a philosopher's cast of characters and for the relationship between these characters and lives outside of the philosophy. The Socrates encountered in a Platonic dialogue is not a simple biographical portrait or representation, but there is a connection between the character of Socrates and a life that unfolded outside of Plato's writings. Moreover, Plato creates his character as an ethical and political act; that is, he wanted his character to influence how we live and think. Deleuze's concept encourages us to describe this complex set of relationships as follows. For Plato, the life of Socrates embodied certain qualities. While rare these qualities were not embodied by Socrates alone; at the very least, future lives could express these qualities as well. Plato extracted these qualities from the life of Socrates and reinscribed them within his system. This reinscription took the form of a creative act: the production of the character Socrates, a character that can only be understood through a consideration of its relationship to the rest of Plato's system. Hopefully, it will not simply be the other characters within a dialogue that encounter the character Socrates. Hopefully, readers will encounter this character. A genuine encounter results in the reader's life actualizing new tendencies, or in a modification of the ratio of tendencies the reader's life already actualizes.

2.4   The question of evaluation

This exposition of Deleuze's metatheory invites the question of evaluation or justification. How can an Idea, a problem, or plane of immanence be evaluated? What should be clear is the extent to which the familiar criteria – coherence, correspondence, solvability, sense – will not do. For Deleuze, every great philosophy coheres; every great philosophy is consistent. The challenge is that of discerning a philosophical system's coherence – its unique rigor or consistency. By identifying philosophies as problems rather than solutions, and problems as extra-propositional, the notion of correspondence is short-circuited. For the Deleuzian, nothing is sillier than approaching a philosophy as if it were a sentence such as "the cat is on the mat," or "there is snow outside."

Since philosophical systems are the articulation of problems, and the articulations *are* the solutions, there is, within Deleuzian metaphilosophy, no room for the notion of unsolvable problems. A problem only exists within its solutions or "the problem always has the solution it deserves".[75] What about the still-prevalent tendency to bifurcate philosophical discourse into meaningful and meaningless, scientific and pseudoscientific discourse? This should receive a Deleuzian diagnosis. When a critic attacks a philosophical text as nonsense, he or she is actualizing the concept of the academic. Deleuze's conceptual persona of the academic – the counterfeit philosopher – is designed to capture such tendencies and intervene against them. Far from an opposition to the university, this intervention reflects Deleuze's deep commitment to producing difference within the space of the university. The character's defining qualities are an inability to get over a philosopher's chosen taste (i.e. how a philosopher writes); an inability to move past taste to reach style (i.e. past the words to the acts of thought comprising the philosophical system); a tendency to claim what the most cursory glance at the history of philosophy belies, that there is such a thing as *a* way of writing philosophy; an inability to reach the level of abstraction that would be required to define philosophical rigor (the character uses the term "rigor" but without any robust, abstract definition of conceptual consistency); an interest in elevating the few texts he or she is comfortable with into an exclusive canon. For Deleuze, the "sense" of a philosophical text is the immanent, complex theme or problem. *If only* the task of understanding a philosophy's sense were as easy as measuring its author's taste against the norms of professional writing.

In his outstanding book on "French philosophies of difference," Todd May takes up the question of Deleuze's metaphilosophy and the practice of evaluation.[76] There he suggests philosophical planes, despite being nonrepresentational, can be evaluated by playing them off of one another. In other words, planes can be compared and evaluated relative to one another, albeit not as competing representations. While this is entirely plausible, I think it represents a bit of a short-cut through the theme of Deleuze and evaluation.

Simply in terms of the language he employs, Deleuze's treatment of the practice of evaluation consists of at least four distinct moments. These moments are logically rather than chronologically distinct: *Empiricism and Subjectivity, Bergsonism,* and *Difference and Repetition* contain a redefinition and relocation of the values of true and false. *Empiricism and Subjectivity, Difference and Repetition* and *What Is Philosophy?* contain numerous passages in which this redefined notion of truth is advanced in a manner that places the value of false off to the side. "True" begins to operate independently of the opposition between true and false. In *What Is Philosophy?* the devaluation of the distinction between true and false occurs alongside a proposal for different criteria. Finally, and I would argue most importantly, *Nietzsche and Philosophy* replaces the question of values with that of the value of values. Instead of asking "What is this philosophy's value?" we have to ask "Which one would evaluate or read a philosophy in this particular manner?"

The first moment occurs when Deleuze insists that, when it comes to philosophy, the values of true and false apply to problems exclusively.[77] Of course this invites the question "When is a problem false?" The question receives a couple of different answers. In *Empiricism and Subjectivity* the distinction between true and false is contained in a few, brief allusions to the rhetoric of Bacon's epistemology. How coercive is the problem; how much does the problem force the real to give up the goods?[78] In the introduction I suggested this is Deleuze's way of introducing the issue of power into the subject of evaluation. What can a philosophy do? What can we do when we incorporate a philosophy into our life?

When we move from *Empiricism and Subjectivity* to *Bergsonism*, we see the values of true and false take on metaphysical significance. Like Plato's butcher (a reference to the *Phaedrus*), the philosopher knows how to determine whether a question carves up the real properly.[79] In Bergson's work, to carve well is to discern the heterogeneous tendencies comprising individual perceptions, lives, and species. For Deleuze, the bad cut either divides the real into different worlds *or* fails to divide beings into different sides or directions. The values of true and false correspond to two commitments within Deleuze's metaphysics: immanence and the idea of individuals as concrete mixtures of heterogeneous tendencies (i.e. as actualizations of a differential structure). These ontological commitments can only be understood as simultaneously ethico-political commitments. What effect does the commitment to transcendence have on our lives and on the social? What happens when we fail to recognize the tendencies we actualize? What happens to our life when the ratio of tendencies we actualize remains the same? What risks accompany alterations of this ratio?

The second moment of evaluation is comprised of passages in which Deleuze appears to call into question the very practice of evaluating philosophical systems. This is best understood as Deleuze's way of highlighting the shortcomings of most criticism. Once again, there is the idea that when "false" or "wrong" is applied to all or part of a philosophy it represents a failure to reach the problem. Sometimes this failure reflects the "malicious stupidity" of the academic. Sometimes it reflects the fact a problem only exists within its solutions: "the solutions necessarily come to conceal the problem."[80] Naturally this means the solutions are not recognized as solutions.

When Deleuze relegates "false" to the margins, when he speaks of every philosophy as producing the truth, when he describes philosophies as self-justifying, his goal is to foreground this relationship between problem and solution, plane and concept: "A concept always has the truth that falls to it as a function of the conditions of its creation."[81] Why is there "no point in wondering whether Descartes was right or wrong?" Because "Cartesian concepts can only be assessed as a function of their problems and their plane."[82]

What *Empiricism and Subjectivity* adds to this picture is the idea objections miss their mark for multiple reasons. Objections miss the mark because they fail to grasp the structure of the philosophical system. But objections also miss the mark because the system already anticipates and deflects them. Having enumerated the common charges leveled against Hume's philosophy Deleuze writes "The reader should not be surprised to find in the text itself the literal refutation of all these objections – despite the fact that the objections come after the text."[83] Once again, the central message is that objections are misinterpretations stemming from a failure to recognize the problem. Nevertheless, the statement contributes something to the idea that philosophical systems could be self-justifying. Not just Hume but every philosopher anticipates criticisms beforehand and issues something along the lines of a response. Just as Freud protects the standing of his theories through the notion of intellectual resistance (i.e. built into his interpretations is the idea most will reject them), so philosophers create a conceptual persona representing every future critic (the soul unable to master the body, the person unable to free their mind from prejudice, etc.).

Deleuze's third treatment of evaluation is one in which the devaluation of the opposition between true and false goes hand in hand with the creation of different values: "thought as such produces something *interesting*."[84] The categories of "the new, remarkable, and interesting" replace "the appearance of truth and are more demanding than it is."[85] "Relevancy" and "necessity" (in the sense of urgency and passion) are opposed to "irrelevance" and "stupidity."[86] Deleuze's selection of philosophical and literary mediators (Hume and Artaud, Spinoza and Henry Miller, etc.) has little or nothing to do with approaching a piece of writing as a body of propositions, the categories of true and false in hand.

And Deleuze's mediators, not to mention Deleuze's own philosophy, are not universal "mediums of becoming." They are not necessarily the mediators that a particular person needs; perhaps a different philosophy will show up as a sign. This accounts for an important transition in *What Is Philosophy?*[87] On the one hand, philosophers "have too much to do" to bother with the question of whether a particular plane is the "best." On the other hand, "concepts must relate to our problems, to our history, and, above all, to our becomings."

Deleuze's treatment of the history of philosophy supports this substitution of criteria: "interesting" for "true." Above I described how his critique of the history of philosophy is presented, not as a critique of philosophy, but as the project of unshackling philosophy. This liberation of philosophy is simultaneously the liberation of the philosophical side or the active side of the history of philosophy. The history of philosophy now appears, not as the progression toward an authoritative representation, not as a series of failed attempts at authoritative representation, not as the failure to recognize that authoritative representation is impossible, but as a series of incommensurable problematics and nonfoundationalist surfaces. No less than a Nietzschean text, Plato's dialogues now appear in a nonfoundationalist light. We need not perceive them as a foundation or as a failed foundation. A philosophy does not need to be experienced as true or false.

In his essay "The history of philosophy as a philosophical problem," Guéroult adds a vital component to this picture.[88] Guéroult asks "what does it mean for a group of texts to show up as philosophical?" What he means is show up as philosophical rather than scientific. For the natural scientist, the archives of natural science show up as artifacts, pieces of history. Put somewhat differently, scientific texts can be experienced as out of date. But for Guéroult philosophical texts never become outdated. At best we can say more or less attention is directed toward certain texts over others at particular moments in time. At best we can say certain texts strike an individual as uninteresting.

What does this mean as far as Deleuze's metaphilosophy and the question of evaluation? Anti-foundationalism, deconstruction, antiphilosophy, and so on often rest upon the idea their target is ubiquitous if not inescapable. Philosophers, we are told, have always tried to pass off their constructions as discoveries, their illusions as definitive explanations. For the deconstructionist, even the critique of philosophy risks turning into its opposite (when the critique is seen as occurring on the outside of philosophy). Deleuze's metaphilosophy suggests that while the penchant for foundationalism is stubborn, it can be eliminated.

One can assign philosophy a positive mission – one can put critique in the service of creation – without regressing into foundationalism. For Deleuze the critique of universals, contemplation, and transcendence is indispensable. But after such a critique philosophy can turn to other tasks. These include reactualizations of classic philosophical concepts. What is suggested by Guéroult's essay is that a Deleuzian conversion of the contents of the history of philosophy is not only possible, but that it occurs all the time. Deleuze and Guattari contend the category of "interesting" to be more important than "true." Perhaps we can take this as a descriptive as well as normative statement. Perhaps the authors are not simply proposing criteria but identifying criteria already at play. Did Plato interpret his dialogues as authoritative explanations? Maybe. Maybe not. But the student of philosophy finds himself or herself returning (always returning) to these writings. What prompts such returns? A commitment to the notion of forms? The belief the notion of forms needs to be demystified? The belief the notion of forms needs to be refuted because so many profess allegiance? No, it is the fact that Plato's dialogues appear as interesting, perpetually relevant, always new, never out of fashion. The very way we return to the history of philosophy (not because we think Plato was right, and not because we think Plato needs to be proven wrong) is evidence that deconstruction's "philosophy as logocentrism" is far from inescapable.

Perhaps philosophy as logocentrism is not the fundamental norm of philosophical discourse. For Deleuze it would seem that the true norm is a differential characterized, not by foundationalist claims, but by professed expertise, endless talking, pathetic critical annotations of philosophical texts, an emphasis on prerequisites, exams rather than "scales," the dismissal of certain writings as nonsense, geographic travels rather intellectual journeys. As Deleuze would say, eliminating *this* norm within ourselves requires a vigilant guerilla campaign ("How is this *politics*, this full *guerilla warfare*, to be attained?").[89] This campaign is *Nietzsche and Philosophy's* project of "self-destruction."[90] Not guilt, a symptom of reactive forces, but an effort to bring about the nonreturn of reactive forces (the eternal return as principle of selection). For the philosopher, the project of "active destruction" includes the elimination or mitigation of academic tendencies. Yes, Deleuze's metaphilosophy and metaphysics include a critique of the history of philosophy. But the task of active destruction passes through "interesting" or "useful" planes of immanence rather than anti-foundationalism. Philosophies are encountered, they are signs, they are used as "mediums of becoming," or they are nothing.

Whether the issue is Deleuze's relocation or displacement of truth-value, his rejection of the idea that philosophies are refuted, or his promotion of alternative values ("interesting," "banal," etc.), the theme of Deleuze and evaluation always leads to the question of types ("which one?"). Deleuze's conceptual personae or typology in turn lead us directly to the theme of power – philosophy as the power to create new problems and new concepts. The three moments of Deleuze's treatment of evaluation have a common horizon. This is the fourth moment – the question of the power of philosophy. May's proposal was to measure one nonrepresentational plane by playing it off of another nonrepresentational plane. Deleuzian thought suggests the need to pose the question of type with regards to such a practice. "Which one," "which type," would engage in such a practice? In no way does the question afford a simple answer.

First, we should acknowledge Deleuze distances himself from a certain way of comparing planes. "Is there one plane that is better than all the others, or problems that dominate all others?" Deleuze states "Nothing at all can be said on this point" or that philosophers are too busy doing philosophy to "bother with the question."[91] More importantly, we need to remember the metaphilosophical version of his critique of conversation. The problem with the idea of conversation is it obscures difference in the form of incommensurable problems or systems. If Deleuze insists philosophies contain their own measure, it is because the attempt to find a common measure for two systems results in the reduction of one or both. Locating a mediator, finding a medium of becoming rarely takes the form of comparing two planes in order to find which one is more interesting. Instead of bothering with comparison, one is *bothered by* a particular text. A particular text is encountered or disclosed as a sign.

Nevertheless, it should be said, that Deleuze continually plays philosophies off of one another in the construction of his own system. Concepts from diverse locales are lifted and reterritoralized onto a common plane. As pointed out in Part II, Deleuze has several distinct ways of writing. What each of these compositional forms have in common is that, in Deleuze's eyes at least, they embody philosophical extremism. In his reading of the eternal return, the first selection consists of privileging the extreme over the average. Certain forms of philosophical writing should be seen as comparable to the weak, undeveloped reactive forces that can be eliminated during this first selection. In terms expressed earlier, writing in certain ways rather than others is a small step toward making sure that only philosophy

returns – a small step toward the elimination of academic tendencies. For the question of how to evaluate philosophy, Deleuze substitutes the question "who is concerned with evaluating philosophy
and why?" The values of true and false are replaced by a concern
with the different ways in which we work with the history of philosophy. For Deleuze, each of these ways is measured in terms of the distinction between active forces and reactive forces or the distinction
between philosophy overcoming a limit or being further restrained.
On the one hand, you have philosophical writing or a philosophical
approach to the history of philosophy. On the other hand, you have
academic writing or an academic approach. The first is extreme; the
second average. The first represents commentary going to the limit;
the second commentary being separated from the powers of fidelity
and difference. Deleuze's guide for evaluating philosophy – which is
to say his evaluations of ways of evaluating philosophical systems –
would look something like this:

Philosophical Evaluation/Writing	Academic Evaluation/Writing
1. Portraiture, reactivation, becomings (the absence of explicit objections or reservations)	1. Conversations, slavish book reports, summaries with critical annotations
2. Ridicule, genealogical deflation	2. Serious debate, respectful disagreement
3. Deterritorialization/reterritorialization	3. Comparison/contrast

3   The second metaphilosophical question: what does it mean to think?

Earlier I referred to two questions comprising Deleuze's metaphilosophical register. Exploring Deleuze's answer to the first, "What is a
philosophy?" has introduced us to nearly all of this register's concepts.
Let us now turn to the second question, "What does it mean to think?"
and a final, related concept – "image of thought." Deleuze's affirmation
of philosophy suggests we will find the same structure of critique and
construction, attack and alternative, as we did with the first question.
The assault on the dogmatic image is accompanied by a new theory of
practice and a call for experimentation within life. The "overturning"
of the dogmatic image requires more than "critique;" it requires the
"power of a new politics."[92]

3.1 What is an image of thought?

Proust and Signs, Nietzsche and Philosophy, and *Difference and Repetition* are books in which Deleuze explicitly considers and answers the question of the meaning of thought. At the same time, Deleuze's image of thought should be seen as coextensive with his entire body of work. While "image of thought" is a Deleuzian concept, Deleuze's own "image of thought" is less a particular concept than his overall performance. Similarly, the concept of "image" is designed to capture a general, pervasive feature of a philosophical system. Little surprise, then, that in *What Is Philosophy?*, the notion of Problem, Idea, or plane of immanence is equated with the idea of an image of thought. A philosophical system is the invention and elaboration of a problem. This process embodies a vision of what it means to think: "The plane of immanence is not a concept that is or can be thought but rather the image of thought, the image thought gives itself of what it means to think, to make use of thought, to find one's bearings in thought."[93]

3.2 The idea of a dogmatic image

Deleuze characterizes the "dogmatic" image as a set of presuppositions or pre-philosophical postulates.[94] By describing these presuppositions as subjective and objective, he highlights the extent to which they concern the meaning of "thought" rather than what happens to be true or what happens to exist. The subjective-objective distinction further highlights the extent to which the rhetoric of "overcoming presuppositions" or achieving a "presuppositionless inquiry" can be accompanied by the most common vision of thought. This understanding is common because it is based upon everyday experiences and activities.

No less than any other image of thought, Deleuze presents the dogmatic image as having the structure of a problem or Idea. The dogmatic image is largely "extra-propositional," though inseparable from a philosopher's explicit pronouncements: "The postulates need not be spoken ... they function all the more effectively in silence."[95] The dogmatic image circumvents the distinction between the One and the Many. There is only one dogmatic image of thought: "a single Image in general which constitutes the subjective presupposition of philosophy as a whole."[96] But Foucault is right when he suggests the notion of a dogmatic image should not be conflated with a theme such as the metaphysics of presence. The image is a variety of "small impurities" and "paltry compromises."[97] This is to say the content of the image is difference – in the sense of a diverse set of interrelated postulates. Moreover, against the logic of a self-identical essence and its instantiation, the diverse postulates of the dogmatic image are actualized along heterogeneous pathways. Even in their adherence to a dogmatic image, two philosophical systems can be characterized by nonresemblance. The dogmatic image "has variant forms;" philosophers "do not presume its construction in the same fashion."[98]

Nevertheless, is there not a sense that the notion of a dogmatic image of thought compromises Deleuze's emphasis on discontinuity and creativity within the history of philosophy? In an absolutely vital move, Deleuze stresses the irreducibility of philosophical systems to the dogmatic image. Not only is there nonresemblance in how the dogmatic image is actualized, philosophies are always more than actualizations of the dogmatic image: "philosophers often have second thoughts and do not accept this implicit image without adding further traits drawn from explicit reflection on conceptual thought which react against it and tend to overturn it."[99] As mentioned previously, Deleuze envisions the history of philosophy in terms of disparate directions or tendencies, but feels that only one of these directions deserves the name "philosophy." On the one hand, we have philosophy overcoming a limit or going to its limit through the construction of an original problem and its conceptual elaboration. For Deleuze, philosophy is this process of invention. On the other hand, we have philosophy separated from its power to act, a philosophy diminished or, as Foucault put it "compromised," by a dogmatic image. As with the history of philosophy as a whole, individual philosophies are concrete mixtures. Not a difference between philosophies but a difference within a philosophy: the philosophy and its internal handcuffs. When Deleuze repeats or constructs a portrait of a philosophy, the objective of fidelity is that of fidelity to the philosophical tendency. To repeat a philosophical system is to subject it to the eternal return. The shackles fall away. The philosophy becomes less moderate, more aggressive.

3.3   The dogmatic image and the problem of creativity

But is not the dogmatic image created? The various postulates comprising it are not eternal notions. Why, then, are these postulates not displays of philosophical creativity? The fact that, despite its being a creation, the dogmatic image is opposed to creativity can be approached in a couple of ways. Many of the image's subjective presuppositions are not displays of philosophical creativity because they do preexist philosophy. I mentioned above how the dogmatic image reflects a failure to differentiate philosophy from ordinary experiences:

> The criticism that must be addressed to this image of thought is precisely that it has based its supposed principle upon extrapolation from

certain facts, particularly insignificant facts such as Recognition, everyday banality in person; as though thought should not seek its models among stranger and more compromising adventures.[100]

The invention of a problem should, thus, be distinguished from the reactualization of a preexisting dogmatic image. Not because reactualization is simply the return of the same (the actualizations of the dogmatic image possess the feature of nonresemblance), but because what is being reactualized is banal, everyday.

A somewhat different approach is suggested by *Nietzsche and Philosophy*. There the triumph of reactive forces is said to hinge upon moments of innovation. Instead of being a simple, "mechanical process," the becoming-reactive of forces can only occur through the intervention of two figures (two priests) possessing great artistry.[101] The first invents and directs a fictitious image of force (the "paralogism of ressentiment"); the second invents the notion of guilt and sin. The first priest represents active forces as things distinct from their effects (as transcendent rather than immanent causes); projects this idea of a transcendent force onto a morally neutral subject (everyone has the potential or ability to act in that manner); and assigns values via negation (those who do such things are bad, we don't do such things, therefore we are good). The second priest not only completes but also changes the direction of ressentiment by encouraging individuals to locate the cause of suffering and pain within themselves ("we are all guilty," "all sinners"). Both inventions are fictions, but ones that succeed in turning active forces against themselves: "while it is true that active force is fictitiously separated from what it can do, it is also true that something real happens to it as a result of this fiction."[102] For present purposes what is most important is how Deleuze, in his account of the triumph of reactive forces, accents pivotal moments of innovation and discontinuity. The turning of active forces against themselves requires reactive forces to generate the requisite fictions, and these fictions represent genuine breakthroughs in the progression of reactive forces.

One should insist on a basic isomorphism as far as Deleuze's treatment of repression. On his metaphilosophical register there is the idea of the repression of philosophy; in *Nietzsche and Philosophy* there is the notion of the repression of active forces; in *Anti-Oedipus* there is the repression of desiring-production. What needs to be grasped is the overall logic of this account of repression. First and foremost, what should be appreciated is the extent to which, in Deleuzian thought, repression always receives a positive definition. This should not come as a surprise since Deleuze privileges the notion of institution over law – positive conceptions of the social over negative ones.

Curiously, this means that whenever we encounter the theme of repression in Deleuze's writings we should ask "what inventions (devices or technologies) are being denoted by the term 'repression'?" In *Nietzsche and Philosophy*, the answer is the paralogism of ressentiment and the notion of guilt; in *Anti-Oedipus* there are the postulates comprising the paralogisms of psychoanalysis; within philosophy there are the postulates comprising the dogmatic image of thought, but also, spectacular inventions such as Platonic transcendence and Aristotelian difference. The question "what is being produced?" also has to be asked with regards to the application of these technologies. In other words, the function of the technologies is described less as a "burying" or "elimination" than as a producing. In *Nietzsche and Philosophy*, the separation of an active force from what it can do is equivalent to the active force becoming-reactive. The more general process of active forces becoming-reactive (the negative will-to-power) is a matter of poisoning the healthy with negative passions (guilt, jealousy, etc.). In *Anti-Oedipus*, the paralogisms of psychoanalysis help solidify capitalism's production of passive Oedipal subjects. When it comes to Deleuze's metaphilosophy, the repression of philosophy is historically bound up with the production of philosophical systems. The repression of philosophy is discerned in philosophical systems, in those aspects of them that seem less radical, less extreme than they could be, in part because of the presence of other elements.

The basic elements of this model of repression can be expressed as a set of typological positions and correspondences:

Active Force	Reactive Force	Artist of Repression
The Philosopher	The Academic	Plato and Aristotle
The Master	The Slave	The Two Priests
The Schizo	The Neurotic	The Psychoanalyst

Repression is simultaneously the production of the types in the second column and the process of turning the first column into the second column. The process of repression is only able to go to *its* limits through the creation of a set of fictions. These fictions are described as possessing brilliance ("*Ressentiment* still had to become 'genius'"), as well as artistry ("It was still necessary to have an artist in fiction, capable of profiting from the opportunity and of directing the projection, conducting the prosecution and carrying out the reversal"). As such, the third column begins to resemble the first.

Why is the dogmatic image, as an invention, not a display of philosophical creativity? The first answer to this question was the idea that the dogmatic image was modeled on banal occurrences and acts. The second answer is a resounding "because." But this "because" should not be perceived as a failure to answer (as an instance of begging the question), but as a sign we are dealing with a basic axiom of Deleuze's philosophy – a feature of his system's differential. Once again, we find ourselves witnessing a redirected Platonism. In the *Republic*, Plato establishes a strict hierarchy among the order of particulars. Individual virtuous lives and poetic works are both particulars. But there is a difference in kind between the two particulars. The former are representations of the form justice. The latter are mistakenly perceived by the majority to have something to do with morality. The description of poetry as a copy of a copy – an imitation twice-removed – should not make us lose sight of the pivotal moment of the analogy. The painting of the bed is mistaken for one that can be slept in. Unless the bed in question is one by Rauschenberg, we need to remember we are dealing with an analogy. Plato, of course, was not particularly interested in beds. His persona Socrates discusses beds in order to help a bewildered audience grasp the basic lesson of the doctrine of forms. The lesson is that for many epic poetry appears as a guide to morality when the real guide, the genuine representation of justice, is the life of the philosopher.

The phantasms, simulacra, or counterfeit representations of Plato become in Deleuze the dogmatic image of thought, the commitment to universals, transcendence, analogical conceptions of being, the paralogism of ressentiment, and the paralogisms of psychoanalysis. Deleuze's multifaceted definition of philosophy is at the same time a hierarchical distinction between genuine philosophy and counterfeit philosophy, the type of the philosopher and the type of the academic. The seductive powers of poetic works, become the confusion of philosophy with counterfeit philosophy, desire with Oedipus. A person mistakes a counterfeit bed for a representation; an active force identifies with the fictions of the priest; we buy into one or many of the artificial territories (identities) capitalism provides (the familial triangle of psychoanalysis being only one of these territories).

Where does Deleuze's reversal of Platonism reside? In Deleuzian thought the privileged term is not a representation, imitation, copy, and so on but something radically new. No less than Platonism, however, the

Deleuzian emphasis on novelty can only be understood in relation to a hierarchy of particulars. We should not conflate the production of novelty that defines philosophy, desire, or an affirmative will-to-power with the production of a new technology of repression. That being said this hierarchy or nonconflation can be formulated in a variety of ways. Each demonstrates the inadequacies of simplistic, pseudo-Heraclitean formulations ("difference difference everywhere") of Deleuzian thought.

1. For Deleuze, not every creation is a true creation or some creations do not deserve the name "creation." Platonism positions the epic poetic depiction of morality as a counterfeit morality. In this regards it should be distinguished from the lives and social arrangements that represent the universal to varying degrees. There is a difference in degree between representations, a difference in kind between representations and simulacra. Deleuze's reworking of this scenario involves differentiating genuine from counterfeit novelty. The category of counterfeit novelty is comprised of "inventions" that are in reality re-presentations. The dogmatic image of thought is the "novel idea" that philosophy is made up of the most common, ordinary of acts. Counterfeit novelty also consists of ingenious moves (e.g. the notion of abstract universals) designed to arrest the production of the genuinely new.

2. For Deleuze, all creations are not created equal. In Platonism the hierarchy among particulars is cemented into place through the hierarchy between universals and particulars. The latter are brought into existence. The former have always existed as stable, self-identical principles. In contrast, Deleuze declares "being" to be univocal where part of the common sense of beings is that they are creations rather than representations: to be is to be something that comes into existence, not something that has always existed. The real is a process of creativity, not a process of models being imitated. That being said, there is a hierarchy among creations. Some creations display the nature of the real more powerfully than others. Some creations limit the process of creativity at the same time as they express the process of creativity – hold the real back at the same time as they express it.[103]

3. For Deleuze, creations are symptoms. Nietzsche asks "which one is evaluating, the slave or the master?" with regards to values (particular acts of evaluation). The triumph of reactive forces is the story of these forces going to their limit. But active forces are defined as forces that go to their limit. Does this mean that reactive forces can become active forces? No, it means the expression "a force going to its limit" is essentially ambiguous; it only has a precise meaning relative to more fundamental notions: the distinction between active force and reactive

force, and the distinction between a becoming-active of forces (or affirmative will-to-power) and a becoming-reactive of forces (a negative will-to-power). "Becoming-reactive" is the story of reactive-forces going to their limit, and this is the story of active forces being separated from what they can do. Active forces, however, do not go to their limit through a direct opposition or negation of reactive forces. In the evaluation of the master, negation only appears in the conclusion. A burst of creativity is followed by an affirmation of this creativity. Only then does opposition appear, as an afterward ("how fortunate to not be like them")? For Deleuze, the problem of creativity is such that the expression "creativity" is just like the expression "a force going to its limit." The only way to ensure that it does not function as a slogan or serve to valorize commercial goods is to have its meaning be determined by the question "which one?" In the service of what forces? Is this creation in the service of action or reaction, affirmation or denial?

Whether we consider the dogmatic image of thought, universals, transcendence, and so on as displays of creativity depends upon the formulation. Each formulation has its advantages and disadvantages. When the accent is placed on univocity (#2) we can easily forget the Deleuzian hierarchy. When Deleuzian evaluation is emphasized (#1 and #3) we can easily forget we are dealing with one world and one meaning of being. Truth be told, it is only by understanding Deleuze's notion of repression that we can ensure we do not forget this last point (the univocity of being).

We have seen repression defined as the formation of technologies which, in turn, ensure the production of a particular type of system, body, or subject. But for Deleuze the notion of the dogmatic image of thought, reactive force, or Oedipal subject are abstractions (or abstract machines). The standard way of thinking about repression is the following chronology: first, the existence of a substance; second, the repression of that substance; third, the return of the repressed or recovery of the substance. For Deleuze what is first is a concrete mixture of heterogeneous directions: philosophy and the dogmatic image of thought, the direction of immanence and the direction of transcendence, active forces and reactive forces, desiring-production and Oedipus, the subject group and subjected groups. Portraying Deleuzian repression according to the familiar model is predicated upon complete ignorance of his philosophy of difference. "Repression" corresponds to the second tendency, and it is made up of inventions whose identity consists of opposing the first. As for the first tendency, it is decisively not the second; but its identity is not that of being opposed to the second.

The coexistence of repression and what is repressed encourages us to consider Deleuze's reworking of the idea of recovery or the return of the repressed. A couple aspects of this reworking are essential. One is that the Deleuzian return cannot be the repetition of some content. The first tendency corresponds to radical novelty, genuine creativity, or active creation. The return of the first can only take the form of a production of difference: a new philosophical system, a new actualization, a new way of living. Since the first tendency already existed we have to look at this return not as the uncovering of something buried, but the radicalization of a tendency already present (present as promissory cracks within dominant structures). The final aspect concerns the precise nature of this radicalization. In *Nietzsche and Philosophy*, the active type is not characterized by the total absence of reactive forces. The two types correspond to the two qualities of the will-to-power, and the qualities of the will-to-power (affirmation and negation) are not the same thing as the qualities of force (active and reactive). Active and reactive types, the affirmative and negative will, are two distinct arrangements or relations between active and reactive forces. Affirmation involves reactive forces being acted; this means they play a supporting role to active transformations and bursts of creativity (a healthy type possesses the reactive power of adjusting to circumstances).[104] In place of a return of the repressed, we find in Deleuze the idea of a reworking of the relationship between the two tendencies or the idea of changing the ratio or proportion of the two tendencies. Genuine creativity – including genuine philosophy – involves genuine dangers. The lives of Spinoza and Nietzsche provide very different testaments to this fact. The attainment of "full guerilla warfare" is at the same time a matter of being "a little of a guerilla," "just enough to extend the crack but not enough to deepen it irremediably?"[105]

3.4   The dogmatic postulates and the Deleuzian alternative

The peculiar status of the dogmatic image has led us to posit the following definitions or formulations: not philosophy but the conflation of philosophy with prosaic acts; a creation, but not a display of philosophical creativity; an invention, but one that separates philosophy from its power of invention. What, however, are the postulates making up this image? To paraphrase Foucault, "What are philosophy's compromises and impurities?" Just as important, what is the Deleuzian alternative? What nondogmatic vision of thought does Deleuze provide?

One of these postulates we have already considered at some length. This is the conventional understanding of problems and their solutions. The residence of the problem is believed to be inner-life ("so and so has a question"). Problems, or at least genuine problems, are believed to be solvable. Most likely, this is the same thing as believing the problem possesses one correct solution. At the very least possessing multiple solutions is not believed to be an essential feature of a problem. "Solvable" means the correct solution dissolves the problem ("it is no longer a problem; it has been solved"). As we saw above, the Kantian notion of Ideas as problematics (i.e. horizon defining goals) and the Deleuzian vision of philosophical Ideas or problems requires us to us to think of problems and solutions differently. For Kant the problematic Idea of nature as a well-ordered totality is continuously solved through nonepisodic, empirical judgments. For Deleuze, a philosophy's defining problem is tantamount to a complex curve. This curve can be expressed in more than one way. Moreover, no solution or expression cancels out the problem. The whole of a problem is never fully given. Every philosophy can have a future: if the right contingent encounter occurs, if the philosophy is disclosed as a sign, if the person to whom it is disclosed as a sign tackles the arduous task of engineering a new actualization.

Another postulate represents one of the central targets of Deleuze's ethico-political metaphysics. What Deleuze refers to as the postulate of representation or as the illusion of representation is the conventional understanding of difference and repetition.[106] Routinely, difference means the difference between two objects, beings, bodies, or entities. The objects can belong to different kinds ("this is an apple; that is a chair") or they can be members of the same kind ("I have two apples."). In each case, difference is bound up with the practice of subsuming entities under a concept. Not the Deleuzian concept, of course, but the concept as a taxonomic region. Aristotelianism and theism provide another common form of difference. This is a deeper ontological division into two basic kinds of entities – substance and the other categories, God and the order of creation. The division is so great that we can only legitimately describe them both as "beings" or "things that are" if we recognize that the meanings of these words are different on each side of the divide. The word "being" has two entirely different senses (the equivocal position), or two different but related senses (the analogical position). Difference is also thought through the notion of resemblance. The copy resembles the model; the various copies resemble one another. We say we are holding two apples because the entities in question resemble one another. Lastly, difference is dogmatically related to determination through opposition or negation. What an entity is – what constitutes the identity of a entity – is the fact it is not another entity or that it is not every other entity.

If we tend to speak of difference and repetition, not difference as rep-etition, or repetition as difference, it is because we think of repetition as the repetition of the same. There is repetition when there are chrono-logically distinct instances of the same thing. A movie is repeated in the sense of being given multiple screenings. Or, a movie is repeated when it is remade. How does the term "representation" evoke these various ways of thinking difference and repetition? The film is repeated or re-presented. The copy re-presents the model it resembles. The Platonic notion of a group of particulars representing an Idea or form is at the same time a more general position. What is the ground of an entity's identity? What a being *is* is a re-presentation of an abstract essence or universal. Since these essences or universals (in the non-Deleuzian sense of "essence" and "universal") are the referents of concepts (in the non-Deleuzian sense of "concept") we can say that dogmatic difference and repetition is the reduction of determination to conceptualization. The question of an entity's identity is the question of "which concept?" The question "what essence does this entity represent?" is equivalent to the question "under which concept should this entity be subsumed?" which, in turn, is equivalent to "under which concepts should this entity not be subsumed?"

Granted, the Deleuzian alternative to representation is located prima-rily on the ethico-metaphysical register. Have we not, though, already encountered, on the metaphilosophical register, a different way of con-ceiving of difference? For Deleuze, negative or oppositional definitions of a philosophical system will never give you the system in its funda-mental positivity. While the oppositions can be numerous and refined, the philosophy's defining problem is such that the philosophy is always more than the inverse of another philosophy. The philosophy is even more than the negation of every other philosophy.

Furthermore, we saw above how Deleuze's treatment of the history of philosophy is one in which "difference" does not simply mean the posi-tive difference between philosophies (the difference between problems) or the positive difference between philosophy's history and another his-tory (e.g. the history of art). The principal difference was the difference constitutive of the history of philosophy as well as the difference consti-tutive of individual philosophies. The history of philosophy is comprised of heterogeneous directions. There is the pure, creative, active, imma-nent, or philosophical side of the history of philosophy. And, there is the impure, limiting, reactive, dogmatic, transcendent, or nonphilosophical side of the history of philosophy. Similarly, individual philosophies can be understood as distinct ratios of active and reactive forces. They can be at once displays of creativity and the limitation of creativity, radical invention and conversation. They can be both the extraordinary and the commonplace. Strictly speaking, Deleuzian difference is not the difference between the two constitutive directions, but the first direction. Difference is the creative side of a philosophy or the history of philosophy. The philosophical direction is defined as difference in the sense of the making of difference (the invention of new problems).

What about an alternative to the dogmatic understanding of repetition. Part I included an examination of Hume's notion of habit, and its influence on Deleuze. The idea of the formation of a habit was, more generally, the idea of the formation of the subject. In tandem with passions and principles of association, a constant conjunction or repetition of the same engenders something new – a habitual, structured movement of ideas. In *Difference and Repetition*, Deleuze will number this the first repetition.[107] We should not see this as an endorsement of Hume's specific account of habit-formation or subject-formation. We should see Deleuze's use of the notion of "habit" and the notion "institution" as an endorsement of the idea that subjects and bodies are formed through a synthesis of innumerable, disparate elements. Moreover, Deleuze's use of these terms should not be separated from his consideration of the reorganization of thought and the body. Unlike Defoe's Robinson, Tournier's does not represent or rebuild an old order. A structure of perceiving, desiring, and living is gradually left behind. One structure is replaced by another radically divergent one. In the present context what is most important is that the reference to Hume in *Difference and Repetition* is designed to get us to rethink the opposition between repetition and difference. Hume's discussion of habit formation is one in which what is repeated is difference. The impressions of sensation making up conjunction are heterogeneous. As far as that goes, without the principles of association, there is not even a constant conjunction. There is a repetition of a conjunction only because the disparate elements of one conjunction are related to the disparate elements of another conjunction by the principle of resemblance. The repetition of the same is the synthesis of difference. What is the effect of this synthesis of difference? The synthesis makes or engenders difference in the sense of a new relation or new habit. In Hume's philosophy, the repetition of the same (constant conjunctions) is in fact the story of how difference (the new relation) is made through the organization of difference (the impressions and ideas of sensation).

Have we seen any other ways in which Deleuze loosens *our* habitual association of repetition and sameness? In particular, does Deleuze's metaphilosophical register contain an alternative to the dogmatic configuration of repetition as it did with the dogmatic configuration of difference? In Deleuze's notion and practice of portraiture there is the marriage of repetition and difference, fidelity and innovation. Additionally, we need to consider the content of this repetition. The content is the problem, Idea, immanent cause, differential, abstract machine, concrete universal, concrete essence, or virtual structure. As a distribution of singular and ordinal, remarkable and regular points problems have a shape. Moreover, this shape is not that of a simple polygon such as a rectangle (four singular points connected via four series of ordinal points). The shape is that of a complex curve. That the problem is distinct from a solution is to say that its future is open. Portraiture or reactivation demonstrates this openness. Each philosophical problem affords multiple solutions. Each solution is the actualization of the differential, distribution, or complex curve that defines the problem. The relationship between solutions (or between the portrait and the subject of the portrait) cannot be grasped in terms of resemblance or representation. In portraiture, the novelty of the portrait, its embodiment of difference is as important as fidelity or repetition. What does it mean to say a philosophical problem is one that can be portrayed or reactivated? It means the problem's identity is a function of two processes: differenciation (the problem's disparate actualizations) and differentiation (the problem's differential content). The identity of a philosophical system is never saturated by a particular solution or actualization. A philosophy is its philosophical history – the story of past and future actualizations. A philosophy is the differenciation of a differentiation.

The idea of a virtual content (a virtual difference) repeating itself through the invention of different actualizations is Deleuze's second repetition.[108] The third, or "royal," repetition was suggested by our discussion of the distinct directions embodied by the history of philosophical writing. For Deleuze, the repetition of the history of philosophy and the repetition of an individual philosophy is selective. A Deleuzian repetition of the history of philosophy repeats the philosophical side of that history, not the side representing the separation of philosophy from its creative power. At the very least repetition is the attempt to increase the amount of innovation, decrease the influence of the dogmatic image, transcendence, conversation, debate, and so on. To repeat the history of philosophy is to create problems and concepts. Similarly, the difference engendered through portraiture should be understood as a principle of selection. In Deleuzian terms, a successful portrait is one that unchains a philosophy (one that radicalizes a philosophy by unchaining it). The chains are the limitations inherent in the philosophy's original form, or more generally, in its previous actualizations. On the metaphilosophical register, the third repetition is the return of philosophical creativity. This includes the return of the creative sides of previous philosophies.

The other postulates give a clearer sense of why the dogmatic image is the dogmatic image of thought. Instead of concerning how we think about difference, repetition, problems, or solutions, they concern how we think about thought. In *Proust and Signs, Nietzsche and Philosophy*, and *Difference and Repetition*, Deleuze devotes considerable attention to what he calls the supposed "goodwill" or "good nature" of thought.[109] The idea is that we naturally think, and, thus, do so all the time. What could be a more common occurrence than thought? The "good" in "goodwill" or "good nature" refers to the fact that thought has an innate affinity with the truth. Thought is a natural occurrence, and thought naturally gravitates toward the true. "... the mind as mind, the thinker as thinker, wants the truth, loves or desires the truth, naturally seeks the truth."[110] Political discourse and activism frequently rests upon the assumption of a natural desire for the truth (people are always thinking, and they want to know the truth). Of course, thought can be led astray; its natural course can be impeded – hence the idea or postulate of method.[111] Strengthened through conformity to methodological principles, thought ably deflects the obstacles and distractions (the "objective" presuppositions) that distort its nature.

In the dogmatic image, the exemplary instance of thought is recognition. Deleuze presents this postulate as an implicit view of the subject and as an implicit theory of faculties.[112] Recognition occurs when the faculties (perception, the imagination, memory, etc.) coalesce around a common object. "I am recalling what I perceived." "I am now perceiving what I was imagining." The "I" suggests the faculties are different capacities of an underlying, immutable substance. The object perceived is equivalent to the object recalled and the object imagined; the one perceiving is equivalent to the one recalling and the one imagining. When does thought occur? Answer: whenever a subject recognizes an object ("that is a tree").

Every image of thought includes an image of thought gone astray (an image of the "negative of thought" or "misadventure of thought").[113] If thought is understood to be a matter of recognition, the exemplary instance of failing to think or thinking improperly will be misrecognition. We say "Good morning Theodorus," when it is "Theaetetus who passes by."[114] Understanding thought as recognition, error as misrecognition, is linked to the privilege afforded to the proposition. As Austin stated, "for too long the assumption of philosophers" was that language is primarily a vehicle for statements, and that "the business of a 'statement' can only be to 'describe' some state of affairs, or to 'state some fact', which it must do either truly or falsely."[115]

An image of thought includes a conception of learning. In the case of the dogmatic image learning is understood as an entirely voluntary and transparent affair.[116] "I am now going to think." "I am now going to do philosophy." "I know I am doing philosophy." If learning occurs over time and, as such, is a process, the dogmatic image is the tendency to reduce this process to a particular end. The end is the acquisition of information, and the ability to communicate this information. The end is not the invention of problems, but the invention of solutions to pre-existing problems. In this regard, the model of learning is the classroom examination: "According to this infantile prejudice, the master sets a problem, our task is to solve it, and the result is accredited true or false by a powerful authority."[117]

As with the thought of difference, repetition, problems, and solutions, Deleuze attempts to carry out a complete overhaul of the dogmatic image. This takes the form of criticism, but a criticism that turns into an alternative image. Philosophy should model itself not on the quotidian but the unusual:

> On the one hand it is apparent that acts of recognition exist and occupy a large part of our daily life: this is a table, this is an apple, this the piece of wax, Good morning Theaetetus. But who can believe that the destiny of thought is at stake in these acts, and that when we recognize we are thinking.[118]

Deleuze also appropriates the notion of a presuppositionless inquiry, but he redirects it in the following manner: the critique of presuppositions should extend beyond "objective" presuppositions (beliefs concerning what exists) to "subjective presuppositions" (beliefs concerning the meaning of thought). He intends to inaugurate such a critique and thus initiate a beginning; but this beginning is presented as philosophy's liberation rather than overcoming.

> [T]he conditions of a philosophy which would be without any kind of presuppositions appear all the more clearly...It would find its difference or its true beginning, not in an agreement with the pre-philosophical Image but in a rigorous struggle against this Image, which it would denounce as non-philosophical.[119]

The dogmatic image takes the form of common sense. "We all know" that difference means different objects. "We all know" that propositions have truth-values, not questions. We all know that thought occurs naturally, and continuously. Deleuze's figure of the philosopher refuses to be represented by "common sense." Common sense says "as we all know...," to which the philosopher replies "speak for yourself." Moreover, the philosopher is the one who refuses to position themselves as the voice of "common sense." The philosopher is the one who never says "as we all know" (e.g. the philosopher never appeals to "moral intuitions"):

> It is a question of someone – if only one – with the necessary modesty not managing to know what everybody knows, and modestly denying what everybody is supposed to recognize. Someone who neither allows himself to be represented nor wishes to represent anything.[120]

The task of redefining thought is thus the task of renouncing common sense; it is the task of purifying philosophy (pushing it beyond its "non-philosophical" presuppositions); it is the project of modeling thought on the extraordinary rather than the ordinary ("schizophrenia is not only a human fact but also a possibility for thought").[121]

As an overhaul of the dogmatic image we should expect Deleuzian thought to enact a series of precise substitutions. This is indeed the case. Instead of referring to the "goodwill" of thought, Deleuze describes the thinker as one who is filled with "ill will." Thought is not something we do naturally or spontaneously. Deleuze's definition of thought is such that we are not always thinking. Consequently, thought is rare rather than commonplace. This, of course, is a negative definition of the Deleuzian alternative. The positive side is provided by concepts such as "encounter," "sign." For Deleuze, thought presupposes a contingent, unexpected encounter with an object that forces us to think: "Thought is nothing without something that forces and does violence to it."[122]

What Deleuze calls "signs" are the objects that provide the requisite external pressure. Sensory recognition entails the classification of an entity (we see the kind of thing the entity is) or the identification of one of the entity's quality (we see that the cat is orange). In contrast, the "sign" denotes an aspect of our experience that exceeds recognition. Proust's *In Search of Lost Time* is filled with contingent encounters with objects that seize the protagonist's attention. There is not only the famous madeleine but also the steeples, trees, cobblestones, the noise of a spoon, salon rituals, and a beloved's facial expressions. In each case experience includes the sense of something that must be deciphered. What is it about the taste of the madeleine? Is the beloved's expression a sign of affection or disinterest? Similarly, for Deleuze, we perceive a sign when a situation fills us with emotion (surprise, anger, love, etc.) and forces us to ask "What is happening?" not to mention "What must I do?"

Deleuze's concepts of encounter and sign are linked to a reworking of epistemological modalities described in the introduction. The distinction between contingency and necessity is replaced by a distinction between the possible and contingent-necessity.[123] The latter category is designed to drive home the importance of contingent encounters (we happen upon a sign, we find a mediator or medium of becoming). Only contingency engenders necessity. What does this mean? It means we cannot simply, through an effort of the will, or through a decision to conform to a method, produce necessary thoughts and, more generally, necessary actions. What is a necessary thought? Not a necessary truth (a thought that must be true regardless of place and time).[124] Not the discovery of an explanatory ground. By "necessity" Deleuze means something like the appearance of urgency and passion. Thoughts, words, and deeds can bear the mark of necessity; they strike us as things the "person had to say, had to write, had to perform." Others bear the mark of possibility; it seems as if the person responsible could just as well have done something else (written a different book, expressed themselves differently, etc.).

Part of the dogmatic image is the view that learning is a transparent process. We know when we are doing philosophy; we know when we are learning how to do philosophy. The Deleuzian alternative is the idea of "apprenticeship." The bulk of the apprenticeship happens behind the apprentice's back. In fact, the most important experiences may be the ones we feel are interfering with our vocation or project. Echoing Proust, Deleuze writes "This is why, when we think we are wasting our time... we are often pursuing an obscure apprenticeship until the final revelation of a truth of 'lost time'."[125] What Deleuze devalues are precisely those moments and settings that are consciously and formally devoted to a vocation – in particular, the classroom: "We never know how someone learns; but whatever the way, it is always by the intermediary of signs, by wasting time, and not by the assimilation of some objective content."[126]

Of course it is important to recognize the classroom in question is an abstract, conceptual classroom. We have seen how an absolutely rigorous and substantive question within Deleuze's philosophy is "How can I work in a university and not be an academic?" or "How can I work in a university and still be a philosopher?" or "How can I prevent my classroom from being a classroom?"

To define thought as recognition is to model it on the common-place. For Deleuze "everyday thought" is an oxymoron. What this suggests is in Deleuze's image of thought the negative of thought *will* be associated with the commonplace. And, it suggests, that misrecognition (the dogmatic conception of thought's negative) fails to capture the absence of thought in everyday life. We should imagine Deleuze saying "recognition occurs all the time, but does the same hold for misrecognition?" We should imagine him saying "is there not a more pervasive enemy of thought, one whose ubiquity is the counterpart to thought's rarity?"

> The almost laughable character of the examples usually invoked by philosophers in order to illustrate error (saying "Hello Theaetetus ..." when one meets Theodore ... saying "3 + 2 = 6") is enough to show that this concept of error is merely the extrapolation of puerile, artificial, or grotesque factual situations.[127]

For Deleuze, the history of philosophy displays a profound awareness of the severe limitations of the notions of error and misrecognition. Hence we have the Platonic notion of forgetfulness, the Cartesian critique of prejudice, Kant's notion of paralogism, the Hegelian category of alienation, and Sartre's concept of bad faith.[128] By now it should be expected that Deleuze's move is to claim that the dogmatic image prevents this insight and thus these alternate, negative definitions from going to their limit. Additionally, there is the question of the conception of thought's negative that is needed today. The notions of misrecognition, erroneous proposition, superstition (or unwarranted belief), and objective presupposition (Descartes' notion of prejudgment) provide only limited assistance to philosophy in its creative vocation. As seen in Deleuze's reworking of the notion of repression, he feels the category of alienation (the loss of or movement toward an identity or totality) is an impediment to positive social criticism (i.e. criticism that tells us what the social is rather than what it is not).

Along with the Deleuzian notions of Oedipus, paralogism, and repression, there is the category of stupidity. Thought is unusual; stupidity is all too frequent. Besides being the absence of thought, what can be said about stupidity? In the case of thought a contingent encounter confers urgency or the mark of necessity. Stupidity corresponds to the category of possible. Employing the language of *Nietzsche and Philosophy*, we could say that "average" or "modest" are synonymous with "possible." Lacking the appearance of necessity is tantamount to displaying weakness. The reactive forces expressing themselves are not just weak relative to active forces; they are weak relative to other, more fully developed reactive forces. What characterizes writing purportedly "philosophical" but merely "possible?" The answer: timidity and commercial viability.

The notion of stupidity is developed and given a more political edge in *A Thousand Plateaus*. As discussed in Part II, the major side of the abstract language machine is composed of discursive norms. Often these norms are site-specific. This is why the abstract machine includes, on the other axis, the organization of bodies accompanying a particular utterance. The person working retail is compelled to speak (to not be silent), and moreover, to speak a particular way. "A medium is just ten cents more" versus "I prefer not to" or "perhaps we should form a union." This compulsion should not be confused with the violence of a sign. Instead of engendering thought or necessary speech, one is simply "saying what people say" in that position (the position of cashier, student, instructor, manager, etc.). For Deleuze, redundancy is the hallmark of stupidity: "The problem isn't that some things are wrong, but that they're stupid or irrelevant. That they've already been said a thousand times."[129]

Stupidity is the relaying of a cliché, and according to Deleuze we are awash in clichés: "Nothing but clichés, clichés, clichés everywhere..."[130] Lest we forget, Deleuze's character the academic corresponds to the production of a specific order of clichés. Plato cautions us against mistaking the sophist for the philosopher, epic poetry for genuine virtue. The Deleuzian redirection of this theme privileges fabrication (or creativity) over the representation. We are warned against mistaking clichés for concepts. Most of all, Deleuze instructs us that, minus a vigilant campaign, we will relay countless generalities, fashionable jargon, not to mention those platitudes that pass for significant objections: "Misunderstandings are often reactions of malicious stupidity. There are some who can only feel intelligent by discovering 'contradictions' in a great thinker."[131]

A final feature of the Deleuzian image remains. This is his reoccurring use of the term "faculty." Thought, for example, is defined as a faculty, as are perception, imagination, memory, sociability, and language.

Earlier I described how Deleuze connects the practice of the recognition to the faculties – to them interacting in a specific fashion. All take on the same object ("I am now remembering what I saw yesterday; I am going to speak about what I am seeing."). In contrast, thought is defined as the absence of this harmony or accord. The faculties become "unhinged."[132] What is perceived is not what is spoken of is not what is imagined, and so on. This scenario, however, entails neither the absence of order or interaction.

The faculty of perception makes possible recognition, but also the experience of signs. An object emits a sign when we perceive it as troubling, confusing, even demanding (demanding of us a response). Deleuze describes such an experience with a paradox: the perception of the imperceptible. This simply means what is perceived exceeds recognition. The "transcendental" or "involuntary" use of the faculty of perception goes beyond the limit set by the "empirical" or "voluntary" use. Additionally, the imperceptible or the sign is described as what can only be perceived. In other words, one can only perceive a sign (not imagine or recall it). The perception of a sign can then detonate a transcendental use of another faculty which can in turn detonate another faculty and so on. Each faculty grasps what only it can grasp, an object ungraspable when the faculty is in the service of recognition. Can the order of faculties be reversed? Can the faculty of imagination, for example, pull the trigger on perception. Deleuze's answer is no, and we should take this as basic commitment to exteriority or the Outside.[133] Every transcendental instance of a faculty is traceable back to a violent, unsettling encounter between ourselves and other bodies.

Should we think of the sequence of faculties as something akin to the Deleuzian method? No. At best we can think of it as what Deleuze substitutes for the dogmatic idea of method. The origin of the sequence is a contingent encounter, and in his work on Spinoza, Deleuze suggests there is an art to arranging or seeking encounters.[134] In particular, we become aware that certain venues are more or less conducive to encounters, just as we become aware that certain venues are more or less likely to engender a particular passion (fear, hatred, love, joy). At the same time, one never simply decides to have an encounter ("now I am going to perceive a sign").

The faculties interact to form a definite series, and the order of faculties can vary from series to series. The only constant is that the faculty of perception always serves as the first term. If the idea of method is associated with a clear, desired outcome, the results of a transcendental series is uncertain: "nothing can be said in advance, one cannot prejudge the outcome of research."[135] Prior to this research one cannot enumerate the faculties that will be making up the various series. A particular faculty might be entirely dependent on recognition; it may not possess a transcendental (or irregular) exercise. Other unknown faculties may be discovered.

What is the precise status of thought in this picture? Is thought simply another name for the production of each series, or is it a specific faculty? Deleuze pursues the second avenue. This raises the question of the object of thought: what is it that only thought can do? At one point Deleuze suggests the transcendental exercise of specific faculties could entail creativity. Mind you, the transcendental instance of every faculty is creation in the sense of coming into existence (being forced into existence) rather than being innate. The same will hold for thought; it too is dependent upon the perception of a sign: "Creation is the genesis of the act of thinking within thought itself. This genesis implicates something that does violence to thought, which wrests it from its natural stupor and its merely abstract possibilities."[136] The issue, though, is whether a faculty entails an additional instance of creativity. Does the transcendental use entail the creation of something besides the transcendental use itself? Here Deleuze suggests that the faculty of language might, at its limit, involve something akin to silence.[137] This suggests Deleuze's and Valery's definition of literature as a language within language. "Silence" would be language's equivalent to perception's sign. Just as the sign is referred to as imperceptible, so literature, the power of language taken to its limit, could be referred to as "silence." The same passage finds Deleuze suggesting the transcendent object of the faculty of sociability might be anarchy. Here the twin-senses of the word "anarchy" enable it to serve as both terms of the paradox. The sign is imperceptible; anarchy is antisocial. But the imperceptibility of the sign is only the fact that it is not given through recognition; the absence of the social only measures the distance sociability travels from its current form. The transcendental object of sociability is anarchy in the sense of a revolutionary transformation of social life.

Perhaps, then, the object of thought will also be an object invented. The obvious candidate for this object is the philosophical problem, Idea, or plane of immanence along with their conceptual elaboration. In this way, the notion of constructing the object of thought would represent a zone of indiscernability between the two questions of Deleuze's metaphilosophical register: What does it mean to think? What is a philosophy? The former is the creative act which defines the latter. At the same time, it should be said, that in both *Proust and Signs* and *Difference and Repetition*, the reader finds language suggesting the faculty of thought may not construct its own object. What I have in mind is Deleuze's contention that the object of pure thought is an essence or absolute difference.[138] Of course the philosophical problem or Idea is a differential. Historically philosophical systems have been a mixture of directions – philosophical and dogmatic, inventive and reactive. More importantly, Deleuze considers the "philosophical" side of these systems comparable to the values of a differential equation (i.e. as a complex, unfolding distribution of singular and ordinal points). Nevertheless, when he describes thought's object as an essence one feels the object in question is not a product of thought. The essence or difference in question seems to be something other than the essence or internal difference of the philosophical system. In this scenario, what is thought and what can only be thought, would be the virtual side of a being. This second interpretation of the object of thought would also represent a zone of indiscernability. This time the metaphilosophical question "what does it mean to think?" would blend in with metaphysical question "what is the real?"

How can we reconcile these two formulations of the object of thought? One avenue was developed in Part II. There one class of philosophical concepts were described as concepts of the virtual or concepts of sense. But these concepts cannot be regarded as straightforward representations. The virtual exists within its actualizations; sense subsists on the surface of bodies. Concepts of the virtual are creations because they remove the virtual from its actualizations (the concept is not another actualization of its object). Moreover, the creativity of the concept exceeds this process of separation. Every concept is defined by its endoconsistency and exoconsistency (its participation in a plane of consistency). Thus, concepts of the virtual and sense confer consistency onto their objects. In the transcendental exercise of thought an immanent cause, a virtual structure (i.e. an incorporeal sense, a problem, an essence, an Idea, or a concept) is lifted from its actualizations and rendered consistent by being incorporated within another Idea – a philosophical Idea.

There is an additional way of reconciling the two formulations of the object (the object as essence and the object as invention), and it rests upon three important claims. The first is that the dogmatic image, in particular the privilege it affords recognition, is inherently conservative. Recognition of objects includes the recognition of the values attached to that object.[139] The dogmatic image is thus connected to an entirely passive conception of the philosopher: "we see the philosopher remaining, in the last resort, a thoroughly civil and pious character, loving to blend the aims of culture with the good of religion, morality, or the State."[140] The second is that Deleuze *also* equates stupidity with deference toward norms. The only thing "stupid thought discovers" is the "reign of petty values or the power of the established order."[141] Together these first two claims make abundantly clear that, for Deleuze, true thought, genuine philosophy is hostile and an irritant. Amplifying the Platonic characterization of the philosopher as social gadfly, Deleuze writes "Philosophy does not serve the State or the Church, who have other concerns. It serves no established power... A philosophy that saddens no one, that annoys no one, is not a philosophy. It is useful for harming stupidity, for turning stupidity into something shameful."[142] The third and pivotal claim is that the dominant order has a virtual side. Deleuze makes this clear when he describes Marx as demonstrating the existence of "Social Ideas" or concrete universals.[143] The economy is a "differential virtuality" in the sense of a set of abstract relations of production and positions (a property-owner, an owner of labor-power) that is then differentiated (or actualized) in diverse ways across the social field. If "in the last instance" the economy is the principal determinate, it is because the economy is not one determinant among others, but rather the immanent cause of the social. Similarly, Foucault, applying Deleuzian metaphysics, depicts disciplinary power as a collection of disparate technologies (the organization of space, the distribution of bodies, modes of classification, practices of writing such as the table) that have congealed into an abstract formula and problem: How can a multiplicity be organized into a system that maximizes obedience and utility?[144] Different institutional spaces actualize this virtual structure in distinct ways and for distinct purposes.

Only one conclusion can be drawn from these three claims. For Deleuze, if the object of thought is the virtual, the thought of the virtual can in no way resemble the contemplation of the virtual. Why? Because philosophy or thought are inherently aggressive toward the established order, and the category of the virtual includes the virtual side of this order (e.g. the abstract machines of capitalism, disciplinary power, and control). For Plato, the thought of universals is inexorably tied to the hierarchical differentiation of particular modes of life and social organization. Nevertheless, the doctrine of forms is sometimes spoken of independently of the ethical and political commitments essential to Platonism. Deleuze is acutely aware of the possibility that some will take his definition of thought to be the contemplation of virtuality or concrete universals: "Clearly, at this point the philosophy of difference must be wary of turning into the discourse of beautiful souls: differences, nothing but differences, in a peaceful coexistence in the Idea of social places and functions."[145] Referring to his account of capitalism's virtual side he adds "... but the name of Marx is sufficient to save it from this danger."[146] The fundamental message here is that, for Deleuze, the thought of the virtual must at the same time be a politics of the virtual. For the philosopher, this politics of the virtual includes the production of a philosophical system incapable of "peaceful coexistence." That is, the philosopher attempts to construct an Idea hostile to entrenched Social Ideas or problems.

4 Ethico-political metaphysics

The absolute necessity of conjoining the expression "ethico-political" to that of "metaphysics" is becoming increasingly clear. Deleuze's definition of thought can only be the thought of the virtual or the thought of difference if this means something other than the simple contemplation of virtuality and difference. Let us approach this issue with a simple, straightforward question: "What is the Deleuzian notion of difference?"

There are, I would contend, three influential strategies as far as answering this question.[147] The first attempts to locate Deleuzian difference between one of his portraits and its subject-matter. Deleuzian difference has been characterized as Bergsonian difference. Deleuzian difference has been characterized as Nietzschean difference. The second strategy involves presenting Deleuze's notion of difference as something cobbled together from diverse philosophical sources. Such an approach encourages us to consider Deleuze's monographs as a piecemeal appropriation and formation of his philosophy of difference. This tactic is partially inspired by passages of *Difference and Repetition* in which Deleuze weaves progressive narratives out of the philosophies of his mediators (Nietzsche is presented as radicalizing the Spinozist conception of univocity; Hume, Bergson, and Nietzsche provide repetitions one, two, and three).[148] The third strategy is to reject the idea that there is *a* concept of difference within Deleuze. A gap or discontinuity is claimed to exist, either between Deleuze's "solo" and cooperative efforts, or between *Difference and Repetition* and *Logic of Sense*.

For the most part, the first two approaches have provided the strongest, most helpful, scholarship in the area of Deleuze's philosophy. At the same time, I want to draw attention to a peculiar feature of Deleuze's writing they obscure. In particular, I want to draw attention to the composition of his early portraits. On the one hand, each monograph is a thoroughly positive, focused study of an individual philosophy. As a portrait, nearly every word concerns the subject (i.e. the particular philosophical system being portrayed). One can see how this would invite each of the first two approaches. Either one of these self-contained portraits represents the formation of Deleuzian difference, or each of the portraits provides us with a distinct component of Deleuzian difference. On the other hand, it needs to be said that folded into each portrait are other portraits.

Sometimes the principal portrait explicitly references a second. So, for example, when Deleuze folds his reading of Spinoza into his portrait of Nietzsche the former is mentioned by name ("It is difficult to deny a Spinozist inspiration here").[149] In other cases, it is simply familiarity with the second portrait that enables the reader to detect the fold.

Implicitly or explicitly, Deleuze's readings engineer and draw attention to a series of becomings within philosophical systems. The portrait of Bergson includes a becoming Spinoza, a becoming Leibniz, and a becoming Hume; the portrait of Nietzsche includes a becoming Spinoza and a becoming Bergson; the portrait of Spinoza includes a becoming Nietzsche. Deleuze's knack for locating precisely the passage in the first system capable of operating as a threshold of indiscernability is disturbing.[150] More disturbing is the fact that the process of foldings and becomings does not conform to the chronology of Deleuze's publications. For example, the portrait of Spinoza folded into *Nietzsche and Philosophy* as well as *Bergsonism* predates the publication of *Expressionism in Philosophy*.

What this means is that the experience of reading the monographs back to back does not conform to the image suggested by the first two approaches. Belying the first is the fact that each portrait contains other portraits. How can Deleuze's difference be Bergson's difference if his account of Bergson's difference contains within it Leibniz's difference and Spinoza's difference? Belying the second (a piece here, a piece there) is the fact that all of the components of Deleuzian difference seem to arrive on the scene at the same time. The sequence of monographs do not resemble the two, small evolutionary narratives in *Difference and Repetition*. If Nietzsche is required to radicalize the Spinozist reworking of univocity (as suggested in *Difference and Repetition*) then you can rest assured that Deleuze's portrait of Spinoza will already, tacitly, push Spinoza's philosophy in the required direction.

Is there an image that does capture our experience of the sequence of monographs? Yes, this is Bergson's image of the cone of memory – an image Deleuze incorporates into his book *Bergsonism*.[151] Imagine all of the portraits – the whole of Deleuze's philosophical memory – coexisting in a virtual state. This whole is then actualized through the production of the distinct monographs. Each monograph includes the whole, but at the same time a particular memory or portrait will stand out. Folded into the book on Nietzsche is the portrait of Spinoza; at the same time, the book on Nietzsche is severely focused on Nietzsche's thought – it is a portrait of Nietzsche alone. Is this way of approaching the monographs – each monograph is a solitary portrait, and at the same time, every portrait – a violation of our common sense as readers? Absolutely. Of all of Deleuze's commentators, it is Foucault who best captured the simultaneously distinct and interpenetrating quality of Deleuze's portraits: "a theater of mime with multiple, fugitive, and instantaneous scenes in which blind gestures signal to each other... In the sentry box of the Luxembourg Gardens, Duns Scotus places his head through the circular window; he is sporting an impressive moustache; it belongs to Nietzsche, disguised as Klossowski."[152]

The third approach involves locating a fundamental tension within Deleuze's philosophy of difference. Žižek, for example, proposes we consider Deleuze's work with Guattari a cowardly attempt at dodging a fundamental impasse within his earlier work: "...was Deleuze not pushed toward Guattari because Guattari presented an alibi, an easy escape from the deadlock of his previous position?"[153] What is this supposed deadlock or impasse? The fact that Deleuze's thought of difference is comprised of two incompatible formulations: "Does Deleuze's conceptual edifice not rely on *two* logics, on two *conceptual* oppositions, that coexist in his work?" Both of Žižek's questions represent a failure to achieve the level of abstraction necessary for grasping Deleuzian thought. On the one hand, we can say there are far more logics of difference than two within Deleuze's work. The best reply to Žižek's second question is "Only two?" On the other hand, we can say that Žižek is guilty of seeing double. He sees two logics rather than one because he fails to grasps the principle of unity (the differential) lying beneath Deleuze's multiple formulations of difference. This is due to the fact he takes the distinctions between actual and virtual, corporeal mixture and incorporeal sense, to be *the* distinctions of Deleuze's metaphysics. I have already suggested this ignores the specific manner in which Deleuze redirects Platonism and is the correlate of reducing Platonism to the contemplation of universals or the distinction between universals and particulars. The name "Guattari" is thus Žižek's alibi; his way of avoiding the difficult labor of reading.

How, then, should we approach the question of Deleuze's philosophy of difference? Since Deleuze's conception of difference involves something differing from itself, I suggest we consider how the concept itself differs from itself. Let us consider difference one of Deleuze's characters – a character with a penchant for disguise. As with concepts in general, defining Deleuze's concept of difference requires following it through its numerous appearances. At the same time Deleuze's philosophy of difference is a redirected Platonism (i.e. Deleuze redirects his conception of Platonism). His conception of Platonism turns on two distinctions: Idea and representation, representation and simulacrum. Consequently, we should look for two salient distinctions within Deleuze's metaphysics. In Deleuze's conception of Platonism greater emphasis is placed on one of the distinctions. The distinction between Idea and representation exists to secure a more fundamental distinction between particulars. Plato's motivation is depicted as the hierarchical differentiation of particulars. For this reason, we should look at one of Deleuze's distinctions as securing another. A metaphysical distinction will secure an ethical-political distinction.

4.1   The figure of difference in Deleuze's portrait of Hume

For the sake of exposition I am going to largely bracket those areas where one portrait incorporates another (those areas where one portrait becomes indistinguishable from another). This will enable us to consider the series of portraits in a more linear fashion. Deleuze's portrait of Hume is found in his first three books – *David Hume: His Life and Work* (1952), *Empiricism and Subjectivity* (1953), and *Instincts and Institutions* (1953) – along with a subsequent encyclopedia entry "Hume" (1972). His portrait of Bergson is found in two early essays "Bergson, 1859–1951" (1956), "Bergson's Conception of Difference (1956)", as well as in the book *Bergsonism* (1966). The portrait of Nietzsche is simply the book *Nietzsche and Philosophy* (1962). Deleuze's Spinoza is found in the books *Expressionism in Philosophy* (1968) and *Practical Philosophy* (1970).

As in most of the portraits, the one of Hume contains multiple notions of difference. If Deleuze uses the word "difference" and stresses his use of the word, there is no simple referent. The most obvious form of difference is contained in Deleuze's discussion of the externality of relations. But, in fact, even the doctrine of externality contains two "differences." On the one hand, "difference" refers to the terms of a relation. The content of one term can never adequately account for the act of relating it to another – the act of moving between this term and another.[154] The second term is never contained in the first; no relations are analytic. At the same time, "difference" refers to the relation itself.[155] The relation or habitual association is a function of not only the sensible (the repetition of a conjunction of impressions) but also the passions and principles of association. The subject is a system of habits or relations formed through the synthesis of heterogeneous elements. Because the habits are irreducible to the sensible (the content of impressions) it makes sense to refer to their formation as *the production* of difference. The repetition of the same (a constant conjunction of impressions x and y) produces something new (something not found within an impression), namely the habit of moving from an impression of x to the idea of y. Under the influence of the passions and associative principles, the repetition of the same makes a difference where the difference is the subject (a system of habits).

The idea of difference as the production of something new (the making of difference) connects the notions of habit and relation to the institution. The relation is new because it is irreducible to the content of the terms related. There is an impression of x and an impression of y; there is not an impression of a necessary connection between x and y. The institution is new because it represents the social's irreducibility to human nature. To envision society as a network of institutions rather than of laws is to envision it as thoroughly positive.[156] By definition, an institution cannot be explained without remainder as the repression of natural instincts, and by definition an institution cannot be understood as a direct, natural way of achieving instinctual gratification.

As mentioned earlier, we should not ignore the metaphilosophical form of difference that appears in *Empiricism and Subjectivity*. Deleuze's reading of Hume is linked to the definition of theory he provides in this reading. A theory is the elaboration of a new problem; Hume's philosophy is incommensurable with all previous systems. Difference is the formation of a habit; difference is the formation of an institution; difference is the formation of a philosophical problem. We should also remember Deleuze's interest in both the notion of habit and institution is linked to the idea of undoing habits and institution – undoing and remaking subjectivity and the body (remember that the institution is defined as a "model" or "organization" imposed on the body).[157] "Difference" denotes not only the subject and the body (since every subject and organization of the body is constituted) but also the reorganization of subjectivity and the body. Similarly, "difference" denotes every philosophical problem because problems are inventions. What is difference according to Deleuze's Hume? Difference is the difference between the terms of a relation; difference is the novelty of every subject (their irreducibility to the sensible); difference is the novelty of every organization of the body (their irreducibility to "human nature"); difference is the novelty of every philosophical system (their irreducibility to preexisting problems); finally, difference is the production of new subjects, new bodies, and new philosophies.

4.2   The figure of difference in Deleuze's portrait of Bergson

In his portrait of Bergson, Deleuze is critical of what he calls external and/or dialectical conceptions of difference.[158] Bergsonian difference is not the difference between objects – the difference between well-defined entities. Similarly, "difference" is not the negative determination of an object. The "dialectic" refers to the idea that an entity's identity is determined by it not being other entities (what x *is* is not everything else). Deleuze locates an alternative formulation or logic of difference in Bergson's work. The distinct moments of this logic can be discerned within and between Bergson's individual texts.

The first move in this logic is to relocate external difference (difference as the difference between) within individual objects. Bergsonian intuition represents a peculiar form of abstraction. Instead of discovering a principle of identity behind difference, it involves discovering heterogeneous principles ("tendencies" or "directions") beneath the appearance of identity: "A difference of nature is never between two products or between two things, but *in one and the same thing* between the two tendencies that traverse it."[159] In *Time and Free Will*, the two tendencies are two forms of multiplicity. On the one hand, we have quantitative multiplicities. These are made up of distinct, self-contained elements (hence Bergson calls them "discontinuous multiplicities" or "multiplicities of juxtaposition"). Additionally, the elements are, if not homogeneous, perceived as homogenous or as the same kind of thing. What matters is there are a particular number of apples in the basket, or a particular number of students in the classroom. On the other hand, we have qualitative multiplicities. These are described as "continuous multiplicities," "multiplicities of fusion," or "multiplicities of interpenetration," in that their elements lack clear borders. Each element overlaps with the preceding and subsequent element. Although nondiscrete or nonnumerical, the elements are characterized by heterogeneity. A qualitative multiplicity is a temporal process involving the perpetual creation of novelty. Famously, Bergson associates the first type of multiplicity with space. The second multiplicity is given the name "duration" and is initially associated with inner-life. In this respect, inner-life would seem to be comparable to Heraclitus's river. However, by the end of *Time and Free Will*'s second chapter the distinction between duration and space has been relocated. Instead of corresponding to the distinction between subject and object, self and world, inside and outside the two multiplicities become two selves (or two levels of inner-life). Eventually, in the third chapter of *Time and Free Will*, the two multiplicities become two tendencies comprising our concrete existence. The first tendency corresponds to moments of passion, freedom, and novelty. The second corresponds to clichéd responses and sentiments.

If *Time and Free Will* divides subjectivity into two radically different multiplicities, *Matter and Memory* will divide the given (or concrete experience) into the radically different principles of perception and memory. For Bergson, perception is thoroughly in the service of action (i.e. he demolishes the idea that perception is a matter of a subject distinct from the world contemplating that world). Human perception is a matter of needs and interests filtering out or subtracting most of the world in order to give us the experience of distinct, relatively stable objects.[160] Unlike *Time and Free Will*, in *Matter and Memory* the material world is described as a whole in which every part is continuously acting and being acted upon by all other parts (which is to say there are no discrete, self-identical parts).

What Bergson calls pure memory can be thought of as a comprehensive, unbroken biography of the experiences making up our daily life.[161] Actual perception is a product of the first tendency (perception) summoning the second to its aid. The whole of memory contracts to a degree reflecting our level of engagement in the world (the extent to which we are absorbed in activity); those memories most useful assume the position of centers or nuclei. In this more or less concentrated, more or less centered form the whole is inserted into perception.[162] Concrete or "complete" perception is "only defined and distinguished by its coalescence with a memory-image we send forth to meet it."[163] Pure perception and pure memory are virtual tendencies that only exist to the extent they are actualized in concrete mixtures.

The second step Deleuze identifies consists of identifying difference with one of the tendencies. Difference is not the difference between duration and space or qualitative multiplicities and quantitative multiplicities. Rather difference is duration; difference is a qualitative multiplicity, which is to say the continual production of the new.[164] Difference is not the difference between memory and matter, but the difference between the innumerable planes of memory (each plane a particular degree of concentration or relaxation). The third moment within this logic of difference turns upon this same notion of a virtual

whole (the totality of memory images) actualizing itself via differenciation (the different planes inserted into perception). If Bergson initially
restricts the image of the virtual to our personal, biographical memories, as early as the fourth chapter of *Matter and Memory* he begins to
grant it greater, ontological significance.

A famous and challenging feature of Bergson's work is his theorization of matter. As mentioned earlier, following *Time and Free Will*,
matter is claimed to possess the characteristics of duration or a qualitative multiplicity (continual change and "confused" or nondiscrete
elements).[165] Duration becomes equivalent to the real, which is to say
the real is taken to be a continual process of innovation. An even more
challenging, even notorious move, is Bergson's characterization of the
disparate tendencies – matter and its counterparts of duration, memory,
or spirit – as coexisting degrees of a Whole or One. Instead of classifying
Bergson as a dualist or as a monist, Deleuze (and after Deleuze, William
May, and John Mullarkey) regard Bergson's dualism and monism as two
aspects of one, integrated conception of the real. Moreover the monistic
and dualistic aspects correspond to the distinction between virtual and
actual.[166] A virtual whole actualizes itself and does so by differenciating
itself into tendencies that are different in kind.

Deleuze's philosophy is increasingly thought of as a philosophy of
the virtual. The portrait of Bergson affords a precise summary of the
category's essential features.[167] The virtual is an immanent cause rather
than transcendent or efficient cause. The virtual is distinct from the
actual, but it does not exist apart from the actual. This means the distinction between actual and virtual cannot be a distinction between
two things. Rather, the distinction must correspond to two sides of the
same thing. The existence of the virtual entails the thing's irreducibility to the actual.

The category of the virtual does not correspond to the category of
the possible. The distinction between actual and virtual is not the distinction between the real and the possible. The possible is opposed to
the real ("while not real it is logically possible"). To be precise, what is
real is deemed possible (a collection of possibles) but not every possible is real. Realization – the process through which a possible becomes
real – is a process of limitation. Certain possibilities are realized, others are not allowed to become real. Realization is also characterized by
resemblance. In this respect the distinction between a possible and
the realization is structured by the Platonic image of essence and its
representations. Granted, in this case, what occupies the position of
"essence" is not real. Nevertheless, the real is thought *as if* it already

existed as a possible or reservoir of potential. For Bergson, the notion of a preexisting form that is represented, a preexisting possibility that is realized, a preexisting potential that is tapped into, a set of antecedent conditions that exhaustively determine a subsequent event all constitute a denial of real time.

The virtual is difference in the sense of differenciation. In contrast, the category of the virtual encourages us to look at what is actual as a genuine creation. The actual is not an image or representation of the virtual. Actualization is the differenciation of a virtual rather than the representation of a possible. The virtual is also characterized by difference because the multiple actualizations or lines of differenciation are characterized by nonresemblance.

The final form of difference within Deleuze's portrait of Bergson is the method or practice of intuition itself. Intuition is the effort to disclose difference in kind, duration, qualitative multiplicities, or novelty. But the reduction of difference to differences of degree, duration to space, qualitative to quantitative multiplies, and novelty to the predetermined is not an error as much as a condition. Therefore, intuition does not simply disclose difference; it makes difference in the sense of overcoming a limit: "Whereas the other directions are closed and go round in circles, whereas a distinct 'plane' of nature corresponds to each one, man is capable of scrambling the planes, of going beyond his own plane as his own condition."[168] What is difference according to Deleuze's Bergson? Difference is the difference between heterogeneous tendencies (not simply differences of degree but differences of kind); difference is one of these tendencies (duration, a continual, creative process); difference is the differentiation of a virtual whole; and difference is practical antihumanism (the production of a different nature).

4.3   The figure of difference in Deleuze's portrait of Nietzsche

Deleuze contends Nietzsche's thought provides us with a general theory of bodies. In his portrait the figure of difference emerges within and around this theory. By "body" is meant an individual being, but individuals can be compounds (the social body, groups within the social body, political bodies, etc.).[169] Earlier I applied aspects of *Nietzsche and Philosophy* in a way that suggested we include within the theory of bodies individual philosophical systems and the history of philosophy (as in "a body of writing" and "bodies of work"). In what should by now be a familiar gesture, Deleuze asserts that "difference" does not mean a difference between bodies. Rather, "difference" refers to the forces composing individual bodies. A body is not a force-field since "field" suggests a distinction between forces and a medium these forces populate. Additionally, forces compose bodies not through addition but through relation. Bodies are specific relational structures.

Things get interesting when we turn our attention to a pair of forces constituting a particular relation. Why do we consider this pair of forces difference? Is it simply because we have two forces rather than one? Is the relation between two forces comparable to the relation between two apples (two different examples of the same kind of thing). As might be expected, the difference between forces is a much stronger difference.[170] The forces are described as different quantities. Typically, though, we think of quantitative difference as a difference that can be neutralized. For example, take two glasses of water. One contains three cups of water, and the other one cup. If we empty a cup of water from the first glass into the second glass, we are no longer dealing with different quantities. While a difference between two quantities, the difference between forces cannot be canceled out in this manner. This is equivalent to saying that we should not think of the two forces as two instances of the same thing (the two apples) or as differing amounts of the same thing (the glasses of water). The quantities must be thought of, not as different quantities of some common substance ("force") but as different qualities. The two quantities are equivalent to two forms of tendency or force. If active forces are aggressive, reactive forces are timid. If active forces are spontaneous, reactive forces are prudent. Active forces act upon the world, altering it, introducing novelty into it. Reactive forces adapt.

"Difference" means these different forces (different quantities, different qualities). At the same time, "difference" refers to one of these forces. The active force is difference because it is the power of transformation.[171] Throughout *Nietzsche and Philosophy*, Deleuze contrasts Nietzsche's conception of difference with the dialectic meaning determination through negation or opposition.[172] One might expect Deleuze to defend each type of force against such a determination – to insist upon the fundamental positivity of each quality. "Being an active force is more than not being a reactive force and vice-versa." Instead, Deleuze integrates the dialectic into the distinction between types of force. Negativity is taken to be a property of reactive forces. In this manner, the distinction between active and reactive forces is made to correspond to two logics of difference.[173]

These two logics of difference are also logics of value. Nietzsche dramatizes the two forms of difference and evaluation by associating each with a particular conceptual persona. The active force or figure of the master acts and then affirms their act. Central for Deleuze is the fact that this affirmation in no way rests upon or involves a comparison with how others act. When the master does draw a comparison, it is as an afterthought. The master's identity is not an oppositional identity. With the reactive force or figure of the slave, the starting point is not action but the critique of active forces. The slave's self-affirmation only occurs following a denunciation of the other, and an oppositional definition ("they are bad, I am not like them, therefore I am good"). Active forces tend to go to the limit of their power to act or create. Reactive forces, too, can go to their limit. But in the case of reactive forces "going to the limit" means denying active forces (separating active forces from what they can do).

Perhaps the most famous aspects of Deleuze's reconstruction of Nietzsche's thought are his treatments of the concepts of will-to-power and eternal return. Just as "will" does not refer to a psychological faculty, so "power" does not refer to an object individuals are trying to acquire. The moment the "will-to-power" is equated with an "I want power," it is reduced to a pursuit of established values.[174] "I want power" means I want to acquire the goods, privileges, and opportunities "everyone" would like to have. For Deleuze, the expression "will-to-power" is synonymous with "power wills." What is it that power wills? Power wills (in the sense of determines) the identity of bodies. The identity bodies have is a function of radically different forces – different quantities that are, at the same time, different qualities. Therefore, what power wills are specific relations between forces. Power determines or is responsible for the relationship between forces.

We need, though, to be careful about this idea that power is responsible for this relation. "Power" is not the efficient cause of the relation. Forces are brought together by chance.[175] Nietzsche's vision of history and the real is one of radical contingency. The influence of Deleuze's reading is in part due to his juxtaposition of contingency and power. The metaphor of the dice-throw is designed to bring together these terms in a concise, evocative manner.[176] When "a roll" means "a roll of the dice;" a certain ambiguity is built into the phrase. On the one hand, "roll" refers to the act of holding, shaking, and releasing the dice. On the other hand, "roll" refers to the outcome of this act. The first is the moment of chance: "Nietzsche identifies chance with multiplicity, with fragments, with parts, with chaos: the chaos of the dice that are shaken then thrown."[177] The game is a game of chance because, at this point, we cannot predict the outcome. The sides of each die correspond to the disparate forces. Forces are not predetermined to exist in their specific relations. What is the significance of the second sense of "roll?" While the game is a game of chance, it is a game that produces determinate outcomes. The metaphor helps us to recognize that chaos and determination, chance and structure are not mutually exclusive. Deleuze expresses this fact by saying the dice-throw brings together multiplicity and unity, chance and necessity. "Necessity" does not mean the relation of forces was predestined; it means contingency necessarily produces determinate results: "What Nietzsche calls *necessity* (destiny) is thus not the abolition but rather the combination of chance itself."[178] Later, Deleuze will begin *Difference and Repetition* with a similar, impressionistic and rigorous call: think of difference not as an "undifferentiated abyss" but as a process combining the indeterminate with determination.[179]

Deleuze defines power as the genealogical element of bodies. We are now in a position to understand what this means. Power corresponds to the overall character of a body formed by chance. Power is therefore the immanent rather than transcendent or efficient cause of a body's identity. As such it is distinct but inseparable from the relation of forces. What does this principle contribute to our understanding of bodies? A body is a dynamic system rather than an immobile "thing." The notion of "power" helps us avoid the reduction of the constitutive process to a snapshot (a frozen image). A body is not a field occupied by forces; a body is an arrangement of forces. A body is not moving in a particular direction (a spatial conception of direction); a body is a particular direction (a temporal conception of direction). The qualities of the will-to-power – affirmation and denial – are the different directions constitutive of the character of bodies. "Affirmation" denotes a becoming-active of forces; "denial" denotes a becoming-reactive of forces. These qualities are differentiated from the qualities of forces because a direction is a particular, overall arrangement of active and reactive forces. A body that is an active type (a process of becoming-active) is not a body devoid of reactive forces. Rather, it is a body in which reactive forces are "acted" or placed in the service of the active forces. A body that is a reactive type (a process of becoming-reactive) is a body in which reactive forces are separating active forces from what they can do. This is accomplished by making the active forces turn against themselves.

Any discussion of difference in Deleuze's Nietzsche is incomplete without some treatment of the doctrine of eternal recurrence. In Deleuze's reading, the principle is interpreted as both a "physical" or "cosmological" principle, and as an "ethical principle." For the real to be an eternal recurrence is for it to be a combination of chance and necessity, contingency and order, multiplicity and systematicity. What returns is not the same, but difference. Repetition is the repetition of difference. Or, the "same" which returns is difference; the "being" which returns is becoming. As seen above it is critical that we do not stop the exposition at this point. This would leave open the possibility that the principle of return was equivalent to an "undifferentiated abyss." Rather than redirecting Platonism, it would simply invert the distinction between universals and the absence of order. But neither Nietzsche nor Deleuze believe the real "simply fluctuates up and down as if it were in the Euripus."[180] The return of difference, the repetition of difference, is at the same the "will-to-power" which is to say the formation of bodies having a specific, albeit dynamic, character. What returns are differential structures.

A Nietzschean or Deleuzian ethics is not a "morality." Because they involve the positing of "higher values" (a realm of transcendent norms), moralities are symptoms of nihilism (the denial of life). At the same time, a Nietzschean or Deleuzian ethics is not "reactive nihilism."[181] The critique of higher values is not taken as an end-in-itself. Rather the critique of higher values is a means to the creation of new values. Critique is in the service of affirmation. "No" is in the service of "Yes." The "no" in question occurs when the power of denial is unleashed on reactive forces – the forces impeding creativity. This project is the ethics of the eternal return. Deleuze defines the normative, eternal return as two principles of selection. The first is the effort to eliminate the average and the timid. A rather common way of defining the return is as a therapeutic act of embracing one's past: "At the time I thought what happened to me was terrible;" "I now realize the role it played in making me who I am today;" "I affirm my past to the highest degree; I choose it to happen again and again and again." I think it is safe to say that Deleuze's reading of the return does not allow this interpretation to return. For Deleuze the first selection resembles Kant's categorical imperative rather than bourgeois therapy ("learn to love yourself").[182] The question is one directed toward the future rather than the past: "This action I am about to perform, would I do it an infinite number of times." The "average" is comprised of acts (small pleasures) that we allow ourselves "just this once." Their elimination is a modest step in the direction of excess and aggressive creativity.

The symptoms of more developed reactive forces (the belief in higher values, reactive nihilism, jealousy, guilt) are immune to the first selection. There is nothing average about the triumph of reactive forces; guilt is an excessive display of active forces being turned against themselves.

The second selection of the eternal return is the more challenging and risky enterprise of engineering an active type. The active type is a specific arrangement of active and reactive forces. Reactive forces are acted; the forces of adaptation and conservation assist rather than stifle experimentation and creation. A reactive force is acted when it inserts a degree of caution into experimentation. The project of becoming-active presupposes the nonreturn of the reactive type. The eternal return is the bridge to the overman. The second selection is tantamount to "self-destruction" (the nonreturn of a body's current arrangement). Guilt prevents active forces from going to their limit. Self-destruction enables active forces to go their limit. "Active negation or active destruction is the state of strong spirits which destroy the reactive in themselves, submitting it to the test of the eternal return and submitting themselves to this test."[183] A fierce enterprise of "destruction" is the prerequisite for the creation of new values in the sense of new ways of living and feeling.

The figure of difference in Deleuze's portrait of Nietzsche goes by the name of the eternal return. The first meaning of "eternal return" gives us the first sense or senses of difference. A body is a contingent formation, but a formation – a structure – nonetheless. What constitutes the identity of a body? Difference. Difference means different forces – qualitatively different quantities. But the word "difference" is also used to privilege one of these qualities over another. And the word "difference" is used to privilege one quality of the will-to-power over another. Active forces make difference. They don't adapt to a preexisting reality; they add something new to reality. Similarly, the affirmative will-to-power (the becoming-active of forces) is the process of reactive forces aiding rather than impeding creation. This is linked to the second meaning of "eternal return." The eternal return is the nonreturn of the average and the nonreturn of the reactive type. "Difference" means the project of making, through active destruction, the active type, where the active type is less a way of being than the production of new, different, nonreactive ways of being. What is difference according to Deleuze's Nietzsche? "Difference" means different forces (different quantities, different qualities); "difference" means one of the qualities of force (the active force is the one that makes difference); "difference" means the different forms of power (the becoming-active and becoming-reactive of forces); "difference" means one form of power (the becoming-active of forces makes difference); "difference" means the production of an active type; "difference" means the higher values, the new sentiments and modes of existence active types create.

4.4   The figure of difference in Deleuze's portrait of Spinoza

In discussing the struggle between immanence and transcendence within the history of philosophy, Deleuze often refers to a feature of Scholasticism: the debate between equivocal, analogical, and univocal conceptions of being. Deleuze's best-known reference to the debate is found in *Difference and Repetition*. He asserts "There has only ever been one ontological proposition: Being is univocal. There has only ever been one ontology, that of Duns Scotus', which gave being a single voice."[184]

Lack of familiarity over the classical debate has led to misinterpretations of Deleuze's univocal position. There *is* a recognition that the themes of univocity and immanence are inseparably linked in Deleuze's philosophy. But this recognition typically takes the form of equating univocity and immanence. This prevents us from seeing Deleuze's reference to univocity as the unpredictable move that it is. The reader who comes to *Difference and Repetition* independently of *Expressionism in Philosophy* should be shocked by Deleuze's assertion that being is univocal. This is because each of the positions within the classical debate shared a deep commitment to transcendence. At most one can say the univocal position was accused (by those occupying the other two positions) as a move in the direction of immanence. A close reading of *Difference and Repetition* and, more importantly, *Expressionism in Philosophy* shows Deleuze is absolutely aware of this fact. Deleuze intends his identification with univocity to be a provocative gesture.

The debate can be construed as a differential comprised of these three abstract formulas; the debate and each formula exists within a diverse array of actualizations.[185] If all three of the classical positions reflects a commitment to a transcendent god, two of the positions – the analogical and univocal – also reflects a commitment to the idea of natural knowledge: in this life, knowledge of God is reached through knowledge of nature. The debate centers around the question of the semantic implications of God's transcendence. The words we use to describe God's attributes we also use to talk about things in the order of creation: "exists," "good," "power," "knowledge." The abstract equivocal position is the belief that transcendence is threatened if there is any relation between the meaning a word has when we apply it to creation and when we apply it to God. The abstract univocal position is the belief that the only thing threatened by a separation of meanings is natural knowledge of transcendence. God and created entities share certain predicates, but this does not threaten transcendence because the predicates in question are neutral or indifferent with regards to the creator/creation, infinite/finite divide. The abstract analogical position is the belief that transcendence *is* threatened by the univocal position, and that natural knowledge of transcendence is threatened by the analogical position: as we move from nature to God, the meanings of our words must shift, but the different meanings are related to one another (they're analogous).

Deleuze's affirmation of univocity is linked to his affirmation of immanence. But pairing the two scrambles familiar codes: the exclusive disjunction "univocal or immanence" is replaced by "univocity and immanence." When Deleuze endorses univocity he is not promoting a preexisting position, he is creating a new one. Deleuze's declaration that being is univocal is a tremendous work of engineering. The author counter-actualizes the abstract tendency of univocity by separating it from its historical actualizations (where it is linked to transcendence), and by reterritorializing it within his own system. This system is an actualization of one of the defining tendencies of the differential that is the history of philosophy: the tendency of immanence. Deleuze makes univocity entail immanence and vice-versa. Moreover, Deleuze constructs a connection between these two terms and the thought of difference. Univocity and immanence are linked to the notion of radical difference. Obviously this difference cannot be a distinction between this world and a transcendent one; that would conflict with immanence. But Deleuze adds that this difference, this difference that exists in the only world there is, is not the difference between things. Rather, it is a difference within each thing.

For Deleuze, Spinoza's *Ethics* is the great precedent for hooking univocity onto immanence, and both onto radical difference. Part of Spinoza's greatness lies in showing how the three *can* come together in one, well-formed act of thought. The connection between univocity and immanence should be tackled first. In Descartes' *Principles of Philosophy*, the author explicitly situates his work in relation to the analogical position within the Scholastic debate: "the term 'substance' does not apply univocally, as they say in the Schools, to God and to other things; that is, there is no distinctly intelligible meaning of the term which is common to God and his creatures."[186] Initially Descartes defines substance as that which relies on nothing else to exist. In this respect there is only one substance; only God exists independently. He adds, however, that we can employ the word "substance" to the order of creation by analogy: as the order of creation depends on the creator, so thoughts depend on minds, and physical properties on corporeal things.[187] What should be clear is that, for Descartes, there are not three kinds of substance: divine, mental, and physical. Rather there are two meanings of the word "substance." The first sense applies to God exclusively. The second applies to entities in the order of creation that, while dependent upon God, are nevertheless the existential foundation for other aspects of reality (thoughts or physical qualities).

Without question, Spinoza is more faithful to Descartes' initial definition of substance than Descartes himself. He defines substance as what is in-itself and conceived-in-itself while refusing to posit any analogical meanings. In this way, Spinoza's work belies the exclusive disjunction Cartesian or anti-Cartesian, but not as an average or timid compromise. In terms of preexisting labels, his philosophy can only be described as an inclusive disjunctive synthesis: Cartesian extremist and anti-Cartesian extremist. Radical fidelity to Descartes' initial definition of substance entails not only that there is one substance, and that this substance is God, but it entails that God is an immanent rather than transcendent cause. Something does exist that possesses the defining features of God. There is something that exists necessarily, that is eternal, that is omnipotent, and that is infinite. That something is nature, where nature is reconfigured as an infinite substance possessing an infinite number of attributes of which we know two: thought and extension.

Deleuze's version of this story is slightly different.[188] First he depicts Spinoza as demonstrating the coherence of the idea of substance possessing multiple attributes. Spinoza *needs* to demonstrate this precisely because his definition of attribute eradicates the distinction between primary and secondary attributes (for Spinoza, the word "attribute" always means the essence of a substance).[189] This requires the formulation of a logic of expression. The essence of a substance can be expressed in multiple, radically different attributes.[190] Just as important, what expresses itself (the substance) and what is expressed (its essence) does not exist outside of its heterogeneous expressions (the attributes). Once Spinoza has shown there cannot be more than one substance with any given attribute, and that a substance possessing every attribute exists (God, an absolutely infinite substance), it follows that there can only be one substance. Since everything else is a mode, and every mode is the mode of a substance, it follows that everything else exists within this one substance. Deleuze succinctly captures this idea by declaring that for Spinoza the attributes are univocal. The classical univocal and analogical positions involved going from the attributes found in the order of creation to the very different attributes of God. In Spinoza's metaphysics, each attribute is one of the infinite ways God's essence is expressed and constituted. The attributes denoted by the words "thought" and "extension" are God's attributes. Each mode (e.g. individual bodies and minds) is a mode under one of these attributes. Whether we are talking about finite thoughts or the attribute of thought, finite extended things or the attribute of extension, the meaning of the words "thought" and "extension" are the same.

How does difference enter into this picture of univocity and immanence? The difference between this world and an external, transcendent God has been wiped out. Similarly, difference can not be different senses of the word "substance," or "attribute." Finally, difference cannot be Descartes' version of "real distinction." What Descartes calls "real distinction" (being able to conceive of x independently of y and vice-versa) is, at the same time a distinction within reality, and this distinction is always a distinction between substances. For Descartes, real distinction is a difference between things.[191] For Spinoza, the attributes are conceptually independent, and this conceptual independence is, at the same time, a radical difference within the real. In fact, the distinction between Spinoza's attributes is greater than the distinction between Descartes primary attributes. For Descartes, mental substances and physical substances interact. For Spinoza, no relationships of efficient causality exist between the attributes: the efficient cause of a thought can only be other thoughts; the efficient cause of an event in the material world can only be an infinite chain of material causes. At the same time, the attributes are not attributes of different substances. The real distinction is found not between separate things, but between different expressions of the same thing. Radical difference is the thought of immanence rather than transcendence, and it is the thought of a radical difference within a thing rather than between things: God is a substance whose essence is expressed in an infinite number of heterogeneous attributes; each modification of God is expressed as a mode under every one of these same attributes; the essence of an individual (be it a person or a rock) is expressed as a mode under the attribute of thought (a mind) and the attribute of extension (a body).[192] Just as the notion of univocity undoes the distinction between nature and another world, so this logic of expression prevents nature's various attributes from constituting different worlds.

Spinoza's conjoining of univocity and immanence represents an extreme departure from the preexisting position of univocity, a position exemplified by Duns Scotus. But the conjoining of univocity with a rethinking of difference and unity does not. Deleuze writes "I believe it takes nothing away from Spinoza's originality to place him in a perspective that may already be found in Duns Scotus."[193] In his classic study of Scotus's thought, Allan Wolter lays out the philosopher's theory of modal and formal distinctions.[194] For Scotus, some of our mind's conceptual distinctions (so-called first intentions) correspond to genuine differences within the real; others (second intentions) are simply distinctions within the mind.[195] The first category includes every conceptual distinction corresponding to separate things. But the category of real difference is irreducible to the difference between separate things. Scotus's philosophy of difference is such that a whole range of differences exist between separate things and distinctions that are simply mental constructs. These are the differences characterized as formal distinctions and modal distinctions.[196] The reader should recognize the clear affinity with Deleuze's own thought of difference. Difference does not have to be a difference between things; it can be a difference within a thing. Deleuze's formulation of Scotus's position is simultaneously a metaphysical variant of his slogan of the middle, of thinking in between:

> Formal distinction is definitely a real distinction, expressing as it does the different layers of reality that form or constitute a being.... But it is a minimally real distinction because the two really distinct quiddities are coordinate, together making a single being.[197]

Scotus's theory is articulated as the solution to a series of distinct problems: What is the difference between the figures of the Trinity? What is the difference between the various attributes of God? What is the difference between a species-essence and its instantiations? Scotus rejects the idea that these differences are simply mental constructs; he rejects the idea they simply reflect a single object's ability to produce different conceptions (the traditional notion of virtual distinction); and, he rejects the idea that the differences correspond to separate things. The combination of the problems and these concepts necessitates a radical rethinking of unity and difference.

How does univocity come into this picture? For Scotus, a modal distinction exists between God's attributes and God's infinity (God's mode). Similarly, a modal distinction exists between attributes of beings in the order of creation and the mode of finitude. Obviously the distinction between God's attributes and God's infinity, or between our attributes and our finitude is not a distinction between separate things. If, however, the distinction was only a mental distinction, then natural knowledge of God would be impossible. For Scotus, our conception of a being infinitely wise is a complex act of thought: experiences of the order of creation provide us with the concept of finite, wise things; we subtract the modality of finite from this concept giving us a concept of wisdom indifferent to the finite/infinite divide; finally, we add to this indifferent concept of wisdom the modality of infinity.[198] The success of this operation (the fact that our conception of God's wisdom is not simply a projection of a human property onto the divine) requires our ability to form a conception of wisdom that is indifferent to the modalities of finitude and infinite. Similarly, we can imperfectly grasp, and speak intelligibly of God's being because of our ability to form a univocal or indifferent conception of being.

Clearly there is no necessary connection between immanence and the idea of a difference within a thing rather than between things. For Scotus, univocity is precisely what enables us to know a transcendent God in this life. What Deleuze's reading of Spinoza illuminates is how in the *Ethics*, "thought" and "extension" are univocal (they have only one correct sense), because the attributes of infinite substance are the very same attributes of finite things. For Spinoza, we should not imagine God as extended in the way we are extended (God is not a person with a body); we should not imagine God as thinking in the way we think (God is not a person who has thoughts). But this doesn't entail one set of attributes for God, and another for finite things. Rather Spinoza folds finite things into God's attributes. God's essence is expressed by the infinite attribute of thought. Our mind is a finite mode under this attribute of thought. God's essence is expressed by the infinite attribute of extension. Our body is a finite mode under this attribute of extension.

The division of Deleuze's exposition of the *Ethics* corresponds to a clear division within Spinoza's metaphysics. On the one hand, we have Spinoza's account of the relationship between substance and its attributes (*Natura Naturans*); on the other hand, we have Spinoza's account of the modal universe (*Natura Naturata*). There is, however, an additional reason for Deleuze's approach. In both *Expressionism in Philosophy*, and *Practical Philosophy*, Deleuze devotes tremendous energy to the theory of modes, precisely because he is interested in redirecting Spinoza's notion of substance. Why is this? One could say that, for Deleuze, Spinoza's immanent cause is not immanent enough. The two levels of expression (substance expressing itself in the attributes; the attributes expressing themselves in modes) feel like the vestige of a vertical, two-world separation of the real. Does this mean Deleuze brackets the first level? Not exactly. Deleuze is best read as trying to push all of Spinoza's categories into the second level: "Substance must itself be said *of* the modes and only *of* the modes."[199] To be an entity is to be a substance; to be a substance is to have an identity that includes a real, albeit nonnumerical distinction. Thus Deleuze engineers a new conception of univocity. Like Descartes he will refer to individual beings as substances. Unlike Descartes and like Spinoza, he will not use the term "substance" to denote a transcendent God. Like Spinoza, whenever he uses the term "substance" it denotes a being that is simultaneously *natura naturans* and *natura natura*, an immanent cause and its effects, a degree of power and the perpetual fulfillment or actualization of this power.

Deleuze's account of the modal universe is above all else a theory of bodies. That Spinoza's work provides plenty of material for a robust consideration of bodies follows from his claim that the mind and the body are the same thing (the same individual) expressed under the attributes of thought and extension.[200] This ensures a strict correspondence between the mind and body. When something happens to one, something happens to the other; when one acts the other acts; when one is acted upon the other is acted upon; when the power of one is increased the power of the other is increased; when the power of one is decreased the power of the other is decreased. At the same time, the fact that the attributes are conceived through themselves entails an absence of efficient causality. Spinoza argues the notion of a God transcending the order of creation and the idea the mind is a cause of the body's actions are two mutually reinforcing figments of the imagination; two mutually reinforcing commitments to transcendence.[201] When Spinoza declares we "do not know what the body is capable of" he is responding to the belief thought is the efficient cause of body's most mundane actions (as if a body were not capable of walking across the room on its own).[202] And, he is responding to the way we regard material events as the effects of immaterial causes: we imagine what happens in nature is the realization of a quasi-personal God's project rather than a materially overdetermined event (a product of an infinite chain of material causes); we interpret our body's actions as the realization of ends established by the mind. For Spinoza, a body's actions can only be explained by what the body is able to do and by what is acting upon it. As pointed out by Warren Montag, it is Spinoza's critique of this second form of transcendence that is the source of contemporary discomfort and evasion.

> His refusal to set the human apart from nature, mind from body, thought from action thus makes him perhaps the most thoroughgoing anti-humanist in the history of philosophy; it is doubtless this that constitutes his heresy for our time and that accounts for the

specific forms of incomprehension and anxiety that his work stimulates today.[203]

I think it is useful to consider Montag's statement when measuring the distance between Deleuze's treatment of Spinoza's theory of common notions and the overwhelming majority of other interpretations. In Deleuze's reading, our first common notions are ideas of properties shared by our bodies and one or more other finite modes.[204] Typically, however, the discussion of Spinoza's category restricts it to the general properties (infinite modes) of the physical world. On such a reading our first adequate idea is that everything physical is either in motion or rest. Deliberate or not, such a reading evokes the figure of a disembodied subject discovering the universal features of the world. The idea of common notions is elucidated without any reference to any corresponding adventure of the body. This despite the fact that in Spinoza's philosophy the mind and the body are different expressions of the same thing (the mind expresses in the attribute of thought what the body expresses in the attribute of extension).[205]

The most striking feature of Deleuze's and Spinoza's account of modes is the extent to which it is the story of our bodies interacting with other bodies, combining with other bodies, incorporating other bodies, and expelling other bodies. Our first common notions are ideas of properties our body shares, not with every body, but some bodies. The formation of these ideas under the attribute of thought corresponds to an encounter between our body and these other bodies under the attribute of extension. Thus for Deleuze, the production of common notions is explained through a theory of encounters. Additionally, Deleuze's account of modes highlights Spinoza's characterization of taxonomic categories as confused, abstract ideas.[206] The common notions cannot be of the form, "you and I have the property of being Human." For Deleuze, the first common notions are ideas of the relationship between our bodies and other specific bodies: "In short, a common notion is the representation of a composition between two or more bodies."[207] They are explanations of the impact particular encounters have on our body's vitality. The final piece in this adventure of a body is provided by Part IV, proposition thirty and Part V, proposition ten of the *Ethics*. Spinoza argues that a prerequisite for action is the evasion of what restricts our power to act (i.e. an evasion of what is disagreeable or uncommon) in favor of what enhances our power to act (what is agreeable or common). A prerequisite for active emotions is the elimination of negative passions in factor of positive passions. Summarily put, for Deleuze, the theory of common notions has less to do with the contemplation of a feature shared by all bodies than with our body learning to organize its encounters in the world.

This story of the body turns upon a particular definition of the body. For Spinoza, a body is not defined by membership within a species or genus. Deleuzian difference reappears around this assertion: "Let's try to imagine how Spinoza saw things. He did not see genera, species, he did not see categories, so what did he see? He saw differences of degrees of power."[208] This power is the power to stay in existence (a body can be more or less vulnerable to having its defining, characteristic relation decomposed). More generally, though, this power is also the power to be affected. A body is what it can do. "What it can do" includes what it can do to other bodies as well as what other bodies can do to it.

As with Nietzschean forces, the various quantities or degrees of power cannot be leveled or rendered equal. There is a qualitative side to two degrees of power. The difference between two degrees of power is not simply a matter of how much ("I can bench press more pounds than you"). Bodies are the radically different ways they are affected. Two bodies grouped under the same species term can be affected by one and the same object in radically different ways ("I am allergic to bee-stings, you are not."). Two bodies grouped under the same species term can do radically different things (the racing horse and the horse that draws the carriage). Bodies grouped under separate species terms can have more in common with one another (i.e. they can be affected in more of the same ways) than with other members of their respective species (the identity of the pet dog is closer to that of a pet cat than that of a wild dog). Power as the power to resist destruction is relative. In the zombie film *28 Days Later*, the director Danny Boyle punctures the frantic narrative with a scene of horses in the field. The moving nature of the scene is best explained through Spinoza's metaphysics. The disclosure of the horses is entirely shaped by our experience of being in the middle of plague; the horses embody a segment of nature that is untouched, unthreatened. Whatever we might think of the superiority or inferiority of horses relative to humans, their bodies are safe while ours are in peril. Spinoza's metaphysics also enables us to understand this peril. What does it mean to become a zombie? For Spinoza, severe alterations of our body can be akin to a living death.

> For I do not venture to deny that the human body, while retaining blood circulation and whatever else is regarded as essential to life, can nevertheless assume another nature quite different from its own.

> I have no reason to hold that a body does not die unless it turns into a corpse; indeed, experience seems to teach otherwise. [209]

Deleuze refers to Spinoza's project as a "practical philosophy," and he encourages us to put it into practice. This will involve learning to see the world in terms of power (what Deleuze calls the practice of "ethology") rather than abstract ideas (or "natural kinds"). Repeatedly Deleuze emphasizes the need to live the propositions of Spinoza's philosophy ("It is not enough ... to think this theoretically"), and the difficulty of pulling this off (one must "train one's self").[210] In this context, Deleuze repeats Spinoza's contention that we do not know what a body can do? Deleuze's philosophy appropriates this statement (initially a challenge to the idea that the mind is the body's motor) and turns it into a slogan of praxis.[211] The addition of the word "beforehand" in the following passage adds a Bergsonian inflection to Spinoza's theory of the body: "That is why Spinoza calls out to us in the way he does: you do not know beforehand what good or bad you are capable of; you do not know beforehand what a body or a mind can do, in a given encounter, a given arrangement, a given combination."[212]

We do not know what thought can do. We do not know what the body can do. Deleuze's philosophy suggests we attempt to find out. This will involve fulfilling the power of affection in different ways. Central to this project is the organization of encounters in such a way that what diminishes our power and elicits negative passions (sadness, hatred, envy) is evaded. The positive passions (joy, love) have to be increased; our power to act must be increased. Then we can act, that is, have emotions that are actions (active joy) rather than passions (passive joy). Is Deleuze's practical slogan the all-too-familiar imperative of "realizing your potential" or "being all you can be?" Absolutely not. These two clichés express the project of constructing docile bodies. The imperative to "be all you can be" is the imperative to be obedient. The imperative "realize your potential" is the imperative to get a better grade next time. Just as the marketplace slanders the notion of revolution, and advertising firms slander the notion of concept (concept as marketing strategy), so any number of clichés can pass for a true politics of experimentation and creativity.

The formula "realize your potential" does not work for an additional reason. Deleuze's metaphysics often seduces commentators into a discussion of potentiality. The virtual is routinely equated with potentiality. But Deleuze consistently separates the notion of power from potential. In those few instances where he uses the word the notion is reworked so that it is not accompanied by its familiar connotations: "All *potential* is act, active and actual."[213] To think of power as potentiality suggests the existence of a certain amount of power in reserve ("though I have the power to do it, I am not doing it currently"). But Spinoza directly challenges the notion of power as unrealized potential. For example, the omnipotence of God or nature is completely expressed in what is the case. You grasp God's power by looking at its effects (nature as *natura naturata*), not through a counterfactual ("If God had wanted to do he could have...").[214] Power does not reside in abstract rights ("I could do this...") but in what bodies actually do. In *Nietzsche and Philosophy*, the paralogism of the priest and the slave has as its foundation "the fiction of a force separated from what it can do."[215] The priest distinguishes between an active force and what that force does; then, what the active force does is described as the decision of a neutral subject. The priest tells the slave a story about creative lives: "We could do what they are doing, but we don't, and, therefore we are good."[216] For Spinoza, political freedom is not measured through a counterfactual ("We're free because we have the legal right to form a union") but in what bodies actually do (their degree of passivity or creativity).[217] For Spinoza, the fact people continually talk is not a sign they are continually choosing to realize their potential; it displays the material pressure to talk: "experience teaches us that nothing is less within men's power than to hold their tongues."[218]

Thus Deleuze declares that the power to be affected is not a potential; there is no power in reserve: "This power is not a simple logical possibility for it is actualized at every moment by the bodies to which a given body is related."[219] The lesson of this passage is twofold. First, if we think of the body as potential, it encourages us to regard the body as a self-enclosed unit apart from its environment. But for Spinoza, what we think of as an individual entity is itself a combination of an infinite number of bodies, and this body of bodies is continually interacting with other bodies.[220] The power that is a body is continually actualized and reactualized by acting upon other bodies, and by being acted upon by other bodies.

The second lesson resides in the distinction between power and "logical possibility." Deleuze's use of the phrases "logical possibility" and "actualized" encourages us to consider this way of thinking power along with the summons to practice ethology side-by-side with the distinction between the possible and the virtual. "We do not know beforehand what a body can do?" We should try to figure out what the body can do. If we think of this "figuring out" as the realization of potential then the solution is not a creation. To regard an act or event as the realization of a possibility is to regard it as the representation or realization of a logically prior principle. The logic is one of resemblance: "my body was not swimming an hour ago, but the potential was there, and I am about to realize that potential." Realization is governed by limitation as well as resemblance. A certain set of possibilities are allowed to pass into existence; others are prevented from passing into existence. I am swimming now and, thus, not throwing a brick. Nevertheless, the possibility of throwing a brick is there.

For Deleuze, the notion of potentiality or possibility is inherently conservative. Instead of perceiving the real as created, we regard it as the realization of a set of prior categories, essences, or possibilities:

> The idea of the possible appears, when, instead of grasping each existent in its novelty the whole of existence is related to a preformed element, from which everything is supposed to emerge by simple "realization."[221]

We think of the body's potential by retroactively projecting what the body is currently doing into a fictitious realm of logical possibilities or potential actions. "I am swimming" equals "the possibility of swimming was there before." Notice the possible is, first and foremost, a way of describing what already is. One could even say that thinking in terms of possibilities and their realization is the tremendous restriction of our sense of possibility. "What is was already a possibility" becomes "what is possible is what is already the case." The answer to the question "What can a body do?" would already exist. All we would have to do is identify or recognize the solution. But, for Deleuze, what the body is doing now is a solution and a created solution. The power to be affected is an immanent cause, inseparable from, but also distinct from affections. This formal and real distinction between power and its fulfillment is found in the fact that the fulfillment does not represent or resemble the power. A problem does not exist independently of its solutions, but the solutions do not resemble the problem to which they are solutions. Different solutions will have to be created. Answering, continuing to answer, the question of what the body can do is something that can only be done with our bodies. Similarly, answering the question of what thought can do can only be done with philosophy where philosophy is not the realization of a possibility. The question is not answered by occupying a position in a preexisting debate, but through the creation of thought.

Deleuze's portrait of Spinoza invites us to rethink difference. Difference is not the difference between entities. Difference is not the difference between nature and a transcendent cause or between what the body is doing and a transcendent cause. "Different" does not mean different species. The "real distinction" between attributes is not the determination of substance as an empty genus through a variety of species. Regarding entities as units of force has nothing to do with, and at times runs directly counter to, taxonomic classification. Finally, difference is not the realization of a different possibility – the realization of a reserve of potential. What is difference according to Deleuze's Spinoza? Difference is the real or formal distinction (a distinction within the real that in no way involves the division of the real into different kinds of entities, a distinction within an entity that in no way makes that entity two entities); difference is the difference between a power to be affected and the fulfillment of that power; difference is each fulfillment (a current fulfillment was not already a possibility or potential, no fulfillment resembles the power to be affected); finally, difference is the making of new difference (new fulfillments of the power). Spinoza's distinction between units of power and their various fulfillments is an ethics devoted to making difference (fulfilling the power to be affected in new ways). The project is not a matter of realizing the mind's or body's potential. The project is one of creating new thought, a new body, a new collective body. That is to say, the project is one of creating a new organization of thought (philosophy) and a body without organs.

4.5 Summary: counterfeit difference, genuine difference, and ethico-political difference

Deleuze's portraits bring three terms of his metaphysics into sharp focus. First, we have the notion of counterfeit, inauthentic, or concealed difference. Numerous ways of thinking difference fall under this category:

Counterfeit or secondary difference

1. Difference is the difference between entities.
2. Difference is the difference between nature and principles transcending nature: difference as a vertical or two-world conception of the real.
3. Difference as different senses of the word "being."
4. Difference as determination through opposition or negation: A's identity is a function of it being not B, or of it not being everything that is not A.

5. Difference as specific difference: the different species of a genus, the different members of a species, the members of different species.
6. Difference as numerical difference: three apples, object A is bigger than object B, A is bigger now than it was before.
7. Difference as the difference between what is real and possible or what is actual and what is potential.
8. Difference as representation: the difference between a model and its representations, the different representations of a model.
9. Difference as the difference between two internally related terms or between two parts of a preexisting or future whole: the different parts of an organism.
10. Difference as an undifferentiated, chaotic flux beneath every appearance of identity: difference as the absence of order or structure.

The second term is Deleuze's notion of genuine or radical difference. Here too, there are multiple formulations.

Genuine or primary difference

1. Difference as the subject, a system of habits: difference is the production of a relation where every relation is a habitual association formed between two heterogeneous terms.
2. Difference as the institution: the irreducibility of each organization of our bodies to a simple principle of human nature.
3. Difference as a real, but nonnumerical distinction within every being: difference as the difference between an immanent principle of power (the power of affection, the will-to-power) and how it is fulfilled, difference as radically different tendencies (duration and space, qualitative multiplicity and quantitative multiplicity, memory and matter, active and reactive forces).
4. Difference as one side of this distinction within every being: difference as the immanent cause (the power of affectivity, the will-to-power), difference as one of the tendencies (duration or the continuous production of heterogeneity, the active force that produces difference).

Ethico-political difference

As in Deleuze's account of Platonism, the metaphysical distinction is there to secure another, ethico-political one. This second distinction is *the* fundamental distinction of Deleuze's system: the difference between a dominant organization and the production of a new one. The actualizations of this abstract formula are as follows: the difference between the current subject (a system of intellectual habits) and a new one, the difference between established institutions (or organizations of the body) and a new one, difference as the difference between the human condition and the overcoming of that condition. Bergson's intuition is a method for undoing the natural reduction of duration to space, differences in kind to differences of degree, life to intellectual, affective, and behavioral habits. Nietzsche's eternal return is an act of self-destruction the outcome of which is an active type. Spinoza's ethics involves fulfilling the power to act in new, more active ways.

4.6 This world of forms: *difference and repetition* and *the logic of sense*

The books *Difference and Repetition* (1968) and *Logic of Sense* (1969) are not instances of Deleuzian portraiture. In each book, references and voices abound. Moreover, in *Difference and Repetition*, the systems that served as the models for his portraits are now lined up in two, short progressive narratives. Deleuze describes Nietzsche's eternal return as a more radical vision of repetition than Hume's notion of habit or Bergson's notion of memory.[222] He describes Spinoza as taking the doctrine of univocity beyond Duns Scotus (pushing univocity toward immanence). Nietzsche is described as pushing it to its limit.[223] Additionally, *Difference and Repetition* contains sustained moments of criticism (of the dogmatic image of thought, of analogical conceptions of difference, of determination through negation).

While not portraits, we can say that each book introduces us to an additional mediator. In *Difference and Repetition*, Deleuze's medium of becoming is the early history of calculus: "there is a treasure buried within the old so-called barbaric, or pre-scientific interpretations of the differential calculus."[224] This prescientific calculus is primarily the calculus as it appears in Leibniz's metaphysics. If calculus "becomes scientific" by severing the notion of differential from metaphysical assumptions, Deleuze is interested in the metaphysical treasure this process leaves behind. Additionally, Deleuze makes clear that his return to Leibniz is in fact a return to the post-Kantian return to Leibniz. In particular, Deleuze's return to Leibniz is a return to Salomon Maimon's Leibnizian reformulation of Kant's distinction between appearance and the conditions of appearance.[225]

When it comes to *The Logic of Sense*, Deleuze's principal medium of becoming is Stoic physics. The return to Stoicism is a return to a specific feature of Stoic physics. The real is irreducible to what exists, because in addition to things which exist there are things which subsist.[226] "Something" rather than "what exists" is the category equivalent to the real. Those things which exist (bodies) are something; those things which subsist (incorporeals) are also something. As with Spinoza's metaphysics, Stoicism scrambles familiar codes by being both a radical materialism and an ontological commitment to incorporeals. On the one hand, the definition of "body" (that which can be a cause as well as effect) greatly enlarges the extension of the term (days and nights, seasons, utterances, music, books are all bodies). On the other hand, the category of "something" includes nonbodies: place, time, void, and *lekta*. While Deleuze provides an admirable summary of Stoic physics, ethics, and logic, his interest lies chiefly in the distinction between bodies and sense (the *lekta* or "things said"). Deleuze places this distinction in the service of an ethics and politics, where these should not be conflated with Stoic ethics and politics per se. While Deleuze, like the Stoic, distinguishes between negative passions and positive emotions, he does not employ the Stoic notion of fate. Deleuze does encourage us to be worthy of what happens to us, and Deleuzian ethics does involve fostering an attitude of indifference toward specific aspects of the world. But there is nothing in Deleuze's work comparable to the Stoic catalogue of virtues (or preferable things).[227] When Deleuze declares "How much we have yet to learn from Stoicism ...," it is in the context of calling for "guerilla warfare."[228] Granted, Stoicism could be interpreted as something akin to a guerilla campaign against oneself: a war against the passions waged, not in the name of coldness, but joy, caution, and hope.[229] Nevertheless, Deleuze does not conflate the Stoic and guerilla campaigns. Stoicism simply provides Deleuze with a valuable weapon. This is the distinction between bodies and sense.

The figure of difference is the treasure buried in prescientific calculus, and the treasure buried in the Stoic account of bodies and incorporeals. Curiously, the name Deleuze gives to his project of return, retrieval, and redirection is transcendental empiricism. Expressions such as "empiricism," "a superior empiricism," "a transcendental empiricism," and "a superior transcendental philosophy" repeatedly appear in Deleuze's writings. They occur in his portraits of Hume, Bergson, and Nietzsche as well as *Difference and Repetition* and *The Logic of Sense*.[230]

For the sake of exposition we can understand the notion of transcendental empiricism as three gestures. First, there is Deleuze's critique and reformulation of the transcendental deduction. Second, there is his formulation of a positive conception of difference (difference is not simply the absence of identity). The third consists of Deleuze moving the transcendental deduction in a metaphysical direction. I will now lay out these three steps in a more linear fashion than that found in Deleuze's writings.

Kant's transcendental deduction was an attempt to show the existence of synthetic *a priori* judgments (the existence of truths not derived from the law of noncontradiction, but nevertheless universal and necessary). The judgments in question concern the categories of understanding. While the categories apply to experience (making them synthetic) they are not derived from it (enabling them to be universal and necessary). The categories are the necessary conditions of possible experience. An object that failed to conform to the categories would not be an object of experience (it would not even be recognizable as an object).[231] The notion of the synthetic *a priori* is secured by depicting experience as a function of intuitions and the categories – a function of the passive faculty of sensibility and the active faculty of understanding.

Two of Maimon's criticisms are relevant for present purposes.[232] For Maimon, the Kantian picture of experience duplicates the problem of dualism. How can a material world be created by entirely spiritual being? How can a nonextended mental substance interact with physical substance? How can the faculties of understanding and sensibility interact? In each case a radical difference between two terms frustrates the attempt to position their interaction as an explanatory principle. Additionally, Maimon exacts a certain Humean revenge by challenging the very existence of "possible experience" (as possible experience is defined by Kant). Kant, it is claimed, does not demonstrate that Hume's account of experience is incorrect. Rather, he simply assumes it is incorrect in order to make the synthetic *a priori* possible. What evidence does Kant provide us that experience has the form of the categories? Maimon's redefinition of the transcendental deduction as a search for the conditions of "actual experience" can only be understood in relation to this skeptical challenge to Kant's account of "possible experience." At the same time "actual experience" directs our attention to the concrete. Instead of searching for the properties of any object whatsoever, the issue is the ground of particular concrete givens.

Deleuze, of course, has his own reasons for rejecting the notion of "possible experience." Previously I referred to Deleuze's/Bergson's contention that the category of possibility is a retroactive fiction. We project the given backwards – if not temporally then logically – creating the illusion that it represents the realization of a preformed possibility. Little surprise then that the conditions resemble the conditioned – the ground of the given resembles the given. Even if the given did conform to Kant's "possible experience," it does not legitimate the assertion of resemblance: the claim the condition resembles the conditioned. What is the meaning of "transcendental empiricism?" The "empiricism" refers to the fact that Deleuze is concerned with actual rather than possible experience. For now we can say Deleuze's interest is in actual, concrete givens rather than abstract conditions of possibility. "Transcendental" refers to the necessity to turn away from the given in the direction of the ground. There is something along the lines of a Deleuzian deduction: "We go beyond experience, toward the conditions of experience (but these are not, in the Kantian manner, the conditions of all possible experience: They are the conditions of real experience)."[233]

When conjoined "transcendental" and "empiricism" suggests moving from a concrete given to a ground, where the relationship between the two is one of nonresemblance or heterogeneity. The Deleuzian ground will not be Kant's categories (the conditions of appearance). Nor will it be the phenomenological ground in which the essence becomes the essence of what appears as it appears.[234]

The name Deleuze gives to the ground is "Idea." Transcendental empiricism is a redirected Platonism – a new theory of Ideas. In *Difference and Repetition*, the term "Idea" is used interchangeably with "problem," "problematic," "complex theme," "structure," "sense," "the virtual," "essence," "universal," and "substance." In *Logic of Sense*, the term "Idea" is used interchangeably with "event," "ideal event," "sense," and "incorporeal." The fact Deleuze refers to the ground as "Idea" tells us he is pushing the deduction in the direction of metaphysics. For Plato "appearance" is equivalent to a particular or the world of particulars. Similarly, the Deleuzian account of the given includes a discussion of appearance (how things tend to show up for us) but the "given" is a particular entity.

Where does the perversion of Platonism come in?[235] The Platonic universal is linked to the division of the real into two worlds: a realm of transcendent entities and their representations. Deleuze's Idea, universal, or essence reflects a commitment to immanence. The Idea is an immanent cause. It plays a critical role in the determination of a being's identity, but it does not exist independently of the being. Consequently, the ground of the particular can be thought of as a side of the particular or as subsisting on its surface. The traditional essence groups particulars into a kind. The Deleuzian essence is the essence of an individual. This individual, however, can be as large as an individual society; there is even the Idea of capitalism. In Plato, the relationship between an essence and its particulars is understood in terms of representation, imitation, resemblance, or copying. We know that for Deleuze the relationship between an Idea and its particular is characterized by heterogeneity and nonresemblance. For Plato, the senses and more generally the body impedes our comprehension of the Idea. For Deleuze, what is typically given is simply the interactions of bodies or the actual side of a particular. But atypical corporeal encounters and experiences are required to move or force thought in the direction of the Idea.

At this point we should contrast the Deleuzian Idea with the traditional formulation of substance. In fact, Deleuze equates a reformulated notion of substance ("substance must itself be said of the modes") with his conception of Ideas.[236] In its classical formulation, "substance" denotes a principle of spatial and temporal identity beneath difference. Substance is the metaphysical ground beneath disparate properties, and substance is characterized by permanence over time. Or, substance is constituted by a specific property (a primary attribute). This property is presupposed by the others (the secondary attributes) and remains the same as an entity undergoes various modifications. We can also think of the notion of substance as resting upon the following exclusive disjunction: either substance is the ground of determination or there is no determination.

This dilemma links the classical notion of substance with the Platonic universal. In the *Phaedo*, Plato gives us the option of being the lover or hater of the *logos*.[237] The minimum requirement for being the former is a commitment to species-essences (whether or not we take them to be transcendent). The rejection of species-essences is equivalent to viewing the real as a chaotic flux or river. Either we endorse traditional universals or we can be Heraclitus.

Earlier we saw how Deleuze's image of the dice-throw is intended to break up this particular intellectual habit. A roll of the dice simultaneously involves contingency and necessity, difference and identity. Similarly, the difference that returns in the eternal return (as a cosmological doctrine) is not the undifferentiated but a particular structure. The theory of Ideas in *Difference and Repetition* should be considered a reworking of the notion of substance – a reworking in conformity with the image of the dice-throw. Deleuze's Idea will be the ground of an entity's identity, but this ground is difference rather than a principle of identity. That being said, the substitution of difference for identity on the level of substance is not a substitution of chaos for structure. The Idea is difference where this difference is said to be a particular kind of structure. Deleuze provides us with a positive definition of difference

(difference is not simply the absence of identity). And this positive definition enables the philosophy of difference to be more than the deconstructionist or nominalist gesture ("universals are illusions," "essences are illusions," etc.).

Up to this point, *Difference and Repetition* and *The Logic of Sense* run parallel. As suggested above, where the books diverge is in the language used to describe the ground. This reflects the fact that Deleuze composes each book with a specific medium of becoming. In *Difference and Repetition*, the content of the Idea or ground is defined using ideas borrowed from the early philosophical calculus. In *The Logic of Sense*, the content of the Idea is defined using the Stoic account of bodies and incorporeals. When it comes to Deleuze's language, the books reconverge when the relationship between Idea and particular is defined as a process of "actualization."

Deleuze's philosophical calculus tethers the notion of differential to terms such as "vanishing difference," "limit," and "infinitesimal." The extremely difficult discussion of calculus in *Difference and Repetitions* revolves around two philosophical applications of the calculus. While more or less in the background of *Difference and Repetition*, Deleuze does devote considerable attention to these applications elsewhere.[238] In his reading of Leibniz, Deleuze argues the notion of infinite analysis – a notion belonging to Leibniz's metaphysics – is rendered intelligible through the calculus. Additionally, Deleuze is interested in the way Leibniz, and Maimon following Leibniz, uses the notion of differential to articulate a theory of perception. This theory of perception represents for Deleuze a nonpsychoanalytic way of envisioning the unconscious.

According to Deleuze, a differential structure is characterized by three properties: the absence of determination, reciprocal determination, and complete determination. What this means is that there is an aspect of a differential structure that is undetermined, another aspect displays reciprocal determination, still another displays complete determination. The symbol dx is not a value of x, and, unlike $2x$, it is not determined by the value of x. Rather, dx is a change in the value of x (x has changed by such and such amount). This is what Deleuze means when he says, "in relation to x, dx is completely undetermined, as dy is to y."[239] But dx and dy are not just any changes of x and y, they are incredibly small changes. dx is a change of x so small that it approaches zero (it is a change that borders on being no change at all). Deleuze's interest in the differential is related to the notion's applicability to complex curves. In vertical or horizontal lines, the value x or y remains constant while the other value increases or decreases. In a diagonal, the rate of x's change relative to *y's* change is a constant. But in a dynamic, complex curve this ratio is not a constant. Nevertheless, we can describe what is happening at a particular point of the curve by considering dy/dx (the change of y and x between that point and another so close that the difference between the two tends to vanish or approach zero). The differential is neither dx nor dy but dy/dx. While the dx and dy are not determined by x and y, they do assume a definite value in relation to one another (when y changes this amount, x changes the following amount). What Deleuze means by complete determination is the overall shape of the curve defined by all the values of dy/dx. This set of values will include what are called singular points and ordinal points.

When Deleuze uses the term "singularity" or "singular," it is significant that he is borrowing the term from mathematics rather than logic.[240] "Singular" does not refer to a proposition concerning an individual entity (as in singular versus universal or general propositions). As Deleuze points out the meaning of "singular" or "singularity" in mathematics has an affinity with "remarkable" or "dramatic," while the opposed term "ordinal" resembles "ordinary": "mathematics already represents a turning point in relation to logic. The mathematical use of the concept 'singularity' orients singularity in relation to the ordinary or regular, and no longer in relation to the universal."[241] Deleuze gives as an example the square: four singular points (the vertices), with each singular point extending itself into an ordinal series (a series comprised of an infinite number of points) that takes us to the next singular point.[242] With regards to a curve, a large change of y relative to x, or a small change of y relative to x will make the value of dy/dx approach infinity or zero respectively. In either case one is dealing with a singular or remarkable moment in the life of the curve – the curve takes a sharp turn vertically or horizontally. Various ordinal series ensure the continuity of the curve by taking us from one singular point to another.[243] A differential is completely determined in that it is a precise distribution of singular and ordinal points.

Deleuze identifies two applications of the notion of differential within Leibniz's philosophy. The first concerns the notion of infinite analysis. For Leibniz, the class of true propositions is not divided along the lines of the analytic/synthetic distinction. Rather, for Leibniz every true position is analytic.[244] The predicate "three-sidedness" is contained in the subject "triangle," *and* "crossed the Rubicon" is contained in the subject "Caesar." Hence Deleuze's association of Leibniz with the image of folding and unfolding: "...like you unfold a rug. It's the same thing: explicate, unfold, unroll. Thus crossing the Rubicon as event only acts to unroll something that was encompassed for all times in the notion of Caesar."[245] Moreover, the event of crossing the Rubicon occupies a precise place within an unbroken causal chain. Not only is that particular episode part of the concept of "Caesar," so is the entire world. For Leibniz, the notion of each subject contains within itself the entire world or expresses the entire world from a specific perspective.

Nevertheless, as Deleuze points out, there is a difference between the proposition "triangles have three-sides" and "Caesar crossed the Rubicon." The former is a truth of essence meaning that the inclusion of the predicate can be demonstrated through a finite number of operations. In contrast, the latter can only be demonstrated through an infinite analysis and only God is capable of performing such an analysis. A distinguishing feature of Deleuze's reading of Leibniz is his goal of providing a positive definition of infinite analysis and his desire to rigidly differentiate finite and infinite analysis. An infinite analysis is not a really long finite analysis – one consisting of so many steps that only God can run through them: "Can we say that this is an indefinite analysis? No because, an indefinite analysis would be the same as saying that it's an analysis that is infinite only through my lack of knowledge, that is, I cannot reach the end of it. Henceforth, God with his understanding would reach the end."[246] According to Deleuze, what Leibniz's God grasps is that the infinite analysis does not come to an end. This, however, raises the question of the coherence of the notion of an infinite analysis. For Deleuze, it is Leibniz's mathematics that provides this coherence. Instead of approaching geometric figures as static, instantiations of traditional essences (geometry as an "axiomatics"), Leibniz approaches them as dynamic figures (objects that can grow, shrink, be folded, be cut, be intersected, etc.). This enables him to take two distinct terms (two triangles or a polygon and a circle) and show how through expanding the area of one, the difference between the two vanishes (the second is contained in the first).[247] Similarly, Leibniz's calculus presents us with the idea of one singular, distinctive point leading to another by way of an ordinal series. In both cases, the thought is the same. Two very different terms can at the same time be continuous. And this, according to Deleuze, is the difference between a finite and infinite analysis. The first demonstrates the identity of two terms while the second demonstrates the continuity of two terms. Famously, for Leibniz, the absence of true, synthetic propositions is tied to the fact that the universe displays a maximum of harmony. For Deleuze, the more demanding, precise version of this thesis is that the world is a complex curve in which each singular point passes into an ordinal series connecting it to another singular point.[248]

A second philosophical application of the differential is found in Leibniz's and Maimon's theory of perception – a theory of perception that is, at the same time, a theory of the unconscious. In addition to self-awareness, consciousness is composed of appetites and desires directed toward "global objects" or "global qualities."[249] "I see the tree." "I want a glass of water." Deleuze's use of "global" serves two purposes. On the one hand, it captures a basic character of the given. Not only does the given strike us given (we do not experience it as something we are constructing), it also strikes us as simple or impervious to analysis. On the other hand, "global" suggests a "whole" or composite. For Leibniz and Maimon, self-aware perception and/or desire for a global object has beneath it differential relations between infinitely small perceptions and desires. Beneath my perception of a wave lies countless perceptions of drops of water. The unconscious ground of my desire for a burrito includes a minute hunger for salt and protein.

This conception of the unconscious is differential rather than psycho-analytic.[250] The Freudian topography of the mind turns upon relations of opposition (conflicting impulses). The various impulses are repeatedly personified. Just as individuals fight so we can think of parts of an individual fighting. Just as the censor prevents the writer's message from getting through in its original form, so the agency of repression demands desire distort or conceal itself. In contrast, Deleuze describes the Leibniz-Maimon unconscious as a differential relation between our body and the rest of the environment (the relation is not between two preexisting terms but reciprocally determined terms). dy/dx is the relation between infinitely small variations of my body and infinitely small variations in my proximity. If either side of the differential remains relatively constant while the other changes, a singular point is engendered. An infinitely small change is registered by a change in the content of consciousness: "perception becomes conscious when the differential relation corresponds to a singularity ... It's the molecule of water closest to my body that is going to define the minute increase through which the infinity of minute perceptions becomes conscious perception."[251] The figure of the curve reappears; as a description of life as consciousness and the unconscious (of life as the given and the given's differential ground).

At this point it bears repeating that Deleuze's ultimate aim is not the explication of Leibniz's metaphysics and the Leibnizian unconscious.[252] In fact, it is worth noting that in his own system, Deleuze's use of the word "unconscious" conforms to a statement from *Bergsonism*: "We must be nevertheless be clear at this point that Bergson does not use the word 'unconscious' to denote a psychological reality outside consciousness, but to denote a nonpsychological reality – being as it is in itself."[253] Transcendental empiricism includes an account of experience (of how experience typically conceals the ground), but the ground in question is "being as it is in itself."[254] The ground of the entity is the Idea, where the Idea is difference in the sense of a differential structure.

Deleuze uses the differential calculus as a mediator in order to engineer a precise becoming. As with all becomings this one involves a movement away from a set of familiar, rigid coordinates. In place of the singular proposition, Deleuze speaks of singular points. Or, in place of the distinction between singular and universal Deleuze gives us the distinction between singular and ordinal. The life of an individual entity contains a certain number of singular points connected by ordinal series. In place of identity or the classic notion of substance, Deleuze gives us the notion of consistency (the fact one singular point leads to another by way of an ordinal series). The classic notion of substance evokes the image of a perfect, self-enclosed point traveling across a line of change. The Deleuzian notion of substance or Idea suggests a complex, still unfolding shape or distribution of points. Most importantly, Deleuze undoes the traditional distinction between identity and chaos: either there exists principles of identity beneath difference, or there is a complete absence of order. Deleuze finds in the history of philosophy – in the history of philosophical mathematics – a way of thinking difference as a structure. The Idea is difference but completely determined; a differential is a distribution of singular and ordinal points.

If the figure of difference appears in the definition of an Idea (an Idea is a differential), it also appears in the relationship between Idea and particular. The precise character of this relationship needs to be identified. The Idea is an immanent rather than transcendent cause. This means that the Idea or essence of a particular is one side of the particular. The name Deleuze gives to this side is the "virtual": "the virtual must be defined as strictly a part of the real object."[255] Nothing could be further from the Deleuzian notion of the virtual than virtual reality. "Virtual reality" refers to a representation of a preexisting reality. Thus, the language of "virtual reality" approximates the Platonic distinction between model and copy. For Deleuze, the Idea or virtual is a real side to real objects. "The reality of the virtual consists of the differential elements and relations along with the singular points that correspond to them."[256]

The fact an entity includes an immanent cause should not make us regard the entity as self-caused. Instead of operating as an eternal principle, the Deleuzian Idea is a product of contingent forces; it *is* the difference that returns from the game of chance: "The differential of the Idea is itself inseparable from the process of repetition which defined the throw of the dice."[257] Nevertheless, like the Platonic Idea, the Deleuzian Idea is less about bringing entities into existence than defining their character. But Deleuze stresses the heterogeneity or nonresemblance of ground and grounded, condition and conditioned, virtual and actual. As with Spinoza's attributes, there can be a real distinction within a single substance. "Every object is double without it being the case that the two halves resemble one another."[258]

The nonresemblance of virtual and actual gives us the second version of difference in *Difference and Repetition*. While Deleuze gives the differential content of the Idea the name "differentiation," he refers to the relationship between virtual and actual as a process of actualization or "differenciation." The difference of "differenciation" lies in the nonresemblance of virtual and actual. It also lies in the fact that a virtual structure can receive multiple actualizations, and in the fact that the relationship between these actualizations is one of nonresemblance. In *Difference and Repetition*, an entity is defined as an Idea and its actualization. We are now in a position to appreciate the extent to which we are dealing with a philosophy of difference. To say an entity is the actualization of an Idea is to say an entity is the differenciation of differentiation (or different/ciation).[259]

When out for a walk the Platonist sees the world in a particular way. Others are regarded as making very specific errors. Each error corresponds to a specific distinction – form versus representation and representation versus counterfeit. The first error is not exactly a matter of mistaking the representation for a form. The representation is only understood as a representation if there is an awareness of forms. When one fails to recognize a particular as an imitation, one fails to recognize it as a kind of thing. At the extreme, this would be equivalent to seeing the world as devoid of all form and structure. The second, more egregious error is that of overinflation or a lack of discernment. Individuals are continually purchasing fools gold in the sense of counterfeit conceptions of morality. The discerning individual knows that some particulars are representations, others simulacra.

What does a Deleuzian see when wandering about? For one thing, a world filled with radical novelty. The corresponding mistake is perceiving a being as if they, to all extents and purposes, were given before being given. Regarding an entity as an instantiation of a species-essence or as the realization of a set of logical possibilities is, for Deleuze, equivalent to regarding it as a duplicate of a prefabricated model. Regarding an entity *as if* it were an instantiation or realization is equivalent to regarding it as an imitation. The Deleuzian sees a body or arrangement of bodies as a strictly contingent formation rather than what had to be. The Deleuzian sees bodies, not as self-enclosed units, but as bodies continually interacting with other bodies. Instead of seeing bodies as substances (a self-identical thing persisting over time and beneath change), the Deleuzian regards them as a process defined by singular and ordinal points. The body is not a thing undergoing a process, it is a process – or, rather, the two processes of differentiation and differenciation.[260]

This captures the Deleuzian equivalent of Plato's distinction between form and representation, as well as the mistake of not seeing that a representation is a representation. There is a real distinction between virtual and actual. Regarding the actual as nothing but actual is to regard the entity as distinct from its environment, as an instantiation of a species-essence, and as self-identical in time. But what about Plato's second distinction, the one Deleuze considers the heart of Platonism? Is there a Deleuzian correlate to the distinction between representation and simulacrum, or to the purchasing of fools gold? The answer is yes. The operative distinction here is between heterogeneous actualizations of the virtual. In this case, forgetting the virtual is forgetting the actual is a particular actualization. This has specific implications for our understanding of the social and of our own bodies. And, I would argue that at the end of the day this is Deleuze's real concern. Plato may have spoken of beds, but his concern was justice. Deleuze may have spoken of vegetation, eggs, and dogs but he addressed those of us subsumed under the species-term of human, and his concern was experimentation and transformation.

To forget the virtual in this second sense is to fail to grasp the character of the social. Deleuze's discussion of the social Idea of capital in *Difference and Repetition* should be understood alongside his treatment of the notion of disciplinary power as a diagram in *Foucault*.[261] This makes all the more sense when we consider the influence *Difference and Repetition* exerted on Foucault's *Discipline and Punish*. In the two books, the economy and discipline are described as abstract machines or immanent causes. As such they are a difference distinct from every concrete region of the social; at the same time they cover the social body through difference. The common view that Foucault had a different concept of this stuff called "power" than Marx, that, unlike Marx, he thought this stuff was everywhere, stems from a lack of familiarity with Deleuze's metaphysics. Capital is a differential structure comprised of relations of production, reciprocally determined positions (manager, worker, landlord, renter, etc.), and the abstract formula of extracting surplus value. The differential of disciplinary power is defined as a diverse set of discursive and architectural technologies that, over time, enter into relation, as well as by the "abstract formula" or goal of organizing a multiplicity into a group of docile, efficient bodies. The two social ideas interpenetrate and cover the social according to a logic of differenciation rather than representation or resemblance. Areas of the social (the school, the army, the mall, the factory, the office, etc.) are radically different and are actualizations of the same differential structures. Losing sight of social Ideas results in a specific impasse within social theory. A particular region of the social (e.g. a specific institutional site, a particular form of oppression, etc.) is elevated to the position of center, or every attempt at identifying a structure to the social is decried as reductive. On the one hand we have reductionism, on the other a perpetual, quasi-nominalist critique of reductionism.

To forget the virtual is at the same time to reduce one's body or the bodies of others to a specific organization (e.g. "the body of a good worker," "the body that acts like a girl should, etc.").[262] One is tempted to say that to forget the virtual is to forget that a different actualization of the body is possible, or to say the body's potential exceeds its current actualization. This language is pervasive in discussions of Deleuze's metaphysics. The virtual is consistently equated with potential. But we need to remember Deleuze uses the word "virtual" precisely to avoid the words "possible" and "potential." Different lines of actualization are not preformed ("already there"). Different actualizations are not objects of contemplation. We can grasp possibilities intellectually. A different body (or "body-without-organs") can only be engineered. The vision of difference afforded in *Difference and Repetition* is now in full view: difference is differentiation (the differential structure of the virtual Idea); difference is differenciation (the nonresemblance of virtual and actual along with the nonresemblance of the different actualizations). Most of all, difference is making difference in the sense of the destruction of certain social Ideas, and the creation of new bodies (new actualizations) and new forms of interaction: "The transcendent object of the faculty of sociability is revolution... revolution is the social power of difference."[263]

Let us now return to the earlier point of convergence between *Difference and Repetition* and *Logic of Sense*. Transcendental empiricism is the attempt to locate the ground of experience, where the ground is heterogeneous from experience. To be more precise, transcendental empiricism is the attempt to locate the conditions of an actual entity, where conditions and conditioned are not characterized by resemblance. While ordinary, everyday experience is incorporated into the category of "actual," the actual is as much a metaphysical category as an empirical one (just as Plato's "apparent world" is as much a metaphysical category as an empirical one). In short, the distinction between virtual and actual should not be reduced to the distinction between being and appearance. As discussed earlier, Deleuze replaces the opposition of reality and appearance with the idea of an appearance built into or belonging to the real. Additionally, one is not even tempted to regard certain aspects of the actual as "mere appearance." Unemployment and life in a slum represent specific actualizations of the capitalist Idea. The case-files kept by parole officers belong to a specific actualization of the diagram of disciplinary power.

At this point the two books fork; the different directions correspond to different mediums of becoming. In *Logic of Sense*, the medium or "zone of proximity" is found in a specific aspect of Stoic physics and logic rather than the notion of the differential. The most general feature of Stoicism that Deleuze gravitates toward is the division of the real (of "things that are something") into bodies and incorporeals, existence and subsistence. Within Stoic physics, the necessary and sufficient condition for being a body is the ability to affect and be affected.[264] Consequently the category of the corporeal includes the soul, seasons, times of the day, virtues, the sounds I make when I talk, the inscriptions I produce when I write, and so on. On the most general level, corporeality is Cosmos (a fully rational organism) or Fate (an unbroken and necessary chain of causes). The corporeal totality can then be regarded as a blend (or complete interpenetration) of an active body and passive body. Each of these bodies can in turn be regarded as combinations of the elements (fire-air and earth-water respectively).[265] Eventually one arrives at what we tend to think of as particular bodies. Here the active principle varies as we move from rock to human. The variation takes the form of the type and number of *pneuma*: there is the *hexis* which holds the body together, the principal of nature responsible for development, and the soul (the body responsible for perception).[266] Additionally, once we break the Cosmos into an active body and a passive body, the Stoic theory of bodies becomes an account of various kinds of mixtures: "Mixtures are in bodies, are in the depth of bodies: a body penetrates another and coexists with it in all of its parts, like a drop of wine in the ocean, or fire in the iron. One body withdraws from another, like liquid from a vase."[267] A corporeal mixture can be a juxtaposition (various bodies are simply placed alongside of one another), a fusion (the bodies interpenetrate and become indistinguishable), or a blend (the bodies interpenetrate while remaining distinguishable): two apples, a cake, and the active/passive mixture comprising the Cosmos.[268]

The other side of the real's division is comprised of incorporeals. The defining feature of bodies is their ability to affect and be affected – each body occupies a place within the causal chain of Fate. The feature shared by incorporeals is the absence of causal efficacy.[269] Place does not act upon the cosmos but is simply the space occupied by the cosmos. The cosmos needs space but the space does not act upon the cosmos. In contrast to the Epicurean void (a mobile, empty space presupposed by the motion of bodies), the Stoic void is simply the space required for the cosmos to expand.[270] If the Stoic considers temporal happenings (e.g. the evening) bodies, these happenings occur within time.

So far, the positing of incorporeals seems to turn upon the image of container and content. The container (place, void, time) is required by the content but does not act upon the content. However, Deleuze concentrates on the fourth incorporeal – the *lekton*.[271] The Stoic theory of discourse (a component of Stoic logic) is made up of a dizzying array of divisions. The *lekton* occupies a precise place within this branch – the place where the theory of language incorporates the corporeal/incorporeal division. For the Stoics, speech was a particular kind of body.[272] Speech is air that has been organized or shaped into a definite form (speech versus the bark of a dog). This form can be irrational or rational, meaningless or meaningful. In the case of the latter, the *lekton* is the sense (or "what is said"). Revisiting the Stoic philosophy of language one encounters a variety of ideas associated with the evolution of the philosophy of language. For the Stoics the sentence rather than the word is the principal vehicle of meaning (predicates or "what can be said of something" are incomplete *lekta*).[273] Far from simply being a vehicle for propositions, the category of complete lekta contains a variety of illocutionary forces (not only propositions but also questions, imperatives, oaths, expressions of emotion, expressions of confusion, etc.).[274] While the Epicureans reduced language to a signifier and object, the Stoic introduces a third term. Sense (what is said) is not the referent.[275]

Deleuze's exclamation "How much we have yet to learn from Stoicism..." concerns this distinction between sense and referent. Employing the language of *Nietzsche and Philosophy*, we can say there is an average and extreme, timid and unrestrained way of making this distinction. The average corresponds to one of the basic lessons of analytic philosophy: the predicates "morning star" and "evening star" are distinct things we can say about the same object.[276] In contrast, the version that passes the test of the eternal return includes within it a theory of bodies. For the Stoics, the referent is a body or, more precisely, a mixture of bodies. The body is a mixture because it exists alongside other bodies (juxtaposition). The body is a mixture because it is comprised of innumerable, indistinguishable elements (fusion). And the body is a mixture because it is comprised of a conceptually distinct active body and passive body (the active principle, or *pneuma*, blends with the passive material it organizes).

As previously stated, the notion of *lekton* introduces a third term into this equation. An utterance or inscription is a body. The referent is corporeal mixture. But there is also "what is said" or "sense." What is said of the mixture of bodies by way of the body of speech or writing is not itself a body. As in *Difference and Repetition*, where "sense" was used interchangeably with "problem," "Idea," and "complex theme," Deleuze pushes this theory of language in a decidedly metaphysical direction. Thus, the *lekton* is not simply what is said of a mixture of bodies, but what is happening to the mixture of bodies. Alternatively, the notions of "sense" and "verb" can be turned into metaphysical categories:

> The attribute is not a being and does not qualify a being; it is an extra-being. "Green" designates a quality, a mixture of things, a mixture of tree and air where chlorophyll coexists with all the parts of the leaf. "To green," on the contrary, is not a quality in the thing, but an attribute which is said of the thing."[277]

In *The Logic of Sense*, the Idea is an ideal event, an incorporeal sense, a metaphysical verb, subsisting on the surface of a corporeal mixture. As in *Difference and Repetition*, the relationship between Idea and particular is characterized by nonresemblance: "what is expressed has no resemblance whatsoever to the expression."[278]

To say we need to differentiate the "sense" of a mixture from empirical acts of description is to say we need to separate the ground (or "transcendental field") from consciousness: "We seek to determine an impersonal and pre-individual transcendental field, which does not resemble the corresponding empirical fields, and which nevertheless is not confused with an undifferentiated depth. This field can not be determined as that of a consciousness."[279] Remembering that the Deleuzian unconscious is not a region of interiority but something which exceeds interiority enables us to speak of the Idea as the unconscious of concrete corporeal mixtures. As in *Difference and Repetition* the particular (the entity or mixture) is described as the actualization of a sense or ideal event.

Nevertheless, the relationship between Idea and particular is described somewhat differently in the two books. In *Difference and Repetition*, the ground is characterized as the virtual side of an object. In *Logic of Sense*, the ground is characterized as subsisting on the surface of a mixture of bodies. In *Difference and Repetition*, the ground is associated with being (to be is to be an entity, and to be an entity is to have a virtual side and an actual side). In *Logic of Sense*, the ground is given the status of "extra-being" (reflecting the Stoic division of the category of "something").

Žižek's charge that Deleuze's metaphysics is in fact two metaphysics is essentially the charge Deleuze offers competing conceptions of the ground. The suggestion is that besides the terminological difference, there exists a fundamental tension within Deleuze's theory of Ideas. On the one hand, Deleuze describes Ideas as producing the particulars; on the other hand, Deleuze describes Ideas as effects of particulars.[280] When it comes to *The Logic of Sense*, it seems obvious that the ground or Idea, as an incorporeal, is by definition causally sterile. But we need to be careful for Deleuze defines sense as a quasi-cause. The distinction between bodies and sense is linked to two different "causal orders." In the first, you have a continual process of mixtures remixing. One mixture of bodies is acted upon by another mixture of bodies. Different ideal events are actualized or subsist on a particular body in the course of a day ("drinking water," "driving," "reading," "taking notes," etc.). What Žižek is picking up on is the fact that the word "Idea" or "sense" *is* being used in slightly different ways. In *Difference and Repetition*, the journey of this particular body would be characterized as the actualization then reactualization of a virtual structure (the body's singular and ordinal points). The Idea is serving as the principal of unity (granted a differential unity) for a variety of actualizations. In *The Logic of Sense*, the journey involves a variety of Ideas (or ideal events) being actualized. On the one hand, we have multiple actualizations of a single Idea; on the other hand, we have the actualization of multiple Ideas.

But in his rush to identify a contradiction Žižek misses two obvious points. The first is that beneath the different locations of the term Idea there is no fundamental tension. In both cases, the fundamental message is a pluralist one. A body can be a plurality of actualizations. A body can have a plurality of senses. In both cases, the function of the Deleuzian Idea is to contest a particular way of looking at the body: as an organism (the idea that the body is reducible to *an* organization), as an insular unit apart from its environment, as a classical substance (a principle of identity moving through space), and as an instantiation of a classical essence (as if the body "preexists" its unique history, a history which is a process of interaction or mixture). The second mistake Žižek makes seems to arise from the fact that, while comfortable with *The Logic of Sense*, he seems unfamiliar with the details of *Difference and Repetition* as well as Deleuze's various portraits. For example, in *Nietzsche and Philosophy*, Deleuze does describe the will-to-power as producing the body. But at the same time Deleuze describes chance as producing the body. Far from the same thing, chance and the will-to-power are the two distinct moments of the dice-throw: "Chance is the bringing of forces into relation, the will is the determining principle of this relation."[281] The will-to-power does not produce the body as an efficient cause – the body is created through chance rather than the will-to-power. For Foucault, a nonreductive, genealogical analysis is required to explain the formation of the abstract machine of disciplinary power. Thus, Deleuze's essences, Ideas, universals, and so on are neither transcendent nor efficient causes. Cause means the will-to-power is an essential part of a body's character. If we fail to grasp the will-to-power, we fail to grasp the specific character of the body. We fail to see how the body is in part defined by a general direction – a becoming-reactive or becoming-active of forces. We fail to see how the body is a process of active forces being turned against themselves or a process of reactive forces being acted.

Žižek's reading of Deleuze ("contradictory notions of the virtual") is symptomatic of a more general trend in discussions of Deleuze's philosophy. As described earlier, Deleuze is taken to be a philosopher of the virtual, where the metaphysical notion of "virtual" is stripped of any ethical or political thrust. The only difference with Žižek is that he explicitly defines Deleuze's metaphysics as apolitical: "...one can only regret that the Anglo-Saxon reception of Deleuze (and, also, the political impact of Deleuze) is predominantly that of a 'guattarized' Deleuze. It is crucial to note that *not a single one* of Deleuze's own texts is in any way directly political; Deleuze 'in himself' is a highly elitist author, indifferent toward politics."[282] Deleuze would characterize the statement as an actualization of the tendencies comprising the academic Idea: "Misunderstandings are often reactions of malicious stupidity. There are some who can only feel intelligent by discovering 'contradictions' in a great thinker."[283]

Stripping Deleuze's theory of Ideas of their explicit ethical and political connotations should be seen as just the latest misinterpretation of Deleuze's reversal of Platonism. The importance of such a reversal is declared in *The Logic of Sense* as well as *Difference and Repetition*.[284] The first "major" or "academic" reception of Deleuze's system regards the reversal as a straightforward critique, and nothing but a critique, of the ontological commitments we associate with Platonism. Deleuze is reduced to being a critic of Platonic universals or forms, as if he thinks the most important ethical mission of philosophy is tracking down all the Platonists that are running around. Even a cursory glance at Deleuze's work shows his reversal of Platonism involves the production of a new theory of Ideas, essences, substances, or universals. Moreover, when Deleuze invokes the reversal of Platonism, he points out that a critique of Platonic universals was accomplished long ago. The formula of "reversing Platonism" is sometimes taken to "mean the abolition of the world of essences and the world of appearances."[285] But, "the dual denunciation of essences and appearances dates back to Hegel or, better yet, Kant."

The new, dominant reception displays an awareness of the overwhelmingly positive impulse of Deleuzian thought. Moreover, this interpretation of the reversal involves some recognition of the way Deleuze refashions or redirects Platonic concepts. At the same time, it ignores the fundamental message of Deleuze's reading of Plato. For Deleuze, the "secret" of Platonism is the ethical and political motivation behind the commitment to essences." Reversing Platonism means "bringing the motivation out into the light of day," or tracking it down as "Plato tracks down the Sophist." According to Deleuze, Platonic division is not Aristotelian division.[286] Plato's objective is not the construction of a proper taxonomy or locating the various kinds of things in the natural world. When Plato has Socrates speak of the essence of beds, it is to an audience that is confused and in need of clarification. As described earlier, Deleuze construes Plato's motivation as the desire to hierarchically differentiate particulars into superior and inferior representations, and, more importantly, into representations and counterfeits. The distinction between representation (the philosophical life) and counterfeit (sophistry, poetic depictions of morality) requires the notion of universals.[287]

What does all this have to do with the new interpretation of Deleuze's reversal? The Deleuzian alternative to Platonic Ideas and the Deleuzian alternative to the Platonic distinction between essence and representation is taken to be the heart of the Deleuzian enterprise. Deleuze's motivation for reworking the notion of Idea is left in the dark. Deleuze's motivation for the distinction between actual and virtual, or corporeal mixture and incorporeal event is obscured. Deleuze seemed to think that "the name of Marx" would prevent him from being represented as a "beautiful soul" ("differences nothing but differences in a peaceful coexistence").[288] He was mistaken.

The ethical and political import of *The Logic of Sense* can be seen through a consideration of the notion of quasi-cause. What does it mean to describe "sense" or the "incorporeal" in this manner. First of all, it means that senses or ideal events can follow one another *as if* they were a causal chain. The "as if" refers to the fact that no link in this chain is caused by preceding ones. The various senses simply register the trajectory of a particular body (the process of mixing and remixing).[289] Each quasi-cause is an effect of the corporeal mixture upon whose surface it subsists. Just as important, the ideal event is a quasi-cause in the sense of an immanent cause and heterogeneous ground. One error Plato decries is the failure to recognize the existence of universals. The counterpart in *The Logic of Sense* is the failure to adequately recognize the identity of a corporeal mixture. Put somewhat differently we can observe a mixture of bodies without being aware of "what is happening." To know what is happening we have to grasp the Idea or ideal event the mixture is actualizing. We have to know what this arrangement of bodies "means." "A hold-up is taking place," "the plane has been hijacked," "the man is on trial," and so on.[290]

We have yet to consider the most important way in which the incorporeal of sense is a quasi-cause. In *A Thousand Plateaus*, Deleuze and Guattari detail the role of the ideal event in the realm of politics.[291] Politics involves not only physical action but also a debate over the meaning of a situation. When activists ask "what are our slogans?" the issue is one of defining and transforming a situation. The objective is both a matter of capturing the sense subsisting on the present arrangement of bodies, and to have the bodies produce a new sense. The goal is to have bodies actualize a new Idea (a new ideal event).

A final way in which the Idea as sense operates as a quasi-cause goes to the core of Deleuze's system. Deleuze uses the notion of incorporeals to express his concept of becoming. Deleuze describes Plato's motivation as the hierarchical differentiation of particular modes of existence. The motivation behind Deleuze's reversal or redirection of Platonism is also the hierarchical differentiation of particulars. The distinction between virtual and actual, mixture and ideal event has the function of securing this project in place. In Plato's dialogues, three conceptual personae are the philosopher (or friend of wisdom), the philosopher's friend (the friend of the friend of wisdom), and the sophist. We can think of the lives of the first two as unequal representations of beauty or justice. As for the life of the third, it occupies the place of the simulacrum. In chapters 21 and 22 of *The Logic of Sense* we find the Deleuzian correlates: the philosopher, the actor, and the academic. A glaring declaration of

Deleuze's motivations is found in his description of the academic or "abstract thinker." The academic is described as one who may very well grasp the sense of particular bodies and lives. For Deleuze, an individual can discern the virtual but remain an academic:

> What is left for the abstract thinker once she has given advice of wisdom and distinction? Well then, are we to speak always about Bousquet's wound, about Fitzgerald's and Lowry's alcoholism, Nietzsche's and Artaud's madness while still remaining on the shore? Are we to become the professionals who give talks on these topics? Are we to wish only that those who have been struck down do not abuse themselves too much? Are we to take up collections and create special journal issues?[292]

Deleuze's conceptual persona of the academic answers these questions with a resounding "yes." The actions of the actor and the philosopher embody a different answer. What does it mean for an actor to play a role (at least play a role well)? He or she must grasp a certain ideal event. If the role is that of an alcoholic, the actors need to discern the ideal event of alcoholism subsisting on the surface of different lives. Certain lives have the meaning of alcoholism; certain bodies actualize the Idea of alcoholism. The actor grasps what it means to be an alcoholic – a thousand physical habits and mannerisms. The actor then creates this sense with his or her own body on the stage or screen, but without becoming an alcoholic:

> The actor thus actualizes the event, but in a way which is entirely different from the actualization of the event in the depth of things ... Thus, the actor delimits the original, disengages from it an abstract line, and keeps from the event only its contour and its splendor, becoming thereby the actor of one's own events – a counter-actualization.[293]

A becoming takes this process of counter-actualization further. One should not confuse the actors with the part they play on TV. Playing a part suggests a practice anchored in imitation or representation. But the philosopher or the philosophical actor is the one who gets lost in the part – except that they are not interesting in repeating a preexisting sense. Rather, they locate a particular sense and use it as a reference point for invention. They are compeled to invent or deepen a "crack" or "leak" within their own lives.[294] What cracks is "what one is supposed to do with one's body?" Unlike the academic who contemplates sense or the virtual, the philosopher locates mediators enabling them to construct a body-without-organs. Far from being effortless, or risk-free, the task demands the injection of caution. Once again, we find at the center of Deleuze's system a protagonist: the one who "goes a bit further," who "extends the crack" but not enough to "deepen it irremedially." This is our old friend: the pervert of "Michel Tournier and the World without Others;" the "structuralist hero" of "How Do We Recognize Structuralism?" the creator of new institutions in "Instincts and Institutions;" the operative who knows how to stir things up and stay alive in "The Philosophy of Crime Novels;" the one who "scrambles the planes" and "overcomes the human condition" in *Bergsonism*; the "active destroyer" or "self destroyer" of *Nietzsche and Philosophy*; the one who tries to determine what the body can do (*Expressionism in Philosophy* and *Practical Philosophy*); the schizo of *Anti-Oedipus*, the militant of *Anti-Oedipus*.

Notes

Introduction

1. Gilles Deleuze and Félix Guattari, *Anti-Oedipus: Capitalism and Schizophrenia*, trans. Robert Hurley, Mark Seem, and Helen R. Lane (New York: Viking, 1977), p. 240.
2. Gilles Deleuze and Félix Guattari, *A Thousand Plateaus: Capitalism and Schizophrenia*, trans. Brian Massumi. (Minneapolis, MN: University of Minnesota Press, 1987), p. 3.
3. Gilles Deleuze, *Negotiations*, trans. Martin Joughin. (New York: Columbia University Press, 1995), pp. 88–89.
4. Gilles Deleuze, *Empiricism and Subjectivity: An Essay on Hume's Theory of Human Nature*, trans. Constantine Boundas (New York: Columbia University Press, 1991), p. 107.
5. Ibid., p. 106.
6. Henri Bergson, *The Creative Mind*, trans. Mabelle L. Andison (New York: Philosophical Library, 1946), pp. 21–28.
7. Gilles Deleuze, *Difference and Repetition*, trans. Paul Patton (New York: Columbia University Press, 1994), p. 8.

Part I   Deleuze and Systematic Philosophy

1. Gilles Deleuze, *Negotiations (1972–1990)*, trans. Martin Joughin (New York: Columbia University Press, 1995), p. 31.
2. Gilles Deleuze and Félix Guattari, *A Thousand Plateaus: Capitalism and Schizophrenia*, trans. Brian Massumi (Minneapolis: University of Minnesota Press, 1987), p. 18.
3. Gilles Deleuze, *Difference and Repetition*, trans. Paul Patton (New York: Columbia University Press), pp. 170–6.
4. Gilles Deleuze, *Expressionism in Philosophy: Spinoza*, trans. Martin Joughin (New York: Zone Books, 1992). This logic of expression is developed in chapters 1–2 and 6–8.
5. Spinoza brings together the notion of substance and expression in Part 1 of the *Ethics*: definitions 4 and 6, Proposition 10, and the Scholium following Proposition 10. The treatment of modifications and individuals first appears in Part 2, Proposition 7 along with its Corollary and Scholium. On the difference between a modification and individual see Deleuze, *Expressionism in Philosophy*, pp. 126–7.
6. Deleuze, *Difference and Repetition*, pp. 178–9.
7. Gilles Deleuze, *Bergsonism*, trans. Hugh Tomlinson and Barbara Habberjam (New York: Zone Books), pp. 37–47.
8. Chapter 2 of Henri Bergson, *Time and Free Will: an essay on the immediate data of consciousness*, trans. F.L. Pogson (New York: Dover Publications, 2001).
9. Bergson, *Time and Free Will*, pp. 128–34.
10. Henri Bergson, *The Creative Mind*, trans. Mabelle L. Andison (New York: Philosophical Library, 1946), p. 57.

11. Bergson, *Time and Free Will*, pp. 11–12.
12. Bergson, *The Creative Mind*, pp. 16, 41, 58.
13. Deleuze and Guattari, *A Thousand Plateaus*, p. 25.
14. Gilles Deleuze and Claire Parnet, *Dialogues*, trans. Janis Tomlinson and Barbara Habberjam (New York: Columbia University Press, 1987), p. 13.
15. Ibid., p. 17.
16. Deleuze and Guattari, *A Thousand Plateaus*, p. 83.
17. Ibid., p. 25.
18. This quote comes from Deleuze's January 14, 1974 lecture on *Anti-Oedipus* and *A Thousand Plateaus*. The average is embodied by the argument that being is analogical rather than equivocal or univocal. This lecture and others can be accessed online at "Web Deleuze" where various seminars by Deleuze have been collected. See http://www.webdeleuze.com/php/sommaire.html
19. Deleuze and Guattari, *A Thousand Plateaus*, p. 293.
20. See, for example, the abundance of examples in "Becoming-Intense, Becoming-Animal, Becoming-Imperceptible" from *A Thousand Plateaus*.
21. Gilles Deleuze, *Two Regimes of Madness, Revised Edition: Texts and Interviews 1975–1995*, ed. David Lapoujade, trans. Ames Hodges and Mike Taormina (Brooklyn: Semiotext(e), 2006), p. 127.
22. Deleuze and Guattari, *A Thousand Plateaus*, p. 279.
23. Deleuze, *Negotiations*, p. 102. See also pp. 135–6.
24. Deleuze, *Difference and Repetition*, p. xxi.
25. Deleuze, *Negotiations*, p. 6.
26. Ibid., 102.
27. Ibid., p.6.
28. For an earlier treatment of Deleuze's work on Hume see Jay Conway, "Deleuze's Hume and Creative History of Philosophy," in *Current Continental Theory and Modern Philosophy*, ed. Stephen Daniel (Evanston: Northwestern University Press, 2004).
29. This phrase is the title of section 5 of Hume's *An Enquiry Concerning Human Understanding*.
30. See the opening paragraph of Hume's *Enquiry Concerning the Principles of Morals*, for a clear illustration of this refusal.
31. Gilles Deleuze, *Pure Immanence: Essays on a Life*, trans. Anne Boyman (New York: Zone Books, 2001), p. 35.
32. Bergson, *The Creative Mind*, pp. 58–9.
33. Gilles Deleuze and Leopold von Sacher-Masoch, *Masochism: Coldness and Cruelty & Venus and Furs*, trans. Jean McNeil (New York: Zone Books, 1991), p. 45.
34. Deleuze, *Difference and Repetition*, p. 59.
35. Gilles Deleuze and Félix Guattari, *Kafka: For a Minor Literature*, trans. Dana Polan (Minneapolis: University of Minnesota Press, 1986), p. 27.
36. Gilles Deleuze and Félix Guattari, *Anti-Oedipus: Capitalism and Schizophrenia*, trans. Robert Hurley, Mark Seem, and Helen Lane (New York: Viking Press, 1977), p. 8.
37. Deleuze and Guattari, *A Thousand Plateaus*, p. 18.
38. Deleuze, *Negotiations*, p. 5.
39. Deleuze and Guattari, *Anti-Oedipus*, pp 78–9.
40. Ibid., pp. 70–1, 100–1, 127.

41. Deleuze, *Negotiations*, p. 5. Deleuze and Parnet, *Dialogues*, p. 13.
42. Deleuze and Guattari, *What is Philosophy?* (New York: Columbia University Press, 1994), pp. 7–8.
43. Deleuze and Guattari, *Anti-Oedipus*, p. 115.
44. Deleuze and Guattari, *What Is Philosophy?* p. 7.
45. See Gilles Deleuze, *Empiricism and Subjectivity: An Essay on Hume's Theory of Human Nature*. Translated by Constantine Boundas (New York: Columbia University Press, 1991), pp. 46–8, as well as Gilles Deleuze, *Desert Islands and Other Texts (1953–1974)*, ed. David Lapoujade, trans. Mike Taormina (Brooklyn: Semiotext(e), 2004), p. 19.
46. This is the conclusion of section 161 of the *Enquiry Concerning the Principles of Morals*.
47. Deleuze, *Empiricism and Subjectivity*, p. 47.
48. Ibid., pp. 44–7.
49. Deleuze and Guattari, *Anti-Oedipus*, p. 8, 33.
50. Deleuze, *Desert Islands and Other Texts*, p. 20.
51. See section 154 of Hume's *Enquiry Concerning the Principles of Morals*.
52. Deleuze, *Desert Islands and Other Texts*, p. 20.
53. Ibid., 21.

Part II Theatre of Operations

1. Commentaries on Deleuze by Constantin Boundas, Paul Patton, Todd May, Rosi Braidotti, and the special attention afforded Deleuze and Guattari's work by Sylvére Lotringer and *Semiotext(e)*, are notable and indispensable exceptions.
2. The most succinct and forceful discussion of our responsibility to acknowledge dominant interpretations is chapter 2 of Jean-Paul Sartre, *Anti-Semite and Jew*, trans. George J. Becker (New York: Schocken Books, 1948).
3. Gilles Deleuze, *Proust and Signs: The Complete Text*, trans. Richard Howard (Minneapolis, MN: University of Minnesota Press, 2000), p. 4.
4. For a discussion of the philosopher as *atopos* see Pierre Hadot, *Philosophy as a Way of Life*, trans. Michael Chase (Oxford: Blackwell Publishers, 1995), pp. 158–9.
5. Deleuze, *Proust and Signs*, p. 95.
6. Ibid.
7. Ibid., p. 7.
8. Gilles Deleuze and Félix Guattari, *What Is Philosophy?*, trans. Hugh Tomlinson and Graham Burchell (New York: Columbia University Press, 1994), pp. 2–3, 61–83.
9. Gilles Deleuze, *The Logic of Sense*, trans. Mark Lester and Charles Stivale (New York: Columbia University Press, 1990), pp. 150, 157–8.
10. Gilles Deleuze and Félix Guattari, *Anti-Oedipus: Capitalism and Schizophrenia*, trans. by Robert Hurley, Mark Seem, and Helen R. Lane (New York: Viking, 1977), p. 15.
11. Ibid., p. 76.
12. Gilles Deleuze and Félix Guattari, *A Thousand Plateaus: Capitalism and Schizophrenia*, trans. Brian Massumi (Minneapolis, MN: University of Minnesota Press, 1987), p. 177.

13. Deleuze and Guattari, *A Thousand Plateaus*, p. 178.
14. Ibid.
15. This statement is from Foucault's 1973 lectures in Rio de Janeiro in *Power: Essential Works of Foucault, 1954–1984, Vol. III*, ed. James D. Faubion, trans. Robert Hurley, Paul Rainbow, and Colin Gordon (New York: New Press, 2000), p. 17.
16. Louis Althusser, *The Future Lasts Forever: A Memoir*, trans. Richard Veasey (New York: The New Press, 1993), pp. 182, 220, 223.
17. Sylvére Lotringer, "Doing Theory," in *French Theory in America*, eds. Sylvére Lotringer and Sande Cohen (New York: Routledge, 2001), p. 152. Guattari's critique of postmodernism is advanced in "The Postmodern Impasse" and in the interview "Postmodernism and Ethical Abdication," in *Soft Subversions*, trans. Sylvére Lotringer (Brooklyn, NY: Semiotext(e), 1996), pp. 109–17.
18. See Andreas Huyssen, "Mapping the Postmodern," in *Feminism/Postmodernism*, ed. Linda Nicholson (New York: Routledge, 1990), pp. 234–77.
19. Rudolf Carnap, "The Elimination of Metaphysics through Logical Analysis of Language," in *Logical Positivism*, ed. Alfred J. Ayer (Glencoe, IL: The Free Press of Glencoe, 1959), pp. 78–80.
20. Alfred J. Ayer, "Reflections on 'Language, Truth, and Logic'," in *Logical Positivism in Perspective*, ed. Barry Gower, pp. 23–34 (London: Croom Helm, 1987), p. 33.
21. A second Rorty exists alongside of the one I have just presented. In the essay "Deconstruction and Circumvention," Rorty argues against what he perceives as the Heidegerrian and Derridean inflation of foundationalism into a ubiquitous, inescapable center "radiating evil outwards," and suggests that the notion of overcoming philosophy be replaced by a vision of "lots of little pragmatic questions about which bits of that tradition might be used for some current purpose," Richard Rorty, "Deconstruction and Circumvention," in *Essays on Heidegger and Others: Philosophical Papers Vol. 2*, pp. 85–106 (New York: Cambridge University Press, 1991), p. 104.
22. Jacques Derrida, "Différance," in *Margins of Philosophy*, trans. Alan Bass, pp. 1–27 (Chicago: University of Chicago Press, 1982), p. 3.
23. Ibid., p. 7.
24. The critique of the picture theory of ideas is contained in definition 3 and the scholium following proposition 43 in Part 2 of Baruch Spinoza's *Ethics*.
25. See, for example, Spinoza's *Ethics*: Part 2, proposition 15.
26. Deleuze and Guattari, *What Is Philosophy*, pp. 15–34.
27. Richard Rorty, *Consequences of Pragmatism: Essays, 1972–1980* (Minneapolis, MN: University of Minnesota Press, 1982), p. xviii.
28. See Carnap, "The Elimination of Metaphysics through Logical Analysis of Language."
29. See Jacques Derrida, "Signature Event Context," in *Margins of Philosophy*, trans. Alan Bass (Chicago: University of Chicago Press, 1982), pp. 307–30.
30. Slavoj Žižek's, *Organs without Bodies: On Deleuze and Consequences* (New York: Routledge Press, 2003), is one, glaring example of this mistake.
31. Deleuze and Guattari, *What Is Philosophy?*, pp. 85–113.
32. Jay Conway, "Deleuze's Hume and Creative History of Philosophy," in *Current Continental Theory and Modern Philosophy*, ed. Stephen Daniel (Evanston, IL: Northwestern University Press, 2004).

33. Gilles Deleuze, *Empiricism and Subjectivity: An Essay on Hume's Theory of Human Nature*, trans. Constantin Boundas (New York: Columbia University Press, 1991), pp. 37–40.

34. Ibid., p. 99.

35. Gilles Deleuze and Claire Parnet, *Dialogues*, trans. Janis Tomlinson and Barbara Habberjam (New York: Columbia University Press, 1987), pp. 57–8.

36. Deleuze and Parnet, *Dialogues*, pp. 36–51;

37. See the essay "Whitman" in Gilles Deleuze, *Critical and Clinical*, trans. Daniel W. Smith and Michael A. Greco (Minneapolis, MN: University of Minnesota Press, 1997), p. 56.

38. See Willard Van Orman Quine, "Two Dogmas of Empiricism," in *From a Logical Point of View* (Cambridge, MA: Harvard University Press, 1964), pp. 20–46.

39. Willard Van Orman Quine, "Epistemology Naturalized," in *Ontological Relativity and Other Essays* (New York: Columbia University Press, 1969), pp. 69–90. See as well, Quine, "Two Dogmas of Empiricism," p. 45.

40. The conclusion of this text should be read alongside of the introduction to Richard Rorty's *The Linguistic Turn: Essay in Philosophical Method (With Two Retrospective Essays)*, ed. Richard Rorty (Chicago: University of Chicago Press, 1992) and Richard Rorty's *Consequences of Pragmatism: Essays, 1972–1980* (Minneapolis, MN: University of Minnesota Press, 1982) in order to see the extent to which Rorty keeps open the question of philosophy's future, relevance, and desirability.

41. Deleuze and Guattari, *What Is Philosophy?*, p. 140.

42. Henri Bergson, *The Creative Mind*, trans. Mabelle L. Andison (New York: Philosophical Library, 1946), pp. 58–9.

43. Bergson, *The Creative Mind*, pp. 17–8.

44. Gilles Deleuze, *Bergsonism*, trans. Hugh Tomlinson and Barbara Habberjam (New York: Zone Books, 1988), pp. 15–7.

45. Deleuze and Guattari, *What is Philosophy?*, p. 139.

46. Ibid., p. 22.

47. John Austin, *How to Do Things with Words* (Cambridge, MA: Harvard University Press, 1962).

48. Deleuze and Guattari, *What is Philosophy?*, p. 22.

49. Rorty, *The Linguistic Turn*, p. 39.

50. Ibid., p. 14.

51. Ibid., p. 34.

52. Ibid., p. 32.

53. Deleuze and Guattari, *What Is Philosophy?*, pp. 6, 117.

54. Gilles Deleuze, *Two Regimes of Madness, Revised Edition: Texts and Interviews 1975–1995*, ed. David Lapoujade, trans. Ames Hodges and Mike Taormina (Brooklyn, NY: Semiotext(e), 2006), p. 313.

55. Ibid.

56. The distinction between two answers – an easy and scholarly one – runs through Deleuze's course on Leibniz. See Gilles Deleuze, "Les cour de Gilles Deleuze," in *Web Deleuze* http://www.webdeleuze.com/php/sommaire.ht ml (January 1, 2009).

57. Deleuze and Guattari, *What is Philosophy?*, pp. 163–99.

58. Deleuze and Guattari, *What Is Philosophy?*, pp. 163–4.
59. Deleuze and Guattari, *What Is Philosophy?*, p. 127–8.
60. Willard Van Orman Quine, "On Empirically Equivalent Systems of the World," in *Erkenntnis*, pp. 313–28, 9: 3 (1975), p. 313.
61. Deleuze, *Difference and Repetition*, pp. 183–4.
62. Deleuze and Guattari, *What Is Philosophy?*, pp. 21, 144, 159.
63. Marx makes this point in the first and tenth thesis.
64. Deleuze and Guattari, *What Is Philosophy?*, p. 140; Deleuze, *Two Regimes of Madness*, pp. 233–6.
65. Bergson, *The Creative Mind*, p. 16.
66. Ibid., pp. 23–8.
67. Deleuze, *Two Regimes of Madness*, p. 233.
68. Ibid., pp. 233–4.
69. Ibid., p. 234.
70. Ibid.
71. Deleuze, *Bergsonism*, pp. 18, 97–8 as well as Gilles Deleuze, *Nietzsche and Philosophy*, trans. Hugh Tomlinson (Minneapolis, MN: University of Minnesota Press, 1983), p. 62; Deleuze, *Expressionism in Philosophy*, p. 222; Gilles Deleuze, *Spinoza: Practical Philosophy*, trans. Robert Hurley (San Francisco: City Lights Books, 1988), p. 97; Deleuze, *Difference and Repetition*, pp. 211–2.
72. Deleuze, *Two Regimes of Madness*, p. 233.
73. Deleuze, *Difference and Repetition*, pp. 91–6. Deleuze's discussion of Karl Marx's, "The Eighteenth Brumaire of Louis Bonaparte," in *The Marx-Engels Reader* (New York: W.W. Norton and Company, 1978) is mediated by the essay "The Resurrection of the Romans." See Harold Rosenberg, *The Tradition of the New* (New York: McGraw-Hill, 1965), pp. 154–77.
74. Karl Marx, *The Marx-Engels Reader*, ed. Robert C. Tucker (New York: W.W. Norton, 1978), p. 595.
75. Ibid., p. 597.
76. Slavoj Žižek develops this notion in his popular essay "Repeating Lenin." See Lacan Ink, http://www.lacan.com/replenin.htm (January 1, 2009).
77. Deleuze, *Bergsonism*, p. 105; Deleuze, *Difference and Repetition*, pp. 209–11.
78. Walter Benjamin's "Theses on the Philosophy of History," in *Illuminations: Essays and Reflections* (New York: Schocken Books, 1968), pp. 253–264.
79. Deleuze and Guattari, *What Is Philosophy*, p. 118.
80. Ibid., p. 21.
81. Ibid., p. 23.
82. Ibid., p. 159.
83. Ibid.
84. See for example, Deleuze and Guattari, *Anti-Oedipus*, p. 10. On the philosophical implications of Marx's notion of fetishism (the way it reworks the opposition of being and appearance) see Etienne Balibar's *The Philosophy of Marx*, trans. Chris Turner (New York: Verso, 1995), pp. 60–2.
85. Henri Bergson, *Matter and Memory*, trans. N.M. Paul and W.S. Palmer (New York: Zone Books, 1991), pp. 28, 183–5.
86. Spinoza's *Ethics*: Part 1, the scholium following proposition 15; Part 2, propositions 22–28.
87. Deleuze and Guattari, *What Is Philosophy*, pp. 159.
88. Ibid., pp. 19–20.

89. Ibid., p. 22.
90. Ibid., p. 167.
91. The distinction between two answers – an easy and scholarly one – runs through Deleuze's course on Leibniz. See Gilles Deleuze, "Les cour de Gilles Deleuze," in *Web Deleuze* http://www.webdeleuze.com/php/sommaire.html (January 1, 2009).
92. Deleuze, *Difference and Repetition*, pp. 30–5, 133.
93. Deleuze and Guattari, *What Is Philosophy*, pp. 134–7.
94. Drawing heavily upon the work of Russell and Frege, Deleuze and Guattari argue logic inscribes the concept within a "circle of reference" by defining it as an extension, intension, and comprehension. Concepts are represented as terms paired up with independent variables (or "arguments" in the mathematical sense), to form a logical function. A simple example would be that of the concept "Venus" that, upon being conjoined to the variable/argument x gives us x is Venus or Vx. Substituting any object for x gives us a proposition possessing a "reference" (or truth-value). The extension of the concept is a set each element of which is an object that, when substituted for x, gives us a true proposition. In the case of the propositional function Vx this set consists of one object. The intension (or subsets) of the concept are conditions that, when satisfied, make us consider an object an element of this set. For example, Frege famously described "morning star" and "evening star" as two intensions of the same object. If an object is recognized as one or the other, it will be the object comprising the extension of the concept of Venus. Finally, the comprehension of the concept is the essential predicates of the objects in the set: "Venus (the evening star and morning star) is a planet that takes less time than the earth to complete its revolution." In this way, the property of reference – in the sense of a proposition's truth-value – is clearly the "circle" within which the concept's other properties are defined. Extension is an "exoreference" in that it concerns identifying which objects yield true substitution instances. Intension is an "endoreference" in that it tells us what to look for in an object to determine whether it would yield a true instantiation. Comprehension involves delineating through additional logical functions the essential predicates of objects yielding true instantiations.
95. Ibid., p. 128.
96. Gilles Deleuze, *Negotiations (1972–1990)*, trans. Martin Joughin (New York: Columbia University Press, 1995), p. 126.
97. Deleuze and Guattari, *What Is Philosophy?*, p. 128.
98. Ibid., p. 119.
99. See for example Kathy Acker, *Blood and Guts in High School* (New York: Grove Press, 1984), p. 125. The passage Acker re-creates in the medium of literature is found in Deleuze and Guattari, *Anti-Oedipus*, p. 116.
100. Richard Rorty, *Philosophy and the Mirror of Nature* (New Jersey: Princeton University Press, 1979), pp. 166–8.
101. Rorty, *Philosophy and the Mirror*, p. 168.
102. Deleuze, *Empiricism and Subjectivity*, p. 28.
103. "Michel Tournier and the World without Others" is privileged in the following texts: Alice Jardin's *Gynesis: Configuration of Woman and Modernity* (Ithaca, NY: Cornell University Press, 1985); Constantin Boundas's "Foreclosure of the Other: From Sartre to Deleuze," and "Deleuze:

Serialization and Subject-Formation," in *Gilles Deleuze and the Theater of Philosophy*, ed. Constantin Boundas and Dorothea Olkowski (London: Routledge, 1994), pp. 99–116; Dorothea Olkowski's, *Gilles Deleuze and the Ruin of Representation* (Berkeley, CA: University of California Press, 1999); Stephen J. Arnott's "Solipsism and the Possibility of Community in Deleuze's Ethics," in *Contre temps* 2 (2001): 109–23; James Brusseau's *Isolated Experiences: Gilles Deleuze and the Solitudes of Reversed Platonism* (Albany, NY: State University of New York Press, 1998); Pelagia Goulimari's "A Minoritarian Feminism? Things to Do with Deleuze and Guattari," in *Hypatia* Vol. 14:2 (Spring 1999); and Moira Gatens's "Through a Spinozist Lens: Ethology, Difference, and Power," in *Deleuze: A Critical Reader*, ed. Paul Patton (Oxford: Blackwell Publishing, 1997), pp. 162–87.

104. Michel Tournier, *Friday*, trans. Norman Denny (Baltimore: Johns Hopkins, 1997), p. 54. For Robinson's characterization of his journal as philosophical research see pp. 85, 91.
105. Gilles Deleuze, *Desert Islands and Other Texts, (1953–1974)*, ed. David Lapoujade, trans. Mike Taormina (Brooklyn, NY: Semiotext(e), 2004), p. 21.
106. Deleuze, *The Logic of Sense*, p. 308.
107. Ibid., p. 309.
108. Deleuze, *Desert Islands*, p. 21.
109. Deleuze, *The Logic of Sense*, p. 305.
110. Ibid., pp. 315, 319.
111. The discussion of humor and irony is found in Deleuze, *Difference and Repetition*, p. 5. Black humor is employed and defined in Deleuze and Guattari, *Anti-Oedipus*, p. 11.
112. See Jean-Pierre Vernant, *The Origins of Greek Thought* (Ithaca, NY: Cornell University Press, 1982). In letter #73 Spinoza depicts the pre-Socratic *arché* as an immanent cause.
113. Deleuze and Guattari, *What Is Philosophy?*, p. 148.
114. Ibid., pp. 146–50.
115. Ibid., pp. 144–5.
116. Ibid., p. 145.
117. Ibid., pp. 147–8.
118. Plato, *Symposium*, in *Plato: Complete Works*, ed. John M. Cooper and D.S. Hutchinson (Cambridge, MA: Hackett Publishing Co, 1997), pp. 202a–04b.
119. Deleuze and Guattari, *What Is Philosophy?*, p. 148.
120. Plato, *Symposium*, p. 206c–d.
121. This is my interpretation of 210–11d of Plato's *Symposium*.
122. Deleuze and Guattari, *What Is Philosophy?*, p. 146.
123. Ibid., p. 145.
124. Ibid., p. 146.
125. Ibid., p. 143.
126. The others being Sartre, Beauvoir, and Claude Lefort. In a 1951 *Les Temps Modernes* article Lefort expressed their collective concern that Lévi-Strauss was valorizing rigid, quasi-mathematical schemes over sociohistorical analysis and individual experience. See Francois Dosse, *The History of Structuralism Vol. I: The Rising Sign*, trans. Deborah Glassman (Minneapolis, MN: University of Minnesota Press, 1997), pp. 30–1.
127. Deleuze, *Empiricism and Subjectivity*, p. 27.

128. Claude Lévi-Strauss, *Tristes Tropiques*, trans. John and Doreen Weightman (New York: Penguin Books, 1973), pp. 56–60.
129. Deleuze, *Desert Islands*, pp. 170–92.
130. Ibid., 192.
131. Ibid., 191.
132. Ibid.
133. Deleuze and Guattari, *Anti-Oedipus*, pp. 202–9.
134. Ibid., p. 208.
135. Gilles Deleuze, *Negotiations*, p. 125.
136. Ibid., pp. 27–30, 124.
137. Literary critics often do not know what to do with Deleuze. In many cases, they simply repeat his references to literature without a consideration of what this tells us about the way philosophy and literature interact. Even worse, some simply mimic the words Deleuze uses without engaging with the acts of thought or concepts these words embody. A truly rare exception is Timothy Murphy's, *Wising Up the Marks: The Amodern William Burroughs* (Berkeley, CA and Los Angeles: University of California Press, 1998). Murphy develops the category of the amodern – a category contrasted with modernism and postmodernism – through readings of Deleuze and Guattari's political theory, Ralph Ellison's *Invisible Man*, and, as the title suggests, the work of William S. Burroughs.
138. Deleuze and Guattari, *A Thousand Plateaus*, pp. 192–5.
139. In Deleuze's *Foucault*, the categories prevent the assignment of a single, nonheterogeneous meaning to particular institutions and institutions in general. In other words, the categories of Hmslevian linguistics facilitate an institutional analysis that permits the simultaneous recognition of the relatedness and individuality of institutions. See Gilles Deleuze, *Foucault*, trans. Sean Hand (Minneapolis, MN: University of Minnesota Press, 1988), p. 47.
140. Deleuze and Guattari, *A Thousand Plateaus*, p. 194.
141. Ibid., pp. 195–6.
142. See: Deleuze and Guattari, *Anti-Oedipus*, p. 341; Deleuze and Guattari, *A Thousand Plateaus*, p. 204; Deleuze and Parnet, *Dialogues*, p. 36.
143. Spinoza, *Ethics*, Part 2, the note following lemma 7 after proposition 12.
144. Deleuze and Guattari, *A Thousand Plateaus*, p. 204.
145. Deleuze and Guattari, *Anti-Oedipus*, pp. 277–8.
146. See Deleuze and Parnet, *Dialogues*, pp. 36–51; Gilles Deleuze, *Essays Critical and Clinical*, trans. Daniel W. Smith and Michael A. Greco (Minneapolis, MN: University of Minnesota Press, 1997), pp. 56–60.
147. Deleuze, *Proust and Signs*, pp. 112–4, 146.
148. Marcel Proust, *Remembrance of Things Past*, vol. I, trans. C. K. Scott Moncrieff and Terence Kilmartin (New York: Random House Press, 1981), pp. 704–5.
149. For this reason Deleuze attaches importance to Proust's references to Plato's *Symposium*.
150. Proust, *Remembrance of Things Past*, vol. III, p. 935.
151. Deleuze, *Proust and Signs*, p. 22.
152. Deleuze, *Difference and Repetition*, p. xx.
153. Deleuze and Guattari, *A Thousand Plateaus*, p. 192.
154. Deleuze, *Desert Islands*, pp. 81–5.

155. "To be sure, the great majority of novels in the collection have been content to change the detective's way of doing things (he drinks, he's in love, he's restless) but keep the same structure: the surprise ending that brings all the characters together for a final explanation that fingers one of them as the guilty part. Nothing new there," Deleuze, *Desert Islands*, p. 82.

156. Deleuze, *Desert Islands*, p. 81.

157. Ibid., p. 83.

158. Ibid.

159. From Mike Davis, *City of Quartz: Excavating The Future in Los Angeles* (Brooklyn, NY: Verso, 2006), p. 45.

160. Recently reprinted by AK Press: François Eugene, *Memoirs of Vidocq: Master of Crime*, trans. Edwin Gile Rich (Oakland, CA: AK Press/ Nabat, 2003).

161. Deleuze, *Desert Islands*, p. 82.

162. Ibid., 83.

163. Ibid.

164. Incidentally, Foucault's archival materials include Vidocq's memoirs. They are not, however, mentioned in Deleuze's essay where he, more or less sticks, to the books of *La Série Noire*.

165. Michel Foucault, *Discipline and Punish: The Birth of the Prison*, trans. Alan Sheridan (New York: Vintage, 1977), pp. 73–103, 257–92.

166. Duhamel is quoted in Chester Himes' second memoir *My Life of Absurdity: The Later Years* (New York: Thunder's Mouth Press, 1976), pp. 101–5. Himes describes how Duhamel instructed him to read Hammett in order to see how to write a crime novel. Himes' Harlem series are mentioned in "Philosophy and the Crime Novel," in Deleuze, *Desert Islands*.

167. Dashiell Hammett, *Red Harvest* (New York: Vintage, 1992), p. 117.

168. Hamett, *Red Harvest*, p. 157.

169. Ibid., pp. 85, 156.

170. Plato, *Republic* in *Plato: Complete Works*, ed. John M. Cooper and D.S. Hutchinson (Cambridge, MA: Hackett Publishing Co, 1997), p. 598c–d.

171. The notion of minor literature receives its strongest treatment in Gilles Deleuze and Félix Guattari, *Kafka: For a Minor Literature*, trans. Dana Polan (Minneapolis, MN: University of Minnesota Press, 1986). See pp. 16–8.

172. Deleuze and Guattari, *Anti-Oedipus*, p. 15.

173. Deleuze and Guattari, *What is Philosophy?*, p. 29.

174. Deleuze and Parnet, *Dialogues*, p. 6.

175. Deleuze, *Two Regimes of Madness*, p. 380. At times "conversation" is used interchangeably with "discussion;" at other times "conversation" is divided in two. These two forms correspond to the conceptual opposition between discussion and becoming. See Deleuze and Parnet, *Dialogues*, pp. 1–19.

176. Deleuze and Parnet, *Dialogues*, p. xi.

177. Deleuze, *Empiricism and Subjectivity*, p. 106.

178. Deleuze, *Foucault*, p. 15.

179. Deleuze and Parnet, *Dialogues*, p. 1.

180. Deleuze and Guattari, *What Is Philosophy?*, p. 28.

181. Deleuze and Guattari, *A Thousand Plateaus*, p. 197.

182. Ibid., 198.

183. Deleuze, *Two Regimes of Madness*, p. 380.

184. Deleuze, *Negotiations*, p. 129.
185. Julia Kristeva, *Language – the Unknown: An Introduction into Linguistics*, trans. Anne M. Menke (New York: Columbia University Press, 1989), p. 4.
186. Deleuze and Guattari, *A Thousand Plateaus*, p. 7.
187. See Chapter 3 of Ferdinand Saussure, *Course in General Linguistics*, ed. Charles Bally and Albert Sechehaye, trans. Roy Harris (La Falle, IL: Open Court Publishing, 1986).
188. Deleuze, *Negotiations*, p. 28. See also Deleuze and Guattari, *A Thousand Plateaus*, pp. 77–8.
189. Saussure, *Course in General Linguistics*, p. 14.
190. Ibid., pp. 11–2.
191. Deleuze and Guattari, *A Thousand Plateaus*, p. 93.
192. Ibid., p. 7.
193. Ibid., p. 94.
194. Ibid., p. 90.
195. Ibid., p. 88.
196. Ibid., p. 76.
197. Austin characterizes his initial, provisional distinction between performative and constative – between saying and doing – as inadequate for the following reasons: there is no grammatical criterion that would enable us to neatly segregate performative utterances (after all, what sentence could not function as a performative in the appropriate context), there are clear cases of hybridity (utterances that simultaneously describe and perform an action), and, most importantly, there is no reason to consider "saying" or describing a nonaction.
198. Deleuze and Guattari, *A Thousand Plateaus*, p. 78.
199. John Searle, "What Is a Speech Act?" in *Readings in the Philosophy of Language*, ed. Jay F. Rosenberg and Charles Travis, pp. 614–28 (Englewood Cliffs, NJ: Prentice-Hall, 1971), pp. 615, 620–3.
200. Deleuze and Guattari, *A Thousand Plateaus*, p. 76.
201. Ibid., 76.
202. Ibid., 79.
203. Deleuze and Guattari, *What Is Philosophy?*, p. 28; Deleuze, *Two Regimes of Madness*, p. 380.
204. Deleuze, *Desert Islands*, p. 192.
205. Deleuze and Parnet, *Dialogues*, p. 1.
206. Deleuze and Guattari, *What Is Philosophy?*, p. 28.
207. Deleuze, *Negotiations*, p. 137.
208. Deleuze and Parnet, *Dialogues*, pp. 7–8; Deleuze, *Negotiations*, p. 139.
209. Deleuze, *Two Regimes of Madness*, p. 380.
210. Ibid.
211. Deleuze, *Negotiations*, p. 90.
212. Ibid., p. 23.
213. Deleuze, *Empiricism and Subjectivity*, p. 106.
214. For the distinction between schizophrenia and schizophrenics see Deleuze and Guattari, *Anti-Oedipus*, pp. 5, 19, 24, 37, 68, 88, 102, 135–6; for the distinction between both and the revolutionary see p. 341.
215. Ibid., p. 379.

Part III Affirming Philosophy

1. Pierre Hadot, *Philosophy As a Way of Life*, trans. Michael Chase (Oxford: Blackwell Publishers, 1995), pp. 158–9.
2. The central work in this regard is Gilles Deleuze, *Difference and Repetition*, trans. Paul Patton (New York: Columbia University Press, 1994). For the phrases "the reality of the virtual" and *"different/ciation"* see pp. 209, 245.
3. See John Mullarkey, *Bergson and Philosophy* (Edinburgh: Edinburgh University Press: 2000), pp. 138–9; Manuel Delanda, *Intensive Science and Virtual Philosophy* (New York: Continuum, 2002).
4. See Gilles Deleuze, "Bergson, 1859–1941," and "Bergson's Conception of Difference," in *Desert Islands and Other Texts (1953–1974)*, ed. David Lapoujade, trans. Mike Taormina (Brooklyn: Semiotext(e), 2006). The book in question is Gilles Deleuze, *Bergsonism*, trans. Hugh Tomlinson and Barbara Habberjam (New York: Zone Books, 1988).
5. Deleuze, *Difference and Repetition*, p. 59.
6. Ibid., p. 134.
7. Ibid., pp. 67, 166.
8. For Deleuze's reading of Plato see *Difference and Repetition*, pp. 59–68, 126–8; and "The Simulacrum and Ancient Philosophy," published as the first appendix of Gilles Deleuze, *The Logic of Sense*, trans. Mark Lester and Charles Stivale (New York: Columbia University Press, 1990), pp. 253–66.
9. Gilles Deleuze and Félix Guattari, *A Thousand Plateaus: Capitalism and Schizophrenia*, trans. Brian Massumi (Minneapolis, MN: University of Minnesota Press, 1987), p. 203.
10. Deleuze, *Difference and Repetition*, p. 8.
11. From Jacques Derrida, *Positions*, trans. Alan Bass (Chicago: University of Chicago Press, 1981), p. 71.
12. This interview can be found in Gilles Deleuze, *Two Regimes of Madness, Revised Edition: Texts and Interviews 1975–1995*, ed. David Lapoujade, trans. Ames Hodges and Mike Taormina (Brooklyn: Semiotext(e), 2006), p. 176.
13. Gilles Deleuze and Félix Guattari, *What Is Philosophy?* (New York: Columbia University Press, 1994), p. 9; Gilles Deleuze, *Negotiations (1972–1990)*, trans. Martin Joughin (New York: Columbia University Press, 1995), p. 136; Gilles Deleuze and Claire Parnet, *Dialogues*, trans. Janis Tomlinson and Barbara Habberjam (New York: Columbia University Press, 1987), p. 1.
14. Alexandre Kojève, *Introduction to the Reading of Hegel: Lectures on the Phenomenology of Spirit*, ass. Raymond Queneau, ed. Allan Bloom, trans. James H. Nichols Jr. (Ithaca, NY: Cornell University Press, 1980), p. 194. With regards to the notion of the end of philosophy, and the argument that this end presupposes another end – that of history – Kojève's most important lectures were not included in the English-language *Introduction to the Reading of Hegel*. These were subsequently published in the journal *Interpretation*. See in particular: Alexandre Kojève, "Hegel, Marx And Christianity," trans. Hilail Gildin, in *Interpretation: A Journal of Political Philosophy*, 1:1 (Summer 1970), pp. 22, 26–7, 35–8; and "The Idea of Death in the Philosophy of Hegel," trans. Joseph J. Carpino, in *Interpretation: A Journal of Political Philosophy*, 3:2, 3 (Winter 1973), p. 116.

15. The structure of Kojève's argument involves a triangular referent the vertices of which correspond to: (a) the time and place of the end of history, (b) the world-historical individual who brings about this end of history, (c) the author who brings *philosophy* to an end by recognizing and explaining the significance of history's end. In his legendary *École des Hautes Études* lectures and in "Hegel, Marx and Christianity," Kojève's operative trinity is the battle of Jena (October 14, 1806), Napoleon, and Hegel; thus, he positions (or "historicizes") his own work as a post-historical / post-philosophical commentary upon the ends of history and philosophy. In between these pieces (December 4, 1937) Kojève delivered his lecture to the College of Sociology (the group founded by Georges Bataille, Michel Leiris, and Roger Callois). Here the trinity is the Russian Revolution, Stalin, and Kojève. See Denis Hollier ed., *The College of Sociology: Theory and History of Literature* (Minneapolis, MN: Minnesota Press, 1988), pp. 85–7. Kojève positions himself as the figure who brings philosophy to an end (as "Stalin's conscience").

16. Queneau's novel is saturated with references to the Battle of Jena, and the "Sunday" of the title is connected to the problems raised by Bataille in relation to Kojèvian temporality. The charming if vacant protagonist Valentin Bru is concerned, above all else, with figuring out how to kill time. See Raymond Queneau, *The Sunday of Life*, trans. Barbara Wright (New York: A New Directions Book, 1977), pp. 169–70. In 1952 Bataille's *Critique* contained a review of Queneau's fiction by Kojève titled "Les romans de la Sagesse." Bataille's December 6, 1937 letter to Kojève, in which he characterizes himself as unemployed negativity, can be found in Denis Hollier, *The College of Sociology*, pp. xx, 89–93. See also Georges Bataille, *The Accursed Share Vol.1: Consumption*, trans. Robert Hurley (New York: Zone Books, 1989). In *The Accursed Share*, economies are defined as much by useless (or indirectly useful) forms of expenditure.

17. Maurice Blanchot, *The Infinite Conversation*, trans. Susan Hanson (Minneapolis, MN: University of Minnesota Press, 1993), pp. xii, 90–2, 203–8.

18. Claude Levi-Strauss, *The Naked Man*, trans. John and Doreen Weightman (New York: Harper and Row Publishers, 1981), p. 629. The development of Lévi-Strauss' opinion of philosophy can be discerned in the movement between the partial critique found in *Tristes Tropiques* and *The Savage Mind*, to the strident dismissal found at the end of *The Naked Man*. See *Tristes Tropiques: An Anthropological Study of Primitive Societies in Brazil*, trans. John Russell (New York: Atheneum, 1971), pp. 55–60; *The Savage Mind*, trans. George Veidenfield (Chicago: University of Chicago Press, 1962) pp. 247–57; *The Naked Man*, pp. 625–42.

19. Lévi-Strauss, *The Naked Man*, pp. 629, 642. In the chapter "How I became an anthropologist," of *Tristes Tropiques* Lévi-Strauss acknowledges the debt the human sciences owe Freud and Marx, and it is not difficult to imagine what he has in mind. Freud never wavered from linking philosophical discourse to the belief that belonging to the mind means belonging to consciousness. Given this use of the term "philosophy," it comes as little surprise that psychoanalytic thought is represented as a cancellation rather than augmentation of philosophy. The Marx of the *Theses on Feuerbach* calls for an exit from

philosophy where philosophy is associated with a cluster of commitments: the idea that thought is inherently a material force, the notion of autonomous thought, a contemplative model of truth, the goal of representing rather than transforming the world. Etienne Balibar provides a beautiful, nonreductive account of the relationship between Marxism and philosophy in his book *Philosophy of Marx*, trans. Chris Turner (New York: Verso, 1995).

20. Lévi-Strauss, *The Naked Man*, p. 685.
21. Ibid., p. 628.
22. The ambiguous connotation of "philosophy" in Marx's writings can be seen by juxtaposing his *Contribution to a Critique of "Hegel's Philosophy of Right"* (where "philosophy," at least "philosophy in the service of history" denotes the important task of intellectual criticism – a task that is both necessary and insufficient given the goal of social transformation) and the *German Ideology* (where "philosophy" denotes the error of reducing practice to theory, of depicting political struggle as a struggle over ideas). See *The Marx-Engels Reader*, ed. Robert C. Tucker (New York: W. W. Norton and Co., 1978), pp. 56, 60, 147.
23. Jacques Derrida, *Of Grammatology*, trans. Gayatri Chakravorty Spivak (Baltimore: Johns Hopkins University Press, 1976), p. 12.
24. The objection to this claim would appeal to two related assertions in Deleuze's work with Guattari. In *Anti-Oedipus*, capitalism is labeled the end of history and capitalism is linked to the "death of writing." When the authors declare that capitalism is the end of history, they are not saying that capitalism is coming to an end. Capitalism is the end of history in the sense of the meaning of history. But this does not point that capitalism represents the necessary, terminal point of history. Capitalism is a contingent formation. Within this formation, we can retroactively discern a common feature of precapitalist societies: coding or the fact that production is governed by a set of values or beliefs. This feature becomes visible within capitalism through contrast. Decoding is an essential feature of capitalism; the logic of production within capitalism is a quantitative calculus: How much will it cost? How much surplus value can be extracted and realized? Accompanying but not governing this quantitative calculus is a wave of fragmentary belief and value systems. The assertion that writing is dead is a play on the theme of the death of God. The statement is designed to illuminate a peculiar feature of intellectual life: the noise surrounding the classical notion of interpretation, the fanfare surrounding the critique of this notion, occurs within a social formation in which writing and images are consumed unmediated by the question, "What does it mean?" See Gilles Deleuze and Félix Guattari, *Anti-Oedipus: Capitalism and Schizophrenia*, trans. Robert Hurley, Mark Seem, and Helen R. Lane (New York: Viking, 1977), pp. 140, 224–26, 240.
25. See Deleuze and Guattari, *What is Philosophy?*, pp. 100–2, 156–7; and "May 68 Didn't Take Place" found in Deleuze, *Two Regimes of Madness*, pp. 233–6.
26. Deleuze, *Difference and Repetition*, p. 163.
27. See Walter Benjamin, "Theses on the Philosophy of History," in *Illuminations: Essays and Reflections*, trans. ed. Hannah Arendt (New York: Schocken, 1969).

28. Gilles Deleuze, *Nietzsche and Philosophy*, trans. Hugh Tomlinson (Minneapolis, MN: University of Minnesota Press, 1983), pp. 147–9.
29. Gilles Deleuze, seminar on Leibniz, 6 of May 1980. Deleuze's philosophy seminars can be found online at http://www.webdeleuze.com/php/sommaire.html. Further use of seminars will be cited by title and date.
30. Deleuze, seminar on Leibniz, 6 of May 1980.
31. Deleuze, *Difference and Repetition*, p. 165.
32. Deleuze, *Negotiations*, p. 133.
33. Ibid.
34. Deleuze, *Difference and Repetition*, p. 188.
35. Ibid., p. 135.
36. The critique of philosophy as phalogocentric can be found in: Genevieve Lloyd, *The Man of Reason: "male" and "female" in Western Philosophy*; Andrea Nye, *Words of Power: A Feminist Reading of the History of Logic*; and Hélène Cixous' portion of *The Newly Born Woman* (co-written with Catherine Clément), as well as the article by Elizabeth Spelman, "Woman as Body: Ancient and Contemporary Views."
37. Michel Foucault, "Theatrum Philosophicum" in *Language, Counter-Memory, Practice: Selected Essays and Interviews*. Edited by Donfald F. Bouchard (New York: Cornell University Press, 1980), p. 181.
38. Gilles Deleuze, *Proust and Signs: The Complete Text*, trans. Richard Howard (Minneapolis, MN: University of Minnesota Press, 2000), p. 94.
39. Ibid., p. 100.
40. Deleuze, *Difference and Repetition*, p. 132.
41. Ibid., pp. 134, 138.
42. Deleuze and Guattari, *What is Philosophy?*, p. 49.
43. Spinoza, Letter #73.
44. Deleuze and Guattari, *What is Philosophy?*, p. 43.
45. See Jean-Pierre Vernant, *The Origins of Greek Thought* (Ithaca, NY: Cornell University Press, 1982).
46. Deleuze, *Difference and Repetition*, p 134.
47. Ibid., p. 67.
48. Deleuze, *Nietzsche and Philosophy*, pp. 68–71.
49 Gilles Deleuze, *Empiricism and Subjectivity: An Essay on Hume's Theory of Human Nature*, trans. Constantine Baundas (New York: Columbia University Press, 1991), p. 106.
50. Deleuze, *Empiricism and Subjectivity*, p. 105.
51. Deleuze and Guattari, *What is Philosophy?*, p. 18.
52. Ibid., p. 18.
53. Deleuze and Guattari, *Anti-Oedipus*, pp. 76–7.
54. Deleuze, *Difference and Repetition*, pp. 49, 51–2.
55. Henri Bergson, *Time and Free Will: an Essay on the Immediate Data of Consciousness*, trans. F.L. Pogson (New York: Dover Publications, 2001), pp. 128–32; Deleuze, *Bergsonism*, p. 15.
56. Deleuze, *Difference and Repetition*, p. 51.
57. Henri Bergson, *The Creative Mind*, trans. Mabelle L. Andison (New York: Philosophical Library, 1946), p. 129. Deleuze, *Bergsonism*, p. 15.
58. Deleuze, *Empiricism and Subjectivity*, p. 106.

59. Deleuze, *Nietzsche and Philosophy*, pp. 49–52, 84–7.
60. Deleuze, *Difference and Repetition*, p. 168.
61. In "Universal History from a Cosmopolitan Point of View," the notion of purposeful or teleological should be read as regulative. At the beginning of his *Groundwork for the Metaphysics of Morals*, Kant points out that we can never know that we are witnessing a goodwill (an instance of free will or morality). Natural inclinations may be determining our will behind our backs (i.e. unconsciously).
62. I am referring to Socrates critique of the figure of the misologist (Antisthenes?) in the *Phaedo* (89d–90c). The message of this passage seems to be that we can reject the notion of universals as forms, but if we reject the notion of universals as such we eliminate the ground of *logos* or rationality.
63. Deleuze, *Difference and Repetition*, p. 168.
64. Deleuze, *Negotiations*, p. 31.
65. Deleuze, *Difference and Repetition*, p. 157.
66. Slavoj Žižek, *Organs without Bodies: On Deleuze and Consequences* (New York: Routledge Press, 2003), pp. 12–3.
67. Deleuze, *Difference and Repetition*, p. 163.
68. Deleuze and Guattari, *What is Philosophy?*, p. 18.
69. Deleuze, *Difference and Repetition*, p. 163.
70. Deleuze and Guattari, *What is Philosophy?*, p. 28.
71. Ibid., p. 36.
72. These are elucidated in the first three chapters of Deleuze and Guattari's *What is Philosophy?*
73. Deleuze, *Nietzsche and Philosophy*, p. 115.
74. Ibid., p. xi.
75. Deleuze, *Difference and Repetition*, p. 159.
76. Todd May, *Reconsidering Difference: Nancy, Derrida, Levinas and Deleuze* (University Park, IL: Pennsylvania State University Press, 1997), p. 172.
77. Deleuze, *Empiricism and Subjectivity*, p. 106; Deleuze, *Bergsonism*, pp. 15–7.
78. Deleuze, *Empiricism and Subjectivity*, p. 106.
79. Deleuze, *Bergsonism*, p. 45.
80. Deleuze, *Difference and Repetition*, p. 178.
81. Deleuze and Guattari, *What is Philosophy?*, p. 27.
82. Ibid.
83. Deleuze, *Empiricism and Subjectivity*, p. 106.
84. Deleuze and Guattari, *What is Philosophy?*, p. 140.
85. Ibid., p. 111.
86. Deleuze, *Negotiations*, pp. 130–6.
87. Deleuze and Guattari, *What is Philosophy?*, p. 27.
88. Martial Guéroult, "The History of Philosophy as a Philosophical Problem," *Monist*, 53 (1969): 563–87.
89. Deleuze, *The Logic of Sense*, p. 158.
90. Deleuze, *Nietzsche and Philosophy*, pp. 70, 174.
91. Deleuze and Guattari, *What is Philosophy?*, p. 27.
92. Deleuze, *Difference and Repetition*, p. 137.
93. Deleuze and Guattari, *What is Philosophy?*, p. 37.
94. Deleuze, *Difference and Repetition*, p. 131.

95. Ibid., p. 167.
96. Ibid., p. 132.
97. Foucault, *Language, Counter-Memory, Practice*, p. 181.
98 Deleuze, *Difference and Repetition*, p. 131.
99. Ibid.
100. Ibid., p. 135.
101. Deleuze, *Nietzsche and Philosophy*, pp. 124–33.
102. Ibid., p. 127.
103. This way of formulating the Deleuzian real is the thesis of Peter Hallward, *Out of This World: Deleuze and the Philosophy of Creation* (New York: Verso, 2006).
104. Deleuze, *Nietzsche and Philosophy*, p. 111.
105. Deleuze, *The Logic of Sense*, pp. 157–8.
106. Ibid., pp. 137–8, 265–72; Deleuze, *Proust and Signs*, p. 41.
107. Deleuze, *Difference and Repetition*, pp. 70–9.
108. Ibid., pp. 79–85.
109. Deleuze, *Difference and Repetition*, pp. 130–1; Deleuze, *Proust and Signs*, pp. 15–7, 94–5; Deleuze, *Nietzsche and Philosophy*, p. 103.
110. Deleuze, *Proust and Signs*, p. 94.
111. Ibid.; *Difference and Repetition*, pp. 133, 165.
112. Deleuze, *Difference and Repetition*, p. 133.
113. Ibid., p. 148.
114. Ibid., p. 149; Deleuze, *Nietzsche and Philosophy*, p. 105.
115. John Austin, *How To Do Things With Words* (Cambridge, MA: Harvard University Press, 1962), p. 1.
116. Deleuze, *Proust and Signs*, p. 21–2
117. Deleuze, *Difference and Repetition*, p. 158.
118. Ibid., p. 135.
119. Ibid., p. 132.
120. Deleuze, *Difference and Repetition*, p. 130. When, in conversation with Foucault, Deleuze attacks representation in the sense of speaking for others his comments should be situated in relation to similar ones in *Difference and Repetition*. In particular the line in "Intellectuals and Power" about the injustice of speaking for others, should be understood in relation to Deleuze's accounts of recognition and common sense. Is Deleuze prohibiting the activist from speaking about others; is he requiring them to, narcissistically speak only of themselves? Of course not, and both Deleuze and Foucault in their exchange, speak of others and the situations of others. By representation (or "speaking for others") Deleuze means something quite specific. First there is the recognition of established values. As he says on page 135 of *Difference and Repetition*, "What is recognized is not only an object but also the values attached to an object." Then, these values are reinforced through the concealment of divergent experiences. This happens when the norms are cynically or noncynically passed off as common sense ("As we all know"). To see how the idea of the "injustice of speaking for others" is a slogan that opens up a complex set of political considerations (including a consideration of how and when one should speak for others). See Deleuze, *Negotiations*, p. 88.
121. Deleuze, *Difference and Repetition*, p. 148.

122. Deleuze, *Proust and Signs*, p. 95. For further discussion of violence or shock as a prerequisite for thought see also pp. 21, 23; and Deleuze, *Difference and Repetition*, p. 132.
123. Deleuze, *Proust and Signs*, p. 21; Deleuze, *Difference and Repetition*, p. 139.
124. Deleuze, *Nietzsche and Philosophy*, p. 103.
125. Deleuze, *Proust and Signs*, p.22.
126. Ibid.
127. Deleuze, *Nietzsche and Philosophy*, p. 105.
128. Deleuze, *Difference and Repetition*, p. 150.
129. Deleuze, *Negotiations*, p. 130.
130. Gilles Deleuze, *Cinema I: The Movement Image*, trans. Hugh Tomlinson and Barbara Habberjam (Minneapolis, MN: University of Minnesota Press, 2003), p. 208.
131. Deleuze, *Negotiations*, p. 90.
132. Deleuze, *Difference and Repetition*, p. 141.
133. Ibid., p. 144.
134. Gilles Deleuze, *Expressionism in Philosophy: Spinoza*, trans. Martin Joughin (New York: Zone Books, 1992), pp. 275–83; Gilles Deleuze, *Spinoza: Practical Philosophy*, trans. Robert Hurley (San Francisco: City Lights Books, 1988), pp. 31, 48–58.
135. Deleuze, *Difference and Repetition*, p. 143.
136. Deleuze, *Proust and Signs*, p. 97.
137. Deleuze, *Difference and Repetition*, p. 143.
138. Deleuze, *Proust and Signs*, pp. 41–4.
139. Deleuze, *Difference and Repetition*, pp. 135–6.
140. Deleuze, *Nietzsche and Philosophy*, p. 104.
141. Ibid., p. 105.
142. Ibid., p. 106.
143. Deleuze, *Difference and Repetition*, p. 186.
144. Foucault, *Discipline and Punish*, pp. 26, 39, 138, 218, 224–5; See also Gilles Deleuze, *Foucault*, trans. Sean Hand (Minneapolis, MN: University of Minnesota Press, 1988), pp. 36–7.
145. Deleuze, *Difference and Repetition*, p. 207.
146. Ibid., p. 207.
147. The first approach is exemplified by Keith-Ansell Pearson and Daniel Smith, the second by Todd May and Michael Hardt, the third by Slavoj Žižek.
148. Deleuze, *Difference and Repetition*, pp. 35–42, pp. 70–96.
149. Deleuze, *Nietzsche and Philosophy*, p. 62.
150. For Bergson's becoming Leibniz (his discussion of differential equations and curves) and becoming Spinoza (difference as *natura naturans* and *natura naturata*) see Deleuze, *Bergsonism*, pp. 27, 93.
151. Deleuze, *Bergsonism*, pp. 59–60.
152. Foucault, *Language, Counter-Memory, Practice*, p. 196.
153. Žižek, *Organs without Bodies*, pp. 20–1.
154. Deleuze, *Empiricism and Subjectivity*, pp. 98–101; Gilles Deleuze, *Pure Immanence: Essays on A Life*, trans. Anne Boyman (New York: Zone Books, 2005), pp. 37–8.
155. Deleuze, *Difference and Repetition*, p. 70.
156. Deleuze, *Difference and Repetition*, pp. 44–7. Deleuze, *Desert Islands*, pp. 19–20.

157. As mentioned previously, Deleuze's question "useful for whom?" encourages us to think of politics as a struggle between institutions (i.e. modes of organizing the body), see Deleuze, *Desert Islands*, pp. 20–1.
158. Deleuze, *Bergsonism*, pp. 17, 46–7, 75–6.
159. Deleuze, *Desert Islands*, p. 26. This point is also made in pp. 32–6, and in Deleuze, *Bergsonism*, pp. 21–9, and 92.
160. Henri Bergson, *Matter and Memory*, trans. N.M. Paul and W.S. Palmer (New York: Zone Books, 1991), pp. 28, 292–3, 304, 313.
161. Memory records "all the events of our daily life as they occur in time; it neglects not detail; it leaves to each fact, to each gesture, its place and date." See Bergson, *Matter and Memory*, p. 92.
162. Bergson, *Matter and Memory*, p. 220.
163. Ibid., p. 163.
164. Deleuze, *Bergsonism*, pp. 92–3.
165. Besides Deleuze's *Bergsonism*, the most helpful works on this transition are William May, "The Reality of Matter in the Metaphysics of Bergson," in *International Philosophical Quarterly*, 10: 4 (1970); P.A.Y. Gunter, "Bergson's Theory of Matter and Modern Cosmology," *Journal of the History of Ideas*, 32 (1971).
166. See Deleuze, *Bergsonism*, pp. 73–6, 91–4; May, "The Reality of Matter in the Metaphysics of Bergson," pp. 630–41; Mullarkey, *Bergson and Philosophy*, pp. 80–2.
167. Deleuze, *Bergsonism*, pp. 96–8; Deleuze, *Difference and Repetition*, pp. 208, 211–12.
168. Deleuze, *Bergsonism*, p. 107.
169. Deleuze, *Nietzsche and Philosophy*, pp. 6, 39–40.
170. Ibid., pp. 42–4.
171. Ibid., p. 42.
172. Ibid., pp. 8–10, 156–64.
173. Ibid., pp. 119–22.
174. Ibid., pp. 84–5.
175. Ibid., p. 53.
176. Ibid., pp. 25–7, 44.
177. Ibid., p. 26.
178. Ibid.
179. Deleuze, *Difference and Repetition*, p. 28.
180. See Plato's *Phaedo* 90c in *Plato: Complete Works*, eds. John M. Cooper and D.S. Hutchinson (Cambridge, MA: Hackett Publishing, 1997).
181. Deleuze, *Nietzsche and Philosophy*, pp. 147–8.
182. Ibid., pp. 68–9.
183. Ibid., p. 70.
184. Deleuze, *Difference and Repetition*, p. 35.
185. Deleuze describes the abstract machine of the debate between analogical, equivocal, and univocal conceptions of being in his January 14, 1974 lecture on *Anti-Oedipus* and *A Thousand Plateaus*. See http://www.webdeleuze.com/php/sommaire.html
186. This is from principle #51 in Rene Descartes, *Principles of Philosophy* in *The Philosophical Writings of Descartes Vol. II*, trans. John Cottingham, Robert Stoothoff, and Dugald Murdoch (New York: Cambridge University Press, 1984).

187. Descartes' *Principles of Philosophy*, numbers 51 and 52.
188. Deleuze, *Expressionism in Philosophy*, pp. 27–51.
189. Spinoza, *Ethics*: Part 1, definition 4.
190. Spinoza, *Ethics*: Part 1, the scholium following proposition 10.
191. Deleuze, *Expressionism in Philosophy*, pp. 29–39.
192. Ibid., pp. 99–128. For Spinoza's re-location of the logic of expression onto modifications and individuals see the *Ethics* Part 2, proposition 7 as well as the following corollary and scholium.
193. Deleuze, *Expressionism in Philosophy*, p. 49.
194. Allan B. Wolter, *The Transcendentals and Their Function in the Metaphysics of Duns Scotus* (St. Bonaventure, New York: The Franciscan Institute, 1946).
195. Ibid., pp. 14–5.
196. Ibid., pp. 21–30.
197. Deleuze, *Expressionism in Philosophy*, p. 64.
198. Allan B. Wolter, *The Transcendentals and Their Function in the Metaphysics of Duns Scotus*, pp. 53–54.
199. Deleuze, *Difference and Repetition*, p. 40.
200. Spinoza, *Ethics*: Part 2, proposition 21.
201. Spinoza, *Ethics*: appendix to Part 1; Part 3, the scholium following proposition 2.
202. Spinoza, *Ethics*: Part 3, the scholium following proposition 2.
203. Warren Montag, *Bodies, Masses, Power: Spinoza and His Contemporaries* (New York: Verso, 1999), p. xvii.
204. Deleuze, *Expressionism in Philosophy*, pp. 275–6; Deleuze, *Spinoza*, pp. 55–6; see also Spinoza, *Ethics*, II: 39.
205. Spinoza, *Ethics*: Part 2, propositions 11–13.
206. Spinoza, *Ethics*: Part 2, scholium 1 following proposition 40.
207. Deleuze, *Spinoza*, p. 54.
208. Deleuze, seminar on *Anti-Oedipus* and *A Thousand Plateaus*, 14 of January 1974.
209. Spinoza, *Ethics*, IV, the scholium following proposition 39.
210. Deleuze, *Spinoza: Practical Philosophy*, pp. 123–4; see also Gilles Deleuze, seminar on *Anti-Oedipus* and *A Thousand Plateaus*, 14 of January 1974.
211. Deleuze, *Nietzsche and Philosophy*, p. 39.
212. Deleuze, *Spinoza: Practical Philosophy*, p. 125.
213. Deleuze, *Spinoza: Practical Philosophy*, p. 97.
214. Spinoza, *Ethics*: Part 1, scholium 2 following proposition 33.
215. Deleuze, *Nietzsche and Philosophy*, p. 123.
216. Ibid., pp. 123–4.
217. Montag, *Bodies, Masses,and Power*, pp xx-i.
218. Spinoza, *Ethics*, III, the scholium following proposition 2.
219. Deleuze, *Nietzsche and Philosophy*, p. 62.
220. Spinoza, *Ethics*: Part 2 from the first definition following proposition 13 to the scholium following lemma 7.
221. Deleuze, *Bergsonism*, p. 18.
222. Deleuze, *Difference and Repetition*, pp. 70–96.
223. Ibid., pp. 35–42.
224. Ibid., p. 170.
225. Readers of Deleuze are indebted to Daniel Smith for his reconstruction of post-Kantianism and examination of the way Maimon's notion of the

differential informs Deleuzian difference. See his essays "Deleuze's Theory of Sensation: Overcoming the Kantian duality," in *Deleuze: A Critical Reader*, ed. Paul Patton (Oxford: Blackwell Publishing, 1997), pp. 29–56; "Deleuze on Leibniz: Difference, Continuity, and the Calculus," in *Current Continental Theory and Modern Philosophy*, ed. Stephen Daniel (Evanston, IL: Northwestern University Press, 2004), pp. 127–147.

226. Deleuze, *The Logic of Sense*, pp. 4–5; see also Brad Inwood, and L. P. Gerson, trans., *Hellenistic Philosophy: Introductory Readings*, II: 28–9, II: 44 (Cambridge, MA: Hackett Publishing, 1988).

227. Inwood and Gerson, *Hellenistic Philosophy*, II: 94–5.

228. Deleuze, *The Logic of Sense*, p. 158.

229. "There are also three good states [of the soul], joy, caution, and wish." Inwood and Gerson, *Hellenistic Philosophy*, II: 94: 116.

230. That the proposal of transcendental empiricism is a constant, and that the meaning of such an empiricism is a constant, can be discerned in the absolute correspondence between the following passages: Deleuze, *Desert Islands*, pp. 30, 36–7, *Bergsonism*, pp. 23–5, *Nietzsche and Philosophy*, pp. 50–2, *Difference and Repetition*, pp. 173–4, *The Logic of Sense*, pp. 105–6. These passages do not represent a departure from the vision of empiricism espoused in *Empiricism and Subjectivity*.

231. Deleuze's most thorough treatment of Kant's deduction can be found in his seminar on Kant, 14 of March 1978.

232. My account of Maimon's philosophy is based primarily on the one provided by Frederick C. Beiser in *The Fate of Reason: German Philosophy from Kant to Fichte*, "The Context and Problematic of Post-Kantian Philosophy," "The Enlightenment and Idealism," and his introduction to the *Cambridge Companion to Hegel* entitled "Hegel and the Problem of Metaphysics." Also helpful were Paul W. Frank's essays "All or Nothing: Systematicity and Nihilism in Jacobi Reinhold and Maimon" and "Jewish Philosophy after Kant: The Legacy of Salomon Maimon." Deleuze's relationship to post-Kantian philosophy, in particular Maimon, is the theme of a series of incredibly valuable essays by Daniel Smith: "Deleuze, Hegel, and the Post-Kantian Tradition;" "Deleuze, Kant, and the Theory of Immanent Ideas;" "Deleuze on Leibniz: Difference, Continuity, and the Calculus;" "Deleuze's Theory of Sensation: Overcoming the Kantian Dualism." Smith's articles drew my attention to the work of Beiser cited above.

233. Deleuze, *Bergsonism*, p. 23.

234. Leonard Lawler discusses the requirement of heterogeneity or nonresemblance in *Thinking through French Philosophy: The Being of the Question* (Bloomington: Indiana University Press, 2003), pp. 80–1. In his seminar on Kant, 14 of March 1978, Deleuze links the Kantian redefinition of the phenomenon to phenomenology. The classic opposition between being and appearance is rendered secondary to what appears as it appears. In the opening of *Being and Nothingness* (section one of the introduction) Sartre captures with the utmost precision this substitution along with the related redefinition of essence as the essence of an appearance.

235. Deleuze, *Difference and Repetition*, pp. 187–9; Deleuze and Guattari, *What is Philosophy*, p. 49.

236. Deleuze, *Difference and Repetition*, p. 40.

237. Once again I am suggesting that the dice-throw is the Deleuzian counter-part to the *Phaedo* 89d–90c.
238. The differential calculus is discussed in *Difference and Repetition*, pp. 170–82. The two philosophical applications are treated at length in the second and third lectures from the 1980 Leibniz course.
239. Deleuze, *Difference and Repetition*, p. 172.
240. Deleuze, seminar on Leibniz, 29 of April 1980.
241. Ibid.
242. Ibid.
243. Deleuze, *Difference and Repetition*, p. 177.
244. My exposition of this point follows Deleuze, seminar on Leibniz, 15 of April 1980.
245. Deleuze, seminar on Leibniz, 15 of April 1980.
246. Deleuze, seminar on Leibniz, 22 of April 1980.
247. See Deleuze's analysis of Leibniz's essay "Justification of the Calculus of Infinitesimals by the calculus of ordinary algebra" in his seminar on Leibniz, 15 of April 1980.
248. Deleuze, seminar on Leibniz, 29 of April 1980.
249. Deleuze, *Difference and Repetition*, p. 213; see also Deleuze, seminar on Leibniz, 29 of April 1980.
250. Deleuze, *Difference and Repetition*, pp. 173–4; see also Deleuze, seminar on Leibniz, 29 of April 1980.
251. Deleuze, seminar on Leibniz, 29 of April 1980.
252. See the essay "The Method of Dramatization" in Deleuze, *Desert Islands*, p. 115.
253. Deleuze, *Bergsonism*, p. 56.
254. While insightful, Daniel Smith's account of the Maimon-Deleuze and Leibniz-Deleuze connection runs into problems when he tries to hook his exposition of Maimon and Leibniz back onto Deleuze. Instead of moving in the direction of Deleuze's metaphysics, the Deleuzian ground is depicted as simply the ground of experience. Deleuze's philosophy is positioned as a tool for describing lived experience. This despite the fact that Deleuze attacks the idea that philosophy is the practice of representing lived experience. Deleuze, *What is Philosophy*, pp. 141–3.
255. Deleuze, *Difference and Repetition*, p. 209.
256. Ibid., p. 209.
257. Ibid., p. 201.
258. Ibid., p. 209.
259. Ibid.
260. Constantin V. Boundas, "What Difference does Deleuze's Difference Make?" in *Deleuze and Philosophy*, ed. Constantine Boundas (Edinburgh: Edinburgh University Press, 2006), pp. 3–30.
261. Ibid., pp. 186, 207–8; Deleuze, *Foucault*, pp. 37–8.
262. Deleuze, *Difference and Repetition*, pp. 210–1.
263. Ibid., p. 208.
264. Deleuze, *The Logic of Sense*, pp. 4–5; Inwood and Gerson, *Hellenistic Philosophy*, II: 49.
265. Inwood and Gerson, *Hellenistic Philosophy*, II: 20.
266. Inwood and Gerson, *Hellenistic Philosophy*, II: 51.

267. Deleuze, *The Logic of Sense*, pp. 5–6.
268. Inwood and Gerson, *Hellenistic Philosophy*, II: 20: 151, II: 23: 28.
269. For the definition of incorporeal see Inwood and Gerson, *Hellenistic Philosophy*, II: 28, II: 29. For an enumeration of the various incorporeals see *Hellenistic Philosophy*, II: 20: 140–1.
270. On the Epicurean void see Inwood and Gerson, *Hellenistic Philosophy*, I–78, I–79. On the Stoic void see II: 37.
271. Deleuze's analysis of the *lekton* draws heavily upon a small book by Émile Bréhier, *La Théorie des incorporels dans l'ancien stoicisme*.
272. Inwood and Gerson, *Hellenistic Philosophy*, II: 55.
273. Ibid., II–3: 63.
274. Ibid., II: 3: 65.
275. Ibid., I: 74.
276. Deleuze and Guattari treat the analytic approach to the distinction between sense and reference in *What is Philosophy?*, pp. 136–7 as well as in *The Logic of Sense*, pp. 12–3.
277. Deleuze and Guattari, *The Logic of Sense*, p. 21.
278. Ibid.
279. Ibid., p. 102.
280. Žižek, *Organs without Bodies*, p. 21.
281. Deleuze, *Nietzsche and Philosophy*, pp. 52–3.
282. Žižek, *Organs without Bodies*, p 20.
283. Deleuze, *Negotiations*, p. 90.
284. Deleuze, *The Logic of Sense*, pp. 53, 253.
285. Ibid., p. 253.
286. Ibid., p. 254; Deleuze, *Difference and Repetition*, p. 60.
287. Deleuze, *Difference and Repetition*, p. 127.
288. Ibid., p. 207.
289. Deleuze, *The Logic of Sense*, pp. 94–5.
290. Deleuze and Guattari describe a "hijacking" as a radical change of meaning – as the production of a new incorporeal reflecting a reorganization of a host of bodies. See Deleuze and Guattari, *A Thousand Plateaus*, p. 81.
291. Deleuze and Guattari, *A Thousand Plateaus*, p. 83.
292. Deleuze, *The Logic of Sense*, p. 157.
293. Ibid., p. 150.
294. Ibid., pp. 157–8.

Bibliography

Books

Acker, Kathy. *Blood and Guts in High School*. New York: Grove Press,1984.
———. *Bodies of Work*. London: Serpent's Tail, 1997.
———. *Empire of the Senseless: A Novel*. New York: Grove Press, 1988.
———. *Hannibal Lecter, My Father*. Edited by Sylvere Lotringer. New York: Semiotext(e), 1991.
Althusser, Louis. *The Future Lasts For Ever: A Memoir*. Translated by Richard Veasey. New York: The New Press, 1993.
———. *For Marx*. Translated by Ben Brewster. Brooklyn, NY: Verso, 1996.
Austin, John. *How to Do Things with Words*. Cambridge, MA: Harvard University Press, 1962.
Ayer, A. J. *Language, Truth and Logic*. New York: Dover Publications, 1952.
———, ed. *Logical Positivism*. Glencoe, IL: The Free Press of Glencoe, 1959.
Badiou, Alain. *Deleuze: The Clamor of Being*. Translated by Louise Burchill. Minneapolis, MN: University of Minnesota Press, 2000.
———. *Manifesto for Philosophy*. Translated by Norman Madarasz. New York: State University of New York Press, 1999.
Balibar, Etienne. *Philosophy of Marx*. Translated by Chris Turner. New York: Verso, 1995.
Bataille, Georges. *The Accursed Share Vol.1: Consumption*. Translated by Robert Hurley. New York: Zone Books, 1989.
Beiser, Fredrick C. "The Context and Problematic of Post-Kantian Philosophy," in *A Companion to Continental Philosophy*. Edited by Simon Critchley and William R. Schroeder, 21–34. Oxford: Blackwell Publishing, 1999.
———. "The Enlightenment and Idealism," in *The Cambridge Companion to German Idealism*, 18–36. New York: Cambridge University Press, 2000.
———. *The Fate of Reason: German Philosophy from Kant to Fichte*. Cambridge, MA: Harvard University Press, 1987.
———. "Introduction: Hegel and the Problem of Metaphysics," in *The Cambridge Companion to Hegel*. Edited by Fredrick C. Beiser, 1–24. New York: Cambridge University Press, 1993.
Benjamin, Walter. *Illuminations: Essays and Reflections* (New York: Schocken Books, 1968).
Bergson, Henri. *The Creative Mind*. Translated by Mabelle L. Andison. New York: Philosophical Library, 1946.
———. *Matter and Memory*. Translated by N.M. Paul and W.S. Palmer. New York: Zone Books, 1991.
———. *Time and Free Will: An Essay on the Immediate Data of Consciousness*. Translated by F.L. Pogson New York: Dover Publications, 2001.
Blanchot, Maurice. *The Infinite Conversation*. Translated by Susan Hanson. Minneapolis, MN: University of Minnesota Press, 1993.
Boundas, Constantin V. "Deleuze – Bergson: An Ontology of the Virtual," in *Deleuze: A Critical Reader*. Edited by Paul Patton, 81–106. Oxford: Blackwell Publishing, 1997.

—— "Deleuze: Serialization and Subject-formation," in *Gilles Deleuze and the Theater of Philosophy*. Edited by Constantin Boundas and Dorothea Olkowski, 99–116. London: Routledge, 1994.

——. "What Difference Does Deleuze's Difference Make?" in *Deleuze and Philosophy*. Edited by Constantine Boundas, 3–30. Edinburgh: Edinburgh University Press: 2006.

Braidotti, Rosi. *Patterns of Dissonance: A Study of Women in Contemporary Philosophy*. Translated by Elizabeth Guild. New York: Routledge Press, 1991.

Brusseau's, James. *Isolated Experiences: Gilles Deleuze and the Solitudes of Reversed Platonism*. Albany, NY: State University of New York Press, 1998.

Buchanan, Ian, ed. *A Deleuzian Century?* Durham, NC: Duke University, 1999.

Butler, Judith. *Gender Trouble: Feminism and the Subversion of Identity*. New York: Routledge Press, 1990.

Carnap, Rudolf. "The Elimination of Metaphysics through Logical Analysis of Language," in *Logical Positivism*, ed. Alfred J. Ayer (Glencoe, IL: The Free Press of Glencoe, 1959), pp. 78–80.

Cixous, Hélène and Catherine Clément. *The Newly Born Woman*. Translated by Betsy Wing. Minneapolis, MN: University of Minnesota Press.

Conway, Jay. "Deleuze's Hume and Creative History of Philosophy," in *Current Continental Theory and Modern Philosophy*. Edited by Stephen Daniel. Evanston, IL: Northwestern University Press, 2004.

Davis, Angela Y. *Angela Davis: An Autobiography*. New York: International Publishers, 1988.

——. *Women, Race, and Class*. New York: Vintage, 1983.

Davis, Mike. *City of Quartz: Excavating The Future in Los Angeles*. Brooklyn, NY: Verso, 2006.

Delanda, Manuel. *Intensive Science and Virtual Philosophy*. New York: Continuum, 2002.

Deleuze, Gilles. *Bergsonism*. Translated by Hugh Tomlinson and Barbara Habberjam. New York: Zone Books, 1988.

——. *Cinema I: The Movement Image*. Translated by Hugh Tomlinson and Barbara Habberjam. Minneapolis, MN: University of Minnesota Press, 2003.

——. *David Hume, sa vie, son oeuvre*. Paris: Presses universitaires de France, 1952.

——. *Desert Islands and Other Texts (1953–1974)*. Edited by David Lapoujade. Translated by Mike Taormina. Brooklyn, NY: Semiotext(e), 2004.

——. *Difference and Repitition*. Translated by Paul Patton. New York: Columbia University Press, 1994.

——. *Empiricism and Subjectivity: An Essay on Hume's Theory of Human Nature*. Translated by Constantine Baundas. New York: Columbia University Press, 1991.

——. *Essays Critical and Clinical*. Translated by Daniel W. Smith and Michael A. Greco. Minneapolis, MN: University of Minnesota Press, 1997.

——. *Expressionism in Philosophy: Spinoza*. Translated by Martin Joughin. New York: Zone Books, 1992.

——. *Foucault*. Translated by Sean Hand. Minneapolis, MN: University of Minnesota Press, 1988.

——. *Kant's Critical Philosophy: The Doctrine of the Faculties*. Translated by Hugh Tomlinson and Barbara Habberjam. Minneapolis, MN: University of Minnesota Press, 1984.

Deleuze, Gilles. *The Logic of Sense.* Translated by Mark Lester and Charles Stivale. New York: Columbia University Press, 1990.

——. *Negotiations (1972–1990).* Translated by Martin Joughin. New York: Columbia University Press, 1995.

——. *Nietzsche and Philosophy.* Translated by Hugh Tomlinson. Minneapolis, MN: University of Minnesota Press, 1983.

——. *Proust and Signs: The Complete Text.* Translated by Richard Howard. Minneapolis, MN: University of Minnesota Press, 2000.

——. *Pure Immanence: Essays on A Life.* Translated by Anne Boyman. New York: Zone Books, 2001.

——. *Spinoza, Practical Philosophy.* Translated by Robert Hurley. San Fransisco: City Lights Books, 1988.

——. *Two Regimes of Madness, Revised Edition: Texts and Interviews 1975–1995.* Edited by David Lapoujade. Translated by Ames Hodges and Mike Taormina. Brooklyn, NY: Semiotext(e), 2006.

Deleuze, Gilles and Guattari, Félix. *Anti-Oedipus: Capitalism and Schizophrenia.* Translated by Robert Hurley, Mark Seem and Helen R. Lane. New York: Viking, 1977.

——. *Kafka: For a Minor Literature.* Translated by Dana Polan. Minneapolis, MN: University of Minnesota Press, 1986.

——. *A Thousand Plateaus: Capitalism and Schizophrenia.* Translated by Brian Massumi. Minneapolis, MN: University of Minnesota Press, 1987.

——. *What Is Philosophy?* New York: Columbia University Press, 1994.

Deleuze, Gilles and Parnet Claire. *Dialogues.* Translated by Janis Tomlinson and Barbara Habberjam. New York: Columbia University Press, 1987.

Deleuze, Giles and von Sacher-Masoch Leopold. *Masochism: Coldness and Cruelty & Venus and Furs.* Translated by Jean McNeil. New York: Zone Books, 1991.

Derrida, Jacques. "Before the Law," *Acts of Literature.* Edited by Derek Attridge,181– 220. New York, Routledge, 1992.

——. "Cogito and The History of Madness," in *Writing and Difference.* Translated by Alan Bass, 31–63. Chicago: The University of Chicago Press, 1978.

——. "*Différance,*" in *Margins of Philosophy.* Translated by Alan Bass, 1–28. Chicago: University of Chicago Press, 1982.

——. "Force of Law: The Mystical Foundation of Authority," *Acts of Religion,* Edited by Jil Anidjar, 228–298. New York: Routledge, 2002.

——. *Negotiations: Interventions and Interviews 1971–2001.* Edited by Elizabeth Rottenberg. Palo Alto, CA: Stanford University Press, 2002.

——. *Of Gammatology.* Translated by Gayatri Chakravorty Spivak. Baltimore: Johns Hopkins University Press, 1976.

——. *Positions.* Translated by Alan Bass. Chicago: University of Chicago Press, 1981.

——. "Signature Event Context," in *Margins of Philosophy.* Translated by Alan Bass, 307–330. Chicago: University of Chicago Press, 1982.

——. *Specters of Marx: the State of the Debt, the Work of Mourning, and the New International.* New York: Routledge, 1994.

——. "Structure, Sign, and Play in the Discourse of the Human Sciences," in *Writing and Difference.* Translated by Alan Bass, 278–294. Chicago: The University of Chicago Press, 1978.

Descartes, Rene. "Principles of Philosophy," in *The Philosophical Writings of Descartes Vol. II.* Translated by John Cottingham, Robert Stoothoff, and Dugald Murdoch. New York, Cambridge University Press, 1984.

Dosse, Francois. *The History of Structuralism Vol. I: The Rising Sign.* Translated by Deborah Glassman. Minneapolis, MN: University of Minnesota Press, 1997.

———. *The History of Structuralism Vol. II: The Sign Sets.* Translated by Deborah Glassman. Minneapolis, MN: University of Minnesota Press, 1998.

Foucault, Michel. *Archaeology of Knowledge and the Discourse on Language.* Translated by A.M. Seridan Smith. New York: Pantheon Books, 1972.

———. *Discipline and Punish: The Birth of The Prison.* Translated by Alan Sheridan. New York: Vintage, 1977.

———. *Language, Counter-Memory, Practice: Selected Essays and Interviews.* Edited by Donald F. Bouchard. New York: Cornell University Press, 1980.

———. *Madness and Civilization.* Translated by Richard Howard. New York: Vintage, 1965.

———. *Mental Illness and Psychology.* Translated by Alan Sheridan. Berkeley, CA: University of California Press, 1987.

———. *Power: Essential Works of Foucault, 1954–1984, Vol. III,* ed. James D. Faubion, trans. Robert Hurley, Paul Rainbow, and Colin Gordon (New York: New Press, 2000), p. 17.

Franks, Paul W. "All or Nothing: Systematicity and Nihilism in Jacobi Reinhold and Maimon," in *The Cambridge Companion to German Idealism,* 95–116. New York: Cambridge University Press, 2000.

———. "Jewish Philosophy after Kant: The Legacy of Salomon Maimon," in *The Cambridge Companion to Modern Jewish Philosophy.* Edited by Michael L. Morgan, 53–79. New York: Cambridge University Press, 2007.

Gadamer, Hans-Georg. *Truth and Method.* Translated by Joel Weinsheimer and Donald G. Marshall. New York: Continuum, 2004.

Gatens, Moira. "Through a Spinozist Lens: Ethology, Difference, and Power," *Deleuze: A Critical Reader.* Edited by Paul Patton, 162–187. Oxford: Blackwell Publishing, 1997.

Guattari, Félix. *Chaosophy.* Translated by Sylvere Lotringer. New York: Semiotext(e), 1995.

———. *Molecular Revolution: Psychiatry and Politics.* Translated by Rosemary Sheed. New York: Penguin, 1984.

———. *Soft Subversions.* Translated by Sylvere Lotringer. Brooklyn, NY: Semiotext(e), 1996.

Guerlac, Suzanne. *Thinking in Time: An Introduction to Henri Bergson.* New York: Cornell University Press, 2006.

Gower, Barry, ed. *Logical Positivism in Perspective.* Totowa, NJ: Barnes & Noble Books.

Guyer, Paul. "Absolute Idealism and the Rejection of Kantian Dualism," in *The Cambridge Companion to German Idealism.* Edited by Karl Ameriks, 37–56. New York: Cambridge University Press, 2000.

Hadot, Pierre. *Philosophy as a Way of Life.* Translated by Michael Chase. Oxford: Blackwell Publishers, Ltd.

———. *What is Ancient Philosophy?* Translated by Michael Chase. Cambridge, MA: Belknap Press, 2004.

Hallward, Peter. *Out of this World: Deleuze and the Philosophy of Creation*. New York: Verso, 2006.

Hammett, Dashiell. *Red Harvest*. New York: Vintage, 1992.

Hardt, Michael. *Gilles Deleuze: An Apprenticeship in Philosophy*. Minneapolis, MN: University of Minnesota Press, 1993.

Himes, Chester. *My Life of Absurdity: The Later Years*. New York: Thunder's Mouth Press, 1976.

Horkheimer, Max. "Traditional and Critical Theory," in *Critical Theory: Selected Essays*. Translated by Mathew J. O'Connell et al. New York: Continuum, 1982.

Holland, Eugene. *Deleuze and Guattari's Anti-Oedipus: Introduction to Schizoanalyis*. New York: Routledge, 1999.

Hollier, Denis ed. *The College of Sociology: Theory and History of Literature*. Minneapolis, MN: Minnesota Press, 1988.

Hume, David. *Enquiries Concerning Human Understanding and Concerning the Principle of Morals*. Oxford: Clarendon Press, 1975.

Huyssen, Andreas. "Mapping the Postmodern," in *Feminism/Postmodernism*. Edited by Linda Nicholson, 234–277. New York: Routledge, 1990.

Inwood, Brad, and L. P. Gerson, trans. *Hellenistic Philosophy: Introductory Readings*. Cambridge, MA: Hackett Publishing, 1988.

Jameson, Fredric. *Postmodernism, or, the Cultural Logic of Late Capitalism*. Durham, NC: Duke University Press, 1991.

Jardin, Alice. *Gynesis: Configuration of Woman and Modernity*. Ithaca, NY: Cornell University Press, 1985.

Kant, Immanuel. *Groundwork for the Metaphysics of Morals*. Edited by Mary Gregor. New York. Cambridge University Press, 1998.

——. "Idea for a Universal History from a Cosmopolitan Point of View," in *Basic Writings of Kant*. Edited by Allen W. Wood. Translated by Carl J Friedrich. New York: Modern Library, 2001.

Kojève, Alexandre. *Introduction to the Reading of Hegel: Lectures on the Phenomenology of Spirit*. Assembled by Raymond Queneau. Edited by Allan Bloom. Translated by James H. Nichols Jr. Ithaca, NY: Cornell University Press, 1980.

Kristeva, Julia. *Language – the Unknown: An Introduction into Linguistics*. Translated by Anne M. Menke. New York: Columbia University Press, 1989.

Lawler, Leonard. *Thinking Through French Philosophy: The Being of the Question*. Bloomington, IN: Indiana University Press, 2003.

Lévi-Strauss, Claude. *The Naked Man*. Translated by John and Doreen Weightman. New York: Harper and Row Publishers, 1981.

——. *The Savage Mind*. Translated by George Veidenfield. Chicago: University of Chicago Press, 1962.

——. *Tristes Tropiques: An Anthropological Study of Primitive Societies in Brazil*. Translated by John Russell. New York: Atheneum, 1971.

Lloyd, Genevieve. *The Man of Reason: "male" and "female" in Western Philosophy*. Minneapolis, MN: University of Minnesota Press, 1993.

Lotringer, Sylvère. "Doing Theory," in *French Theory in America*. Edited by Sylvere Lotringer and Sande Cohen, 125–162. New York: Routledge, 2001.

Lotringer, Sylvère and Cohen Sande. "Introduction: A Few Theses on French Theory in America," in *French Theory in America*. Edited by Sylvere Lotringer and Sande Cohen, 1–12. New York: Routledge, 2001.

Lyotard, Jean-Francois. *The Postmodern Explained*. Minneapolis, MN: University of Minnesota Press, 1992.

Marcuse, Herbert. *One Dimensional Man*. Boston: Beacon Press, 1991.

Marx, Karl. *The Marx-Engels Reader*. Edited by Robert C. Tucker. New York: W. W. Norton, 1978.

May, Todd. *Gilles Deleuze: An Introduction*. New York: Cambridge University Press, 2005.

———. *Reconsidering Difference: Nancy, Derrida, Levinas and Deleuze*. University Park, IL: Pennsylvania State University Press, 1997.

Montag, Warren. *Bodies, Masses, Power: Spinoza and His Contemporaries*. New York: Verso, 1999.

Mullarkey, John. *Bergson and Philosophy*. Edinburgh: Edinburgh University Press: 2000.

Murphy, Timothy. *Wising Up the Marks: The Amodern William Burroughs*. Berkeley, CA and Los Angeles: University of California Press, 1998.

Nicholson, Linda, ed. *Feminism/Postmodernism*. New York: Routledge Press, 1990.

Nye, Andrea. *Words of Power*. New York: Routledge Press, 1990.

Olkowski, Dorthea. *Gilles Deleuze and the Ruin of Representation*. Berkeley, CA: University of California Press, 1999.

Pearson, Keith Ansell. "Deleuze, Philosophy, and Immanence," in *Deleuze and Religion*. Edited by Mary Bryden, 141–155. New York: Routledge Press, 2001.

Plato. *Plato: Complete Works*. Edited by John M. Cooper and D.S. Hutchinson. Cambridge, MA: Hackett Publishing, 1997.

Proust, Marcel. *Remembrance of Things Past Vol. I – III*. Translated by C. K. Scott Moncrieff and Terence Kilmartin. New York: Random House Press, 1981.

Queneau, Raymond. *The Sunday of Life*. Translated by Barbara Wright. New York: A New Directions Book, 1977.

Quine, Willard Van Orman. *From A Logical Point of View: Logico-Philosophical Essays*. Cambridge, MA: Harvard University Press, 1964.

———. *Ontological Relativity and Other Essays*. New York: Columbia University Press, 1969.

Rajchman, John. *The Deleuze Connections*. Cambridge, MA: The MIT Press, 2000.

Rella, Franco. *The Myth of The Other: Lacan, Foucault, Deleuze, Bataille*. Translated by Nelson Moe. College Park, MD: Maisonneuve Press, 1994.

Rorty, Richard. *Consequences of Pragmatism: Essays, 1972–1980*. Minneapolis, MN: University of Minnesota Press, 1982.

———. *Contingency, Irony and Solidarity*. New York: Cambridge, 1989.

———. *Essays on Heidegger and Others: Philosophical Papers Vol. 2*. New York: Cambridge University Press, 1996.

———. *The Linguistic Turn: Essay in Philosophical Method (With Two Retrospective Essays)*. Edited by Richard Rorty. Chicago: University of Chicago Press, 1992.

———. *Philosophy and the Mirror of Nature*. New Jersey: Princeton University Press, 1979.

Sartre, Jean-Paul. *Anti-Semite and Jew*. Translated by George J. Becker. New York: Schocken Books, 1948.

Saussure, Ferdinand. *Course in General Linguistics*. Edited by Charles Bally and Albert Sechehaye. Translated by Roy Harris. La Falle, IL: Open Court Publishing, 1986.

Scholder, Amy, Carla Harryman and Avital Ronell, eds. *Lust for Life: On the Writings of Kathy Acker*. Brooklyn, NY: Verso, 2006.

Searle, John. "What is a Speech Act?" in *Readings in the Philosophy of Language*. Edited by Jay F. Rosenberg and Charles Travis. Englewood Cliffs, NJ: Prentice-Hall inc., 1971.

Smith, Daniel W. "Deleuze, Kant, and the Theory of Immanent Ideas," in *Deleuze and Philosophy*. Edited by Constantine Boundas, 43–61. Edinburgh: Edinburgh University Press: 2006.

——. "Deleuze on Leibniz: Difference, Continuity and the Calculus," in *Current Continental Theory and Modern Philosophy*. Edited by Stephen Daniel. Evanston, IL: Northwestern University Press, 2004.

——. "Deleuze's Theory of Sensation: Overcoming the Kantian Duality," in *Deleuze: A Critical Reader*. Edited by Paul Patton, 29–56. Oxford: Blackwell Publishing, 1997.

Spinoza, Baruch. *Completed Works*. Edited by Michael L. Morgan. Translated by Samuel Shirley. Indianapolis, IN: Hackett Publishing, 2002.

Spivak, Gayatri Chakravorty. "Can the Subaltern Speak?" in Marxism and the Interpretation of Culture. Edited by C, Nelson and L. Grossberg. 271–313. Basingstoke: Macmillan, 1988.

Tournier, Michel. *Friday*. Translated by Norman Denny. Baltimore: Johns Hopkins, 1997.

——. "Gilles Deleuze," in *Deleuze and Religion*. Translated by Walter Redfern. Edited by Mary Bryden. New York: Routledge Press, 2001.

Vernant, Jean-Pierre. *The Origins of Greek Thought*. Ithaca, NY: Cornell University Press, 1982.

Wahl, Jean. *The Pluralist Philosophies of England and America*. London: The Open Court Company, 1925.

——. *Vers le concrete: études d'histoire de la philosophie contemporaine*. Paris: Vrin, 1932.

Wolter, Allan B. *The Transcendentals and Their Function in the Metaphysics of Duns Scotus*. St. Bonaventure, New York: The Franciscan Institute, 1946.

Williams, Patrick and Laura Chrisman. *Colonial Discourse and Postcolonial Theory (A Reader)*. New York: Columbia University Press, 1994.

Žižek, Slavoj. *Organs without Bodies: On Deleuze and Consequences*. New York: Routledge Press, 2003.

Journal & Online Articles

Arnott, Stephen J. "Solipsism and the Possibility of Community in Deleuze's Ethics." *Contre temps* 2 (2001): 109–123.

Baugh, Bruce. "Deleuze and Empiricism." *Journal of the British Society for Phenomenology* 24:1 (1993): 15–31.

——. "Transcendental Empiricism: Deleuze's Response to Hegel." *Man and World* 25 (1992): 133–148.

Borradori, Giovanna. "The Temporalization of Difference: Reflections on Deleuze's Interpretation of Bergson." *Continental Philosophy Review* 34 (2001): 1–20.

Boundas, Constantin V. "Foreclosure of the Other: From Sartre to Deleuze," in *Journal of the British Society for Phenomenology* 24:1 (1993): 32–43.

Burger, Christa. "The Reality of "Machines," Notes on the Rhizome-Thinking of Deleuze and Guattari," translated by Simon Srebrny in *Telos* 64 (Summer 1985): 33–44.

Deleuze, Gilles. "Les cour de Gilles Deleuze." *Web Deleuze* http://www.webde-leuze.com /php/sommaire.html (January 1, 2009).

Frank, Manfred. "The World as Will and Representation: Deleuze and Guattari's Critique of Capitalism as Schizo-Analysis and Schizo-Discourse." *Telos* 57 (Fall 1983): 166–176.

Friedman, Ellen G. "A Conversation with Kathy Acker." *The Review of Contemporary Fiction* 9:3 (Fall 1989): 12–22.

Goulimari, Pelagia. "A Minoritarian Feminism? Things to Do with Deleuze and Guattari." *Hypatia* 14:2 (Spring 1999): 97–120.

Guéroult, Martial. "The History of Philosophy as a Philosophical Problem." *Monist* 53 (1969): 563–587.

Gunter, P.A.Y. "Bergson's Theory of Matter and Modern Cosmology." *Journal of the History of Ideas* 32 (1971): 525–542.

Kupers, Terry A. Review of *Anti Oedipus: Capitalism and Schizophrenia*, by Gilles Deleuze and Félix Guattari. Translated by Robert Hurley, Mark Seem and Helen Lane. *Telos* 17 (Fall 1973): 242–248.

Lotringer, Sylvère. "After the Avant-Garde," http://www.societyofcontrol.com/library/k-o/lothringer_after_the_avant-garde.txt (January 1, 2009).

——. "Better Than Life – My Life in the 80s." *Artforum* 41:8 (April 2003): 194–197.

May, William. "The Reality of Matter in the Metaphysics of Bergson," in *International Philosophical Quarterly* 10: 4 (1970): 611–642.

Montag, Warren. "Can the Subaltern Speak and Other Transcendental Questions," *Cultural Logic: An Electronic Journal of Marxist Theory and Practice* 1:2 (Spring 1998): 9 paragraphs.

Patton, Paul. "Conceptual Politics and the War Machine in 'Mille Plateaux'." *Sub-Stance* 44/45 (1984): 61–80.

Pearson, Keith Ansell. "The Reality of the Virtual: Bergson and Deleuze." *MLN* 120:5 (2005): 1112–1127.

Piercey, Robert. "The Spinoza-intoxicated Man: Deleuze on Expression." *Man and World* 29 (1996): 269–281.

Quine, Willard Van Orman. "On Empirically Equivalent Systems of the World." *Erkenntnis* Vol.9: 3 (1975): 313- 328.

Siegel, Carol. "The Madness Outside Gender: Travels with Don Quixote and Saint Foucault." *Rhizomes* 1 (Fall 2000), http://www.rhizomes.net/issue1/index.html.

Smith, Daniel W. "Deleuze, Hegel and the Post-Kantian Tradition." *Philosophy Today* 44 (2000): 119–131.

Spelman, Elizabeth. "Woman as Body: Ancient and Contemporary Views." *Feminist Studies* 8:1 (Spring 1982), pp. 109–31.

Stivale, Charles. "The Literary Element in 'Mille Plateaux': The New Cartography of Deleuze and Guattari." *Sub-Stance* 44/45 (1984): 20–32.

Widder, Nathan. "The Rights of Simulacra: Deleuze and the Univocity of Being." *Continental Philosophy Review* 34 (2001): 437–453.

Žižek, Slavoj. "Deleuze's Platonism: Ideas as Real." *Lacan Ink*, http://www.lacan.com/ zizrealac.htm (January 1, 2009).

——. "Repeating Lenin." *Lacan Ink*, http://www.lacan.com/replenin.htm (January 1, 2009).

Index

abstract machine
of academic philosophy, 2, 6–9,
11, 22, 24, 27–30, 35–44, 68, 74,
83–7, 107–24, 133, 138, 142, 148,
150, 152, 154, 159, 168, 170–2,
221–2, 224–5
of capitalism, 27, 38, 78, 134, 82,
86, 106, 161, 172, 176, 200,
216–17, 240 n.24
debate over meaning of being as,
191–2, 245 n.185
defined, 10, 72, 96, 110, 122
dogmatic image of thought as,
155–6, 161
of Deleuze's philosophy, 23–34, 37,
44, 110, 127–8, 205
of disciplinary power, 176, 216–17,
222
of the end of philosophy, 129–32
of the history of philosophy,
136–9
of language, 111–19, 172
literary genres as, 94–8, 101–5
of Oedipus, 161
of opinion, 86
of phenomenology, 71–3
of philosophical discourse, 107–24
philosophical systems as, 46, 145
of revolution, 66
of structuralism, 71–3
see also concept, difference as a
differential, Ideas, Problem
abstraction, practice of, 65–6, 84,
95–6, 100, 102, 110–14, 117–18,
128–9 148–9, 179, 182, 185
Bergson's version, 95, 149, 182, 185
Deleuze's version, 65–6, 84, 95–6,
102, 110, 114, 129, 148, 179
traditional version, 95–6, 100,
111–14, 117–18, 128, 182
academic, the conceptual persona of,
11, 37, 83–7, 110, 121–4, 148, 159,
171–2, 224–5

academic philosophy, 2, 6–9, 11, 22,
24, 27–30, 35–44, 68, 74, 83–7,
107–24, 133, 138, 142, 148, 150,
152, 154, 159, 168, 170–2, 221–2,
224–5
conversation, 8, 25, 36, 86–7,
107–23, 142, 153–4, 165–6, 193,
236 n.175
debate, 1–2, 8, 10, 15, 19, 24–5, 43,
52, 57–8, 86–7, 107–23, 129–30,
129–39, 141–2, 154, 166, 202
discussion, 69, 84–7, 107–23, 236
n.175
exclusive disjunctive synthesis,
37–44
Oedipus and, 27–30
opinion, 83–7, 110, 122
systemic misreading, 2, 6–9, 22,
24, 35, 44, 68, 74, 123, 142, 150,
221–2
Acker, Kathy, 69
active destruction, 152, 190
see also, eternal return
actor, the conceptual persona of,
224–5
see also counter-actualization
acts of thought, concepts and
philosophies as, 45–6, 65–6, 72,
89, 142, 192, 195
compare to difference as
representation
actual, Deleuze's concept of, 3–4, 9,
12, 23, 58–64, 91, 126, 128, 133,
179, 183–5, 204, 208–9, 215–18,
221–4
compare to virtual
actualization, see difference as
actualization
affect, Deleuze and Guattari's concept
of, 56, 67
see also Art
affirmation, 10–13, 44–8, 125, 128–9,
132–9, 154, 161–4, 187–8

CPSIA information can be obtained at www.ICGtesting.com
Printed in the USA
LVOW10*1744230615

443546LV00008B/377/P